Björkgraphy

Björkgraphy

Martin Aston

SIMON & SCHUSTER
A VIACOM COMPANY

First published in Great Britain by Simon & Schuster Ltd, 1996
A Viacom Company

Simon & Schuster Ltd
West Garden Place
Kendal Street
London W2 2AQ

Simon & Schuster of Australia Pty Ltd
Sydney

A CIP catalogue record for this book is available from the British Library
ISBN 0-684-81799-3

Printed and bound in Great Britain by
Butler & Tanner Ltd, Frome and London

Dedicated to my grandmothers Rose and Tessie

Contents

Acknowledgements

Given the priority Iceland places on literature above all other art forms, it's not surprising that biographies are traditionally a literary 'event' – the telling of a life story. On more than one occasion, Björk has supported this notion by saying that she would be happy if her biography was written when she was approaching say, 80 years old, balancing great-grandchildren on her knee, looking back at the overall picture. But now, she says? When you're only thirty-one?

Alas, she must concede that her recording career already stretches back twenty years, a period of time that the remainder of the planet deems worthy of such a story. So while Björk has kept her distance by choosing not to be interviewed afresh for this book, I want to thank her for believing in freedom of expression, and allowing me access to family, friends and musical collaborators.

Special thanks are also due to Ási Jonsson at Bad Taste Ltd., Hildur Hauksdóttir, Árni Matthíasson, Derek Birkett and Netty Walker at Brave Management, Jakob Magnússon, the One Little Indian press department (Joe Kessler, David Peschek and Andrew Campbell), Reptile (for showing me around Iceland), *Mojo* for the picture of Björk in Bangkok, Helen Gummer at Simon & Schuster, Ingrid Connell and Mat Clum for invaluable assistance and/or encouragement. Thanks, too, to those journalists whose interviews I quoted to supplement my own with Björk and associated parties over the years.

Personal thanks to my family – my parents, David, Penny, Katie, Vicki and Christopher, Louis and Tess – and to Angela, Merle, Sara, Mark, Sanne, Meir, Yael, Patrick, Gordon, Maxine, David, Yvette, Rupert, Neil, Yas, Martin, Margriet, Gerrit, Emiel, Joanna, Stuart, Carl, Magnus, Madeline, Mary Pat, Rupert, those I inexcusably left out last time round – Brenda, Richard, Steph, Rod, Elodie, James, Edori, Stephen – and the American clan – the Clum family, Nate, Blake, Lynn, Steve, John, David, Ann, Peter, Paul, Suin, Brian.

The Eruption That Never Lets You Down

'Singing to me is a totally natural thing. It's like going to the toilet or making love – if I don't do it regularly I suffer.'

The Wembley Arena stage is in darkness. Anticipatory screams erupt in small pockets, then build to a swell. A figure skips on, and kneels centre-stage, legs tucked under her body. She has already kicked off her shoes. She hugs herself, a tiny presence in the enveloping midnight of the stage. Slowly, the musicians behind her make their presence felt. It's a quixotic, womb-like sound, a techno-organic lullaby, the kind you might expect to hear towards the end of a show, not at the beginning. In other words, this is not an attempt to pacify or please a standing-and-waiting crowd, to satiate their expectancy with the usual stadia-rock methodology. This is to create a mood, to bring the audience with you. Imagine the noise of half-asleep, as you drift into your subconscious.

Then the figure starts to sing. *'Genius to fall asleep to your tape last night . . . so warm . . . sounds go through the muscles . . . these abstract wordless movements . . . they start off cells that haven't been touched before . . .'*

The track is 'Headphones', and it floats around the arena for a good six or seven minutes. Her voice and the instruments echo and swirl abstractly but with the definite presence of pulsebeats, like tiny hearts with huge microphones attached. This is a world with its own unique, beguiling bewitchment. Call it Björkworld.

It's said that when you reach the age of seven your character is already formed, and will stay the same for the rest of your life. A black and white view, perhaps, but the relationship between yourself and the world outside – people, demands, expectations, responsibilities – is crystallized at that stage more than any other. It's just a question of attitude. Do you see things as a problem, or a challenge? Do you conform to convention, or do you rebel?

At this early stage in her life – she reckons it could have been even earlier, at six – Björk decided that she was destined to stand apart from her peers. 'I remember being in my kindergarten and helping take care of the other children,' she told *Rolling Stone* in 1994. 'Because I insisted on taking care of them. And the second thing I remember really strongly from the same time is me playing with the kids in the street, and we were really excited and really happy and really free.

And then we were just about to do something, I can't remember what it was, and the other five kids decided that we shouldn't do that. And I am like, "Why?" And they said, "Because you are not supposed to, just because you can't." And I always remember that it was a sort of crossroads in my life. Understanding that terrified me. On the one hand are the things you're supposed to do, and on the other hand are the things you want to do, which is a lot more fun, and there's a big canyon between those two. So I said, "Well. I'm doing what I want to do. Fuck you guys." So I went on the side of the canyon, and it was good to be brought up that way, because you have to fight. Like, "Fucking hell, I'm gonna wear pink fur this week!" And I've never regretted it since.'

To really understand the elemental forces that shaped this maverick spirit in her infancy, you have to look at where she originates from. Welcome, then, to the far North Atlantic, and Iceland.

Every media review of Björk has included some reference to the island of her birth – the lure of the unknown plays its part in underlying the singer's particular enigma. Said to be shaped like a duck or even a dragon (though it resembles a ragged sheep from here), Iceland, the most western landmass in Europe, is slightly larger than England, yet has an approximate population of just 260,000 (that's less than the membership of American Express). Ninety thousand of them are located in the capital Reykjavik (or Reykjavikurhofn, meaning 'smoky bay') situated in the south-west corner of the island.

Thus the landscape is dominated not by the concertinaed high-rises but a haphazard amalgam of mountains, glacial ice (5,000 solid square miles of it), geysers, hot water springs, volcanoes and lava – a geophysical architecture second to none. Iceland is distinctly underwhelmed by trees and shrubs (famous Icelandic joke: What do you do if you are lost in an Icelandic forest? You stand up.) Such starkness suggests the end of the world but it's actually the beginning – hence the moonscape similarities, which enticed Apollo mission trainees in their cute buggies. This late arrival on the planet was shoved above water by the intimate rubbing of continental plates; as Björk herself puts it, 'Iceland sits right on the crack that holds the Atlantic Ocean,' a hotspot that means volcanic eruptions and laval action to rival the glacial majesty of its northern exposure. And what a wild, elemental, unpredictable beauty was created – ice and fire, dense rain that can clear in an instant for the sun to flood your eyes, and then ominously return to obscuring grey. Such passionate extremes. A place where the soul, if not always the feet, is duty bound to go walkabout.

But you're on your own when you do; with just two people per square mile, in Iceland no one can hear you scream. There are few main roads to disrupt nature; four-wheel drive is vital for serious investigation, but hiking, boating, bicycling and walking await the hardy, and the more you push on, the more impressive the sights – like the luminescent Blue Lagoon, a by-product of the country's main electricity plant, its rich mineral deposits owning supposed healing gifts. Or the Thingvellir Valley, where the Icelandic parliament was first conceived, and limb-threatening disputes settled (or not), The Great Geyser (at its peak a 600 foot spume, though time has worn its potency); Gullfoss, the Golden Falls, the largest drop in Europe; the blue glint of the Langjökull and Snæfellsjökull glaciers (the latter where Arni Saknusson's journey to the centre of the earth began according to Jules Verne). A place which may require extreme resilience to make the most of but returns an extreme sense of awe and pleasure. But be humbled as you go; these are monuments to forces outside human control. Off the west coast of Iceland, the Westmann Islands gave birth to its thirteenth son, Surtsey, as late as 1963, after two years of volcanic fornication. Not even the landscape here stays the same.

The first to experience the island's savage austerity were gently austere Irish monks, who left home in the eighth century in search of a remote place where they could pray in peace. Their isolated existence was disturbed by Vikings, abandoning Norway for more pragmatic reasons – they disliked the heavy taxes imposed by the monarchy, and so steered clear their wooden boats in search of a temperate zone where their own authority was king. A shame for them, then, that Iceland was their destination, for these seas and climate were not for taming, and fortunes and lives were lost. As legend has it, one such bitter fellow, spying a fjord of solid ice, was moved to christen the country Iceland (or as the natives say, Lydvelid Island), even though the land is hardly ice-bound, unlike Greenland, which has a similarly incongruous name. Legend also has it that Iceland was so named to frighten people off settling, and Greenland was given its name as a decoy.

In spite of the climate, the Vikings settled in. Though they managed to enslave and then wipe out all traces of the Celtic settlers, the new colonists were not as barbarian as history caricatures them, being more farmers at heart than pillagers. In 930AD, they created the world's first known parliament (The Althing) and a concept of democratic society which gave unprecedented equality to women. Their literature, sagas, Eddaic and skaldic poetry are considered a pinnacle of Scandinavian art.

Society prospered until the twelfth century, when escalating feuds over land and power led to one Gissur The White cementing a deal by which the King of Norway would become the King of Iceland and Gissur an Earl. Independence was thus surrendered, but worse was to come. When the Norwegian and Danish crowns were merged and later divided, Iceland fell under Danish rule. Turning Icelandic trade into a Danish monopoly, the new rulers then neglected their charge and years would go by without sight of a supply ship.

Iceland commonly refers to the 700-year foreign rule as 'The Lost Centuries', a period of deprivation, pitifully slow development and isolation – except for some mild mingling and cross-fertilization with neighbouring Greenland, whose Inuit (Eskimo) roots still pop up in the gene-pool, as a certain Björk Gudmundsdóttir can testify. The dominating creed was 'survival of the fittest', alongside a widescale denunciation of Icelandic culture orchestrated by those magnanimous practitioners of the Catholic church and later the Lutherans, who considered music the path to moral decay and Satanic worship. If you ever wondered who imagined that the devil had all the good tunes, now you know. 'They banned singing and dancing as tools of the devil so we don't possess any heritage there any more,' Björk notes, although there is the one traditional Icelandic instrument in existence, the not-very-handy longspit, which is played like a Japanese koto. Unlike instruments, it was hard to suppress the voice, so chants and the written word protected Norse literature (Icelandic language hasn't changed for over 1,000 years).

If Iceland's tradition of telling sagas saved them from cultural extinction, alongside the bare bones of a religion that mixed paganism, mythology and witchcraft, then it was simple quick-thinking that saved them from colonial indistinction. After pressure applied by Icelandic academics studying in Denmark's capital Copenhagen, Iceland was finally given home rule in 1904, and subsequently its own foreign minister in 1918. When the Germans occupied Denmark in World War II, Iceland took the opportunity to form its own republic. Independence is the proudest of virtues in this country.

The next invaders didn't take long to appear; a Cold War-conscious NATO built an American base in the early 1950s. There is more than legend to substantiate the view that Liefur Eiriksson (son of famed Viking ruler Eirik the Red, discoverer of Greenland) landed in America 500 years before Columbus, leading Oscar Wilde to suggest that Icelanders were the most intelligent race in Europe, because they discovered America and kept quiet about it. Sad to say, the Yanks were unwilling to return the favour, and so grudges developed as deep as valleys. 'If those poor sailors had left the base to go for a drink, they would have been slaughtered,' Björk laughed, but to balance this out, the base brought in valuable wealth. With fishing limits simultaneously increased, Iceland jumped from one of the poorest nations in Europe to one of the richest, in around ten years.

Such extremes are natural to a race that witnesses weather changes in matters of seconds. Human nature inclines us to blame the weather for our problems but Icelanders have slightly more justification than most. This island, isolated in the Atlantic, can suffer sleet, snow, rain, sun, sometimes all in an hour (the weather also supports the hardcore Icelandic humour, at the expense of tourists who drive their hired jeeps on to glacier rivers, only to float away . . .). So close to the Arctic Circle, Iceland 'enjoys' near-total sunlight in the summer and near-total darkness in the winter, which are mood-altering environs of the highest order. If the summer is a time of freedom, then winter is a time of depression.

Machines can replicate daylight in winter but Icelanders tend to prefer the act of suicide, or immersion in art, specifically literature, poetry and painting, with music a historical poor forth choice. Icelanders buy and write more books per head of population (sixteen per year) than anywhere else on earth (the local currency, the Kronas, is decorated with poets and artists); the country has nine chess grandmasters (to Britain's two, for example), while there have been three Nobel prize winners out of those 260,000 souls. Oscar Wilde was right – these are brainboxes.

The culture is naturally centred in Reykjavík. The box-style, pre-fab architecture, dotted with multi-coloured, corrugated iron roofs, lends the capital the air of an off-season seaside town, but it has a sophisticated, bohemian soul, a thriving and often radical arts scene to energize its bustling social calendar.

'Artists in Iceland are not pedestrian, they are courageous and I have a theory about that,' the country's president, Vígdís Finnbogadóttir, reflected in 1990. 'I think it is partly because we live in a country that is on the move. We live in a country that we have had to conquer.'

'Take the example of a man who is going to make a film in Iceland,' says Ivar, once bassist of folkjazzpunkniks Reptile. 'He has to be a bit crazy because there is only an audience of 250,000. That's the reason why art becomes radical. You always lose everything you have, like you put your house on the line. No one backs you up.'

'It's a totally crazy culture,' explains Einar Örn, Björk's compatriot and longtime friend. 'You can present absolute rubbish artistically, from any viewpoint or tastepoint, and it's loved. You can present something which has some integrity to it, and it's hated. You can never prejudge what will or won't go down.'

Graham Massey, who co-wrote two songs with Björk on her 1995 album *Post*, played a concert in Reykjavík in 1991 with techno quartet 808 State, thereby experiencing Iceland's cultural tension first hand.

'Everything was so crazy that evening,' he wrote in *Post*, the magazine-format book that Björk published soon after the album. 'There was a keyboard being brought in from the north of the country, an amplifier from forty miles away in the other direction. Everyone pulled together for it to happen and you realized that there was a real creative community. Here you might have small artistic communities but there's not a lot of dialogue. It is very much dictated by the media. It doesn't stand on its own. The various ideas come from outside sources. Whereas the thing with Reykjavík was very functional, it had its own value there. Special people can come out of that because it's quite challenging.'

The 400,000 sheep that co-exist with the humans are less blessed with brainpower – they're just happy munching the trees as well as the grass (but the humans get their revenge by eating the sheep). Iceland has little else it can nurture easily on home soil, so exports are minimal (mainly fish and wool) and imports drastically high. As in Scandinavia, prices are prohibitively high too (a pizza can be £10/$15, a beer £6/$8) yet the standard of living is second only to that of North America. In order to maintain it, it's common to hold two, even three jobs simultaneously, to endure a fourteen hour day. 'Icelandic kids have to earn all their pocket money themselves,' Björk maintains. 'There's a very strong propaganda in Icelandic society of not being a loser and being self-sufficient.'

Self-motivation and self-sufficiency have reduced the archetypal problems of poverty, begging, homelessness, class division and social inequality to a minimum. While unemployment was once non-existent, today it stills stands at a paltry 2 per cent – you can always work in a fish factory.

'People in Iceland still don't know how to have a civilized meal,' Björk said in *Post*. 'It takes them five minutes to eat because they work while they eat. I'm exaggerating here, but there's always this kind of hurry, trying to make the most of your time. There's this workaholism. It's the only way to survive. It's the survival of the fittest, it really is. We are born to exaggerate and do the maximum.'

Extreme weather makes for extreme people – very happy, very sad, very manic, very drunk, very quick to relieve stress, everything 'very'. Nothing is done by halves, including the desire/need to play hard after working hard. A strange lapse in Iceland's post-prohibition laws left beer and lager illegal, and even by the late 1980s, there were only three liquor stores in the country (and all state-owned) but 30,000 Icelanders in the last ten years have had to dry out even if the weather doesn't. Before the laws were reformed in 1989, Friday afternoon queues for alcohol could last forty-five minutes, despite prices that were hiked up by prohibitive taxes.

'People have a lot of money and work very hard, and they think they can't take a break, so they carry on,' says Einar Örn. 'It's in their nature to be manic. You don't go to the pub to have a drink, you go out *drinking*. It's like Icelandic discos: if you go in there, be prepared to fight, no question about it.'

The word in Icelandic for 'get drunk' is also the same as 'to die'. The picture becomes clearer . . .

As the stereotypically healthy, strong Icelandic adult fortifies his or her ego while unloading work and weather stress, the emerging teenager typically does what the establishment culture attempts to prohibit. The social consequences, such as Reykjavík on a weekend night, have to be seen to be believed – Icelandic youth, dressed up to the nines in their flashiest threads (money is spent as fast as it is earnt, as rising inflation ensures that its value ebbs away), congregating in town, drinking and later on perhaps, wrestling in the gutter. Every tourist report on the capital talks of sporadic fighting after midnight, before everyone goes home and the ritual repeats itself next week. Einar Örn: 'People want to look smart, even if they live in shit. Everybody wants to be rich so at least they can look rich. Try talking to these people and they're brainless.'

If the brianlessness of their endeavors looks like a natural result of the brain-strain of living in Iceland, then the intelligensia looks like they've won out. Better to have an escape valve and the advancements that Iceland has made than mediocrity where little is achieved. Take feminism: Iceland hasn't had to make a big play for female equality because it has always been there. In 1980, it became the first country to elect a female head of state, Vigdís Finnbogadóttir. It's said that the respected translator, former school and university teacher and theatre director could trace her unique position to the one-day woman's strike in 1975, where men were left to look after the children. A presidential candidate who stood as a single divorcée, who was one of the first single women in Iceland to adopt a baby, who got elected and has official photos standing with her daughter but without a male consort, is as mindbogglingly revolutionary as it is refreshing (likewise a president who actively attempts to rid her country of its American military base). But then Iceland respects Mother Earth, so it follows that the country respects the female of the species. Where else are women allowed to keep their maiden name?

And where else is there a national holiday when, to increase the population, adultery is actively encouraged? For the same reason, childbirth before marriage, and in the late teens, is not frowned upon but encouraged. Iceland used to have the highest illegitimacy rate in the world until they started counting in Greenland. The instinct and passion for survival for individualism takes on romantic proportions in Iceland; a population which has endured isolation and the loss of home rule tends to concretely believe in the self.

As Björk noted, proudly, 'The United Nations did a survey, some years ago, to a sample of people in all the countries of the world. They asked them a hundred basic questions. One was, "What do you believe in?" Most said Allah, or God, or The Virgin Mary or Buddha. In Iceland, they said, "Myself".'

Iceland's belief system reflects its independence and defiance by absorbing into today's national psyche the ancient Norse sagas of old that survived Catholic indoctrination. The Norse 'bible', the Edda, contains all these myths and legends, telling how the world was born, lived in and how it will die. The state religion is officially Protestant but Icelandic belief in the self is stronger, and thanks to their pagan roots, the presence of elves, fairies and trolls are considered as everyday as the sun in the sky.

'Most people are influenced by the occult, whether they like it or not,' Björk explained. She went on to describe a dual carriageway outside Reykjavíc that actually takes a little detour around a rock because it is believed that elves live under it. When the road was being built, those who tried removing the rock suffered various disasters, at which point a 'translator' between the elves and humans said that they had to stop. 'You see this beautiful, straight asphalt road, which takes this little bend, and then goes straight on again,' says journalist Árni Matthíasson. 'Incredible but true.'

Another time, an agreement was made to allow elves to move away from an area. Did the belief exist as strongly today? Árni Matthíasson believes that, 'It is turning into a tourist thing, making it look like all the nation believe in trolls and elves, which obviously isn't true. But according to [the UN] survey, people in Iceland don't believe in God as such but they do believe in spirits. So it is widespread, and runs deep.'

'In Iceland, it's nothing to make a fuss about,' Björk confirmed. 'I see the cult that comes up from the hippies, and all the occult shops that are abroad, that make such a fuss of it, all this magic and mysteriousness, but it's just normal here. It's not a question of believing, or one of religion. It's just something normal. Everybody has had some kind of experience,' she claims, meaning of ghosts and mediums. 'I mean, my grandmother is with me all the time. I found that out shortly after she died.'

Einar: 'You simply respect a person that does see ghosts or who is clairvoyant. You don't laugh or scoff at them. So while we don't believe in God we do believe in ghosts.'

Björk: 'The landscape hasn't got any definite form, and that's why people are so much into the mystic and paranormal here; they're attracted to such power spots. It's just like Jules Verne wrote a hundred years ago, there's meant to be an entrance to the centre of the earth here.'

That said, the rest of Europe might question the Icelandic belief that mountains are, in fact, trolls. 'They stay awake in the night and if they get caught in the sun they became rock so all the mountains in Iceland are trolls who are late to bed,' Björk kindly explains.

Such is life in an isolated environment, in a land of ice and fire, of extreme light and dark, of sensory excitement . . .

Björk: 'Iceland is my little world, the little village with my relatives and friends, people I love and people I hate. It's a very magical place. Our feeling for magic stems from our recent past: until fifty years ago, Icelanders were still living in the Middle Ages. Actually, they still do: the average Icelander might now have a portable phone and a satellite antenna but his soul still lives in the rural Iceland of the 1750s. Even though I've felt quite misunderstood in Iceland, I've found that quite fascinating!

Magic and realism, pragmatism and individualism – what the rest of Europe sees as atavistic beliefs and modern liberalism. Iceland is a strange catalogue of paradoxes. Where what seems crazy is practically sane. Where what seems sane is born of madcap inspiration.

But despite it all, Iceland's culture has not had much international impact – Nobel prizes and chessplayers aside. Not a widely known fact, this, but abandoning the idea of the usual singular item in favour of the extreme notion of *thirteen* Santa Clauses (the Jolasveinar, or 'Christmas Men', who, says Björk, conduct individual acts of naughtiness like slam doors, play perverted peek-a-boo and steal your food) is novel and hasn't caught on. The British, of course, remember Iceland for its part in the Cold War dispute of the early 1970s, and British culture recognizes the contribution made by Magnus 'I've started so I'll finish' Magnusson, presenter of the long-running brain-box TV quiz *Mastermind*.

The UK's music reference books only offer one Icelandic chart entry, in 1983, when the considerably bland jazz-funketeers Mezzaforte, took 'Garden Party' into the UK Top Twenty singles chart. Indigenous Icelandic pop was never going to get off the ground while there was only one state radio station, which broadcast a stifling combination of cover versions of Western pop, and more archaic MOR showband standards. Fortunately, an alternative came from, of all sources, the American NATO base, which was shunned by Icelandic society but eagerly embraced by rock/pop renegades.

The state TV channel was equally bereft and sad; it broadcast on a part-time basis until 1980 – and then didn't air on Thursdays. It wasn't until the mid-eighties that the country got a second TV station, and their radio stations were bumped up to four. The government even decided to close the NATO radio to protect Icelandic culture, then opened up another station that followed the same programming, a fairly pointless exercise as the taxpayer then had to fund the station, but at least the independence was established.

The NATO presence ensured that The Beatles, The Rolling Stones and the flowering rock fraternity permeated Iceland's cultural defences but the stoic Icelandic spirit held on. *True* independence only arrived when various foraging children of the sixties, modern music's great liberating decade, came into their own in the late seventies. One of them continued to carry the torch, and managed to put Iceland on the map more than any other person or event in the country's history, in a way that sums up all the passions and extremes of that world.

Pronounced Byerk

Hildur Hauksdóttir and Gudmundur Gunnarsson had been an item since she was fourteen and he fifteen. After school, Gudmundur took an engineering degree while Hildur worked for an insurance company and waitressed. Hildur got pregnant at nineteen, and the pair subsequently married. On 21 November 1966, they had a child, a daughter, who they named Björk, meaning 'birch tree'. In the Icelandic tradition of a new-born taking their father's first name and adding 'son' or 'dóttir' (daughter), she became Björk Gudmundsdóttir.

Björk was not a planned event, and the strain of premature marriage and commitment soon told. 'Whether or not it was the right thing to get married, after one year we realized that we really were not prepared,' Gudmundur Gunnarsson says today. 'We ended up drifting away from each other.' Iceland's liberal mores allowed them to do so with relative ease, and the divorce went through when Björk was not yet three.

It was Hildur who most sought an escape from her surroundings, from the contained expectancies of housewife/mother/work – her own mother was a bit of a freewheeling spirit herself, who still headed off into the countryside on camping trips with her paints and easel. 'My mother became a feminist, a rebel, and left her husband to become a hippie and lead a very free lifestyle,' Björk succinctly told *The Face*. 'It was the sixties, and everyone was doing it.'

As a child of the swinging sixties, it seemed apropos that the baby Björk should find music an early, valuable touchstone. When she was one, Hildur remembers that Björk would get goose pimples when she heard a beautiful song. 'She was born musical, I think,' Hildur recalls. 'She started to sing very early. Later on, she was very quick to pick up songs from the radio.'

Hildur remembers that Icelandic lullabies were Björk's first musical acquisition, while she knew all the songs to *The Sound Of Music* by the age of two and a half although she couldn't speak English. As she adapted to the walking-and-taking part of childhood, at family parties Björk would spread a cloth out on the floor as a stage, and perform on it. The born entertainer. 'She had rhythms worked out even then, and a bit of a grown-up voice, although it was still childlike,' says Hildur. 'Already she was different. When she started playing the flute at six, you could hear it in her playing too. She had her own style.'

Her father also recognized her affinity for music: 'You saw that quite early. It was very easy for her to learn. She would hear a song one time and she could sing it. She was very young when she started playing my mother's piano, and there was music in our home, when she would come to visit.'

At the age of five, Björk started attending Barnamúsíkskóli Reykjavíkur, a music school. Fascinated with wind instruments, she played the recorder and soon adopted the flute because her parents couldn't afford to buy an oboe; she played piano, too. But singing seemed a natural form of musical expression, and freed her from the technicalities of learning.

'Singing was very pure for me: it was my own private way of dealing with the other things going on in my head,' the adult Björk admitted. 'I used my voice to think, in the same way that Buddhists use their "Om" chanting. I just always sang the only way I can sing. I love to sing in the wind, in the rain, during the storm, at sea, on a lava flow . . . me against the elements. Where I lived, there were no cars, and we went everywhere by foot, and on the way to my grandparents' house, music school or my mother's house, I would be singing all the time.'

According to the school's director, Stefán Edelstein, 'We didn't teach singing but if she was in a group with other children, she would sing with great joy. And whenever we listened to rhythmic music, she would dance. She was very talented and had a quick mind. But she was sometimes dreamy, as if on another planet. She was like a frog – always hopping around and difficult to catch.'

Björk was fortunate to find the freedom to express herself among her new flat-dwellers in Reykjavík. In her eyes, her mother had started hanging out 'with the wildest lot in Reykjavík,' a gang that all rented a flat together. 'There were ten of them, and I was the only kid.'

Not for the first time, as we shall see, Björk was exaggerating a little. The total number was only seven, including Björk and her baby brother, and though she always referred to the household as a commune, Hildur contests this view. 'It was more a shared house situation, the same as people do today,' she contends.

By this point, Hildur had met Sævar Árnason, an active member of Iceland's nascent rock community, and lead guitarist in Pops, a bluesy, progressive rock outfit in the mould of Cream – Sævar was classified as the Eric Clapton of his generation. They married when Björk was four, and two months after they had a son Arnar (Icelandic for 'eagle'), the extended family unit rented one half of a house while Sævar's sister and twin brothers of Sævar's friend took the other half. Both brothers were also musicians, and so musician friends would invariably congregate at the house, which would have at least resembled a commune in spirit.

'They were always singing and drawing, going wild and barefoot – you know what hippies are like,' Björk contended in turn. 'And being hippies, their favourite people were children, so it was a "let me read you a four-hour-long-story" kinda thing.' Hildur was adamant that her children would have a freedom that her generation had not enjoyed. 'I wanted them to be creative, and not stuck in a boring job for the rest of their lives.'

The result, as Björk recalled, was an absence of discipline, 'just complete anarchy in the most hippie, happy way. It was very positive in that my mother trusted me completely: I was never burdened by her lack of faith in me, or her over-protectiveness. I could do all these things and always believe in a spontaneous way of living. Like, when I decided I was going to eat only bananas for three days, she figured that I would get tired of it soon enough anyway. I remember not wanting to get out of bed unless I could wear a duvet cover, which I wore with a hole cut in my head. Ninety per cent of that hippie stuff is just bullshit but the ideals of that generation were very beautiful and powerful and rebellious for that time.'

Björk saw herself as lucky to have the chance to take care of herself from an early age. Reykjavík was a safe village-style haven (even today, crime in Iceland is extraordinarily rare) but even so, it was unusual for a five-year-old to have a house key around her neck, and walk to school, or take the bus, alone. Björk even claims to have dressed and fed herself from the age of six, 'which meant I became a very organized person. I would have to stand up and get them out of bed if the fridge was empty. And I would be the practical one, the kid who said, "Listen, I've got measles, and I have to go to the doctor, OK?" I went to music school by myself, did the shopping, poked my nose in everything! I was the spontaneous playful child as well as the older, independent daughter . . . I became my own mum very, very early, and I developed a relationship to myself where I was the mum and the child. People see the kid in me; they think I'm innocent and naive and all those things, but being organized and hard-working is completely second nature to me.'

Possibly because the child will always rebel against the parent, or simply because Björk was more determined than her surrounding musician lifestylists, she remembered having enough freedom. 'There came a point when I was about seven or eight, when I saw the absurdity of living in a commune, none of whom wanted to work and who spent their time talking and dreaming and fooling around. For a long time, I thought I was rather cool always having someone around who would tell me stories that lasted six hours, or would push me on the swing, or would paint idealist futurist visions of how we would all set off in a big boat, but one day I told them, "Why don't you just DO SOMETHING!?" All that useless talking! That's something that a lot of people don't see today. My willpower. They only see a thin, small mother who acts a bit weird and think, "aww, how cute". But in reality, I'm made of steel.'

Hildur laughs at her memories of youthful folly – their house painted purple ('I have a purple allergy from it,' Björk contends), the long hair and the Moroccan bracelets which represented individualism in their day, and which her daughter now gently mocks, but adamantly draws the line at Björk's portrayal of an 'idle hippie' culture.

'There were few hippies in Iceland and I definitely wasn't one of them!' she laughs. 'Everybody was listening to hippie music and dressed like hippies but everybody was working in conventional jobs. You can't survive as a hippie in Iceland, you'll freeze to death! You can be very independent when you are young in Iceland because it's not the same as throwing a kid out onto the London streets, but Björk talks about her getting us up in the morning, well, that's bullshit really! We'd drive her to school, and her brother to the nursery, and she didn't know how to cook. I was such a cooking fanatic, I used to take my cookery books to bed with me! When she went to work on a farm when she was around fifteen, I was criticized for not teaching her how to cook. I think Björk bought her own stereo before she even learnt.'

Björk herself admitted in a 1994 interview in *Hot Press* that her upbringing wasn't as bohemian as she made it out to sound, evidence that Björk was sometimes guilty of the child-like habit of embellishment and exaggeration when it came to telling stories. 'They all had proper jobs,' she said. 'My mother made furniture at some point but she also worked in an office doing computers. My stepfather was a full-time blues musician. Everybody worked. Everybody got up early. In Iceland, even the hippies are workaholics.'

Gudmundur, Björk's real father, was the definitive workaholic, and he reckons Björk got that trait from him. Having become a qualified engineer, he had moved over to work in the labour movement in 1975, first in education, then in electricity. In 1986, after a period of teaching, he was made chairman of the electrician's trade union, where he remains today. 'He was an electrician who got fed up with the way the tradesmen are treated in Iceland and became something of a politician,' a proud Björk explained. 'I've inherited their enthusiasm, hard work, and questioning – my parents have always questioned authorities and rules.'

Divorce or no divorce, her parents had remained close, and because Hildur was working, Björk would spend a lot of time with Gudmundur, who was living back at home with his parents. Given that Gudmundur was working too, Björk's grandparents Gunnar and Hallfridur were also involved in her upbringing. Tolerant and artistic themselves, and fond of music, Björk was lovingly indulged at their house.

She was probably liable to play one lifestyle off against the other – to visit her father in barefooted splendour, then try and establish a more organized routine at her home. As a heritage of both parents, Björk was able to grow up with a winning mix of imagination and industriousness.

Somewhere in that hyperactive brain of Björk's there was the judicious ability to separate the positive aspects of her parents' opposing lifestyles. She might have been sceptical and even critical of Hildur's maternal efforts but she still recognized and relished the joys of freedom. While finding Gudmundur's comparative conservatism too limiting, she appreciated the discipline that equally aided creative construction.

Still, being a child, the excitable wildness would win out. Björk once threw the family cat out of the window, 'to see if it could fly, not in a mean way but because I was sorry that he couldn't follow the birds.' She was never destined to be conventional. Dolls bored her; instead, she preferred playing at her grandfather's shop. 'He had these big white rolls of paper which he used to wrap up the lamps he sold. I used to draw on them a lot and make things out of them. I used to make creatures with my grandmothers, of material and bits you should really throw away.'

In *Mixmag*, Björk relayed a story of how, at the age of six, she had developed a fondness for paper and different cardboards, 'and I would tear them into pieces and whatever came out would be pictures, and I would make little worlds. Once, I spent a whole day working on one of these paper worlds. I'd fallen in love with this girl at school, and I took it to her. And I'd never talked to her before. She kind of rolled it apart and it was just a lot of torn pieces of paper with nothing written on them. I suddenly realized it wasn't brilliant, just rubbish really. She just laughed really hard and threw it in the dustbin. It's a sad story!'

Björk took out membership of the Outsider's Club early in life. Her distinctive, oriental-style features, shared in part with her father and thought to come from Greenland's Inuit gene-pool, had earnt her the school nickname of 'China Girl'.

'When I was growing up,' she told *I-D*, 'I always had this feeling that I had been dropped in from somewhere else. That was how I was treated at school, where everybody thought I was unusual because I was Chinese. It gave me room to do my own thing. In school, I was mostly on my own, playing happily in my private world, making things, composing little songs. If I can get the space I need to do my own thing by being called an alien, an elf, a China Girl, or whatever, then that's great. I think I've only realized in the past few years what a comfortable situation that is.'

This was one independent, smart young cookie. Call her Björk, not Bjönkers. 'I got called weird since the age of four. I'd got used to it by five. I made a decision then – I'd either live my life by what people thought of me and to a set of rules I didn't really know or understand, which would make me incredibly unhappy, or I could do just what I wanted. And that's a lot more fun, isn't it?

'What I'm fighting against is narrow-mindedness, which is probably the thing that makes me most mad of all the things in the world, and against stagnation, and people behaving how they're supposed to behave. I think that the kids at school were jealous that I could do whatever I wanted, and that's why they had to call me weird and an alien and strange and something untouchable.' She admitted that she was an introverted spirit but it didn't mean she was unhappy: 'I just liked being on my own. I didn't care what other people thought of me.'

The musical artistry flowed freely but Björk's earliest idols were not pop or rock luminaries but scientists, investigators of the wondrous and the unknown. Albert Einstein was a favourite but a fascination with Britain's premier anthropologist/zoologist David Attenborough turned into a schoolgirl crush. At school, where she was deemed exceptionally bright, Björk excelled at maths, and was fond of collecting insects. 'I have their bodies when they are dead and then I have them to watch because they would be bored if they had to live with me,' Björk recalled playfully, though such turns of phrase would force those less playful to pigeonhole her as 'weird', just as her schoolkid peers did.

She preferred the word 'weird' anyway. She identified with, and would befriend, 'the guys at the back of the class with thick glasses who had insect collections too – they were the people I found really exciting. And I was on the chess team.' By the age of nine, free to dress as she wanted, to be who she wanted, she had started wearing her grandfather's clothes.

Like Saffy, the studious daughter in Britain's epochal nineties sit-com *Absolutely Fabulous*, Björk found science a necessary grounding influence. Home was a playground of possibility but even starryminded children needed some sense of belonging. By the time she was eleven, Björk's father and new wife had had two daughters and a son, an extended family unit of numerous half/stepbrothers and sisters, fathers and mothers, 'so it was my dream when I was eight or nine that David Attenborough would come to Iceland and be standing there holding my hand on top of a hill and explaining it all like it was really simple,' she sighed. 'I had a very happy childhood, but I wouldn't have minded getting a clue why things happened.'

Björk admitted that her scientific bent made her 'a bit over-analytical, a bit over-clever', but it allowed her to weigh up the options. She was smart enough to take on board the strengths of her breast-fed hippie/new age lifestyle – 'I know acupuncture works, for example' – and reject its weaknesses – 'the escapism is what I hate most, like, "Oh, I can't be a tennis teacher because I've got my Mars in Libra".'

In an ironic turnaround of circumstances, as she grew bolder and more comfortable in her skin, Björk found that tolerance for a total-freedom package had its limits even for her family. 'Most of the adults at home hated spontaneity,' she decried. 'They hate you making little cries of delight about things that they consider normal. Take that tape recorder of yours: isn't that fantastic? That something like that exists? I was lucky, my screams were tolerated more because I am a woman, that makes it a little more OK, but often I would start singing, out of the blue, just for the hell of it, without there being a party or the television on . . . The very idea of it! To sing because you feel happy or just to test your voice . . . that's considered madness.'

The free-flow of music competed with the solidity of science for Björk's attentions. As early as the age of four, Björk had written her own tiny songs: articulating gripping scenarios such as her grandmother arguing with the butcher, penning words like, '*I fell on my knee and blood came/I'll never go to the shop again*.' Like a diary, melodies and lyrics were the precious secrets, friends that, she warranted, 'kept me sane through a bit of mad youth.'

Music arrived from all possible directions. At music school, Björk soaked up the classics but decided that the emphasis on old heroes like Bach and Beethoven, 'seemed to have nothing to do with our lives. Playing Beethoven eight hours a day is cowardly – I think the balance should be to play old music one day a year.'

Björk was equally peeved by the conservatism of state radio: 'It only played pop for one hour a week, which meant Abba, so the naval base was really popular,' she recalled. 'Fuck politics. People just want to listen to music.' Björk was lucky in that few children in the 1970s would have had the opportunity that her household could provide. She could appreciate folk-rock via Hildur (Simon and Garfunkel a particular favourite), hard rock via Sævar (Jimi Hendrix and Janis Joplin were his king and queen), jazz and swing via her grandparents, and Western pop music via NATO. But as much as she railed against classical conservatism, she also found herself reacting against the established 'classical' view of rock'n'roll, as donated by her stepfather and clan. By the age of seven, Björk claimed, 'I was convinced that this music was ancient history, that I would do something new. I think that as soon as any form becomes traditional, like guitar, bass and drums, then people start to behave traditionally. It's really difficult to get a band to stay on the edge using the typical set-up because it tends to lapse into a predictable form.'

Right here and now, Björk felt that all types of music should stand a chance, that the politics of taste were counterproductive. 'I grew up with a lot of people who thought that their music was the only right one, and that the others were not so good. Kids can quite easily be voyeurs and I realized early that a good song is a good song if it's got the right intention, if it has true emotion and originality. It doesn't matter if it's by Abba or Stockhausen.'

At home, competition for the record player was intense. 'People sat on the floor and you basically had to queue for it,' Björk recalled. Early rock memories included adoring the sleeve to The Beatles' *Sergeant Pepper's Lonely Hearts Club Band*, and being bewitched by the albino brothers Edgar and Johnny Winter, 'and their weird, red eyes'. But the first record she owned outright was Sparks' 1972 glam-rock opus *Kimono My House*, an album of eccentric, startling glamour, giddy melody, childlike glee and ascerbic wit.

'That was the first time I was like, "I've got a record and I'm going to play it and now you've got to listen to what I like", she recalls with relish. 'i'd really had enough of all those hippie records, all that psychedelic crap, all those guitars and rock'n'roll, so I became like a kid who has to listen to different stuff to her parents. My dad was a bit on the case and probably bought it, but didn't really like it, but I picked it up and listened to it all day, and we were all constantly fighting over what to play. They all thought it was really silly. I played little else for a year, and drove them all mad. It's really for kids as well, you know. A statement like, "*this town ain't big enough for the both of us, and it ain't me who's gonna leave!*" was pretty cool. The singer, Russell Mael, sang like a Japanese geisha, and I loved the way they were into geisha clothes, as I was really into oriental people. I was also right into his brother, Ron Mael's Chaplin image. Kids get very picturesque music, where it's really easy to imagine what's going on, so it was a bit of a fairytale. I was really into them until I read an interview with Russell, a year later, when he said he didn't like kids or animals. That broke my heart.'

As she approached double figures, Björk was to vacillate between polar opposites of security and abandonment. At nine, she took her first trip abroad, to Norway, with her grandparents, where the young'un felt claustrophobic because there were too many trees (and not enough moss). A year later, the household members went their own way; Björk's family bought an apartment in the suburb of Breidholt, on the eastern industrialized side of Reykjavík where the post-war slums were being quickly replaced.

There were compensations for the upheavals; the new apartment was next to a salmon river, she started to occasionally join Sævar's band Pops on stage, 'at the beginning of the evening, before the people got too drunk,' and a window opened when she took part in a radio documentary on her music school. Björk 'was there as the girl that sings,' and for this particular debut chose the pulpy disco anthem 'I Love To Love', a UK number one in February 1976 for teenager Tina Charles, that she'd sung at one of the school's weekly open houses. The song was rhythmic, simple (sample lyric: '*I love to love but my baby just loves to dance*'), memorable, and the property of a teenager Björk could empathize with.

The breath control she had learnt from playing the flute had already lent her voice its distinctive breathiness – it was hard not to be smitten. Her efforts were instantly noticed by Skifan, a local record distributor, who saw an opening for a child star, and subsequently offered Björk the chance to make a record. The Skifan representative, Hildur remembers, 'was not my kind of a person,' so she decided to seek advice from Jakob Magnússon, the frontman of a high-school age band Studmenn which had rapidly progressed up the singles chart.

Magnússon's career curve continued upward; between 1992 and 1995, he was Iceland's cultural attaché in Britain. At the beginning of Björk's trajectory, he recalls Hildur making contact through a mutual friend, and asking if he could spare some time. Days later, he came home to find her mother and Björk sitting on his doorstep. 'Björk had her flute with her, and she played and sung in the most charming way. It was a child's voice but unique, and you could tell immediately she was very talented, and unusually bright. She wasn't so much shy as quiet and gentle, in a world of her own, and obviously a very special kid. She brought some of her favourite records too, I can't remember which, but it was all really progressive pop stuff.'

Magnússon agreed to record a demo tape, which he subsequently shopped around the limited number of Icelandic record companies. He heard nothing back in the first week, and was amazed to get a phone call from the friend who had first introduced him to Hildur, at 2.30 a.m. 'It was the middle of my exams for a start,' he laughs. 'She gave me a hard time over why the deal wasn't sorted out, which I thought was a bit much, and I remember the exam not going too brilliantly the next day! I told Björk's mother that these things tend to take time.'

Magnússon's efforts were detoured when a sudden call from England took him on a lucrative tour of Canada, playing as pianist for the British singer Long John Baldry, but his initial efforts paid off when Fálkinn Records put up the money.

The first hurdle was to decide the musical content, as Björk was already showing signs of the independence that would become evident over the years. 'I was very stubborn and opinionated,' Björk told Q. 'The record label offered me all these songs and I turned them down because they were shit. I got very upset in the end so my mum ran around her hippie musician mates and they all came up with songs for me.'

Backed by Sævar, bassist Pálmi Gunnarsson, drummer Sigurdur Karlsson – the latter pair co-produced the sessions – and guitarist Björgvin Gíslason (she returned the favour when she sung on his 1983 album *Afi*), Björk took two weeks off school ('she was very clever at school so it wasn't any bother' Hildur says) and swept through a handful of Icelandic pop standards, Edgar Winter's 'Alma Mira', Melanie's quasi-nursery-rhyme 'Christopher Robin', Stevie Wonder's 'Your Kiss Is Sweet', The Beatles' melancholy 'Fool On The Hill' ('Alfur 'Ut 'U hól', as it appeared) and even one of her own compositions, the instrumental 'Jóhánnes Kjarval', named after Iceland's first popularist, expressionist painter.

The album *Björk* was released in the autumn of 1977, in time to tap into the Christmas market. Hildur designed the cover, where a crossed-legged Björk sat, suitably surrounded by exotic bric-a-brac of Middle Eastern hue, in Arabic garb ('I remember Björk really liking the clothes' says Hildur in homage to the album track 'Arab Boy' written by Sævar – girl meets Egyptian lad, falls in love, they ride away on his camel.

Only eleven, she already radiated confidence, assured of her place and role in the world, and the music followed suit. As *Record Collector* put it, *Björk* was 'a perfectly listenable, mid-seventies pop album', and as decent a mix of individual expression and industrious pop-making as any eleven-year-old could reasonably expect in Iceland.

Björk's voice is unrecognizable from today's galeforce version but range, expression and tenderness were already intact. Bizarrely, to match her looks, her timbre could easily be mistaken for an Oriental singer. The melodic, concise 'Jóhánnes Kjarval', meanwhile, alternated between jaunty, child-like pop and more relaxed, flute-led passages, belying her youthfulness. 'Fool On The Hill' and 'Alexander Beetle' were plaintive and sweet; the only track that badly jars is the cod reggae/calypso take on 'Your Kiss Is Sweet'; the adult Björk may have happily talked about the album but you can hear why she has never allowed it to be reissued.

'The music was very happy, light-hearted pop, half bubble-gum, half crazy,' Björk recalled. She had enjoyed the experience. 'It was magical, going into the studio at that age, hearing all the tricks you can do,' she told *NME*.

'They really spoiled me, playing me what I'd sung backwards and speeded up so it sounded like Donald Duck. It was quite developed for an eleven-year-old, I guess – people think eleven-year-olds only like Pinky and Porky.'

She meant Pinky and Perky, those sixties-swinging pig string-puppets with musical ambitions. But back in 1977, child stars were distinct novelties, perceived as playing at pop. 'When you're eleven,' she told *The Face*, 'you're not listening to *Sesame Street* any more. I wanted to write music about walking down the street, having visits, laughing, having a swim, the things you do every day.'

Artistic achievement aside, Björk was underwhelmed by the idea of pop stardom. Even at eleven, she understood fame's inherent downside – the jealousies and insecurities, the expectations of others. 'The album was big enough for me to know that I didn't want any of it,' she concluded. 'I hated being recognized in the street and kids wanting to be my friends. You suddenly get a lot of people and only one in twenty sincerely wants to talk to you and the others only want to because it's kinda cool. On the bus, kids were shouting, "Oh she thinks she's better than the rest of us, she sits at the front of the bus." Half of me is completely fine and very, very happy about it, flabbergasted, you know? But the other half of me is: "Alright, it is over now, then?" Because in Iceland, I guess, it's so easy to be famous.'

She subsequently declined the offer to follow up her success, at least with musicians of a different age and songs by another composer.

Cruelly, she saw her backing band as, 'losers in their thirties, past the hottest moment in their life,' and resented being a child amongst unequals. 'I was being treated like a kid, an animal in a zoo,' she told *Details*. 'I wanted to work with people my own age, and write songs that had never been written before. I was always very fascinated by all the people around me, the hippie commune I lived in, the harbour, the farmers. I was on my own a lot and my thing was to write little songs – it was my diary. Like, "*Pete likes raisins too much, Pete likes raisins too much, I think he should actually kiss Shirley today*." They were things that I wanted to happen.'

And what Björk wanted to happen, usually happened. Asked for one anecdote that might sum her daughter up, Hildur recalls New Year's Day, 1979. Björk was just thirteen, a member of the church choir and keen to attend the six o'clock service across town. 'At four o'clock, the weather went completely mad, as mad as it can go in Iceland, the wind at 12 knots, and cars disappearing under snow, up to the roof. I told her that she couldn't go, and she was really unhappy, and we quarrelled, and she went into her room. I started cooking, and when dinner was ready, went to look for her, but she wasn't there. I looked all over, and I got more than worried, but then I thought of calling the church, and there she was. I got really angry but I was very proud too. You had to be powerful to get all that way, though she got a ride for the last five minutes. The police got her home around eleven o'clock. She knew what she wanted, and went for it, and that's her whole story.'

Björk was similarly single-minded when it came to her goals. After recording an album, music school was always going to be an anti-climax as well as a constriction, and she started not turning up to classes. But even this disregard for the rules worked in her favour. 'The school kept telling me I had a lot of talent and all I needed was discipline, so they wouldn't throw me out,' she told *The Face*. 'Which turned out to be a privilege because it meant I could do whatever I wanted.'

She probably would have wandered away for good, if a new, young teacher hadn't opened her mind to the innovations of twentieth century classical modernists like Schoenberg and Stockhausen. At the same time, Björk was finally taking notice of her parents' tastes, and would take Janis Joplin, Jimi Hendrix and Joni Mitchell records into music school; she especially loved the complex, jazzy arrangements of Mitchell's *Hejira* album. Through her grandparents, she picked up on Debussy, 'especially his dramatic little piano pieces,' and numerous jazz greats – Billie Holiday, Ella Fitzgerald, Louis Armstrong.

Björk was starting to see music as a source of experimentation, chance and surprise, and free from conventional boundaries. Icelandic singers weren't meant to be pop stars, or to turn down the chance for further fame, or to pick up on music that belonged to their elders. But Björk had decided that she wanted the chance to be anything she wished – 'to sing, to paint, to become a skateboarding champion, to do something that no one has ever done before, to be a priestess in a mysterious Buddhist temple, and an Oracle woman to whom people would come for advice, and who would solve their problems . . . I really wanted to be all those things, and that's my ideal: that anyone can become anything. That, as a woman, you can be mother and athletic champion and philosopher all at the same time. And no one will say, "No, no, no, you have to choose!"'

But once Björk heard the punk explosion that had broken 1,100 miles to the east, in Britain, there was only one choice that she could really make.

Pönk Rock Lives

3

*T*he sad state of Iceland's licensing laws was a key factor behind the stunted growth of Iceland's bar and club culture, and subsequently the non-availability of live music. With no tradition of Icelandic music and no one willing to start one, the creative energies of the young were channelled into prose and poetry. One exception was former fish-factory worker Bubbi Morthens, Iceland's version of Bruce Springsteen, whose albums have been bought by as many as one in twelve Icelanders. Morthen's blue-collar anthems were largely inspired by bad working conditions in fish factories (one shower for every sixty workers, 50 per cent of wages spent on food, and hardship for many) and proved that there was a demand for music both in Iceland's native tongue and with political content, for something more concrete and real. Then there was Iceland's one true underground hero, Megas, a raw, Tom Waits-style talent, the godfather of Icelandic punk. But the world of Top 40 coverbands was still the rule.

The influence of NATO radio and Western culture had filtered through the fifties and sixties baby-boomers, whose children wanted to make their own mark. Mirroring the rest of Western Europe, the more rebellious sections of Icelandic youth were psyched up for something incisive, and punk's energy, spontaneity and confrontational colour made it the timely vehicle. On top, the notions of anarchy and Do-It-Yourself independence clearly struck a chord with the volcanic Icelandic nature. Unlike the rest of Europe, punk in Iceland was more a rebellion against conservatism and apathy than an overtly political and social revolution; the country was unscarred by class struggle and the poverty trap that the UK, punk's original source point, had endured.

One moment, Björk was appreciating Joni Mitchell with her stepfather; the next she was arguing with him over musical ability and The Sex Pistols, and creating an all-girl alliance to form the deliciously named Spit And Snot. Feeling close to the rhythmic surge of it all, Björk chose to be the drummer. You can picture her now, with a classically mischievous, impish grin, but more determined than if her life depended on it; the shortest of orange crops and even shaved eyebrows, just thirteen, just starting at a new school, Réttarholtsskóli, where she was bound to stand out even more. Fearless, in other words.

Like everyone else in the Western world, punk had an extraordinary knock-on effect, and the Icelandic scene erupted like one of the nearby volcanos. Björk summed up the Icelandic mentality as, 'holding something until it's not possible to hold it a second longer, then they skip it and turn it into something else completely.' And so the emphasis swung from literature to music. 'I think we hold the world record for how many punk bands there were for how many people lived in Iceland,' she claimed. 'But it was very difficult to get English punk records. You'd get one, like a Gang Of 4 record, and everyone would go to that person's house. So all these bands started to play, and we definitely got over the problem of not knowing how to play – that was just mind over matter.'

Björk was proud of Spit And Snot, not only to have written actual songs, but to have stood for something positive. 'We were very tired of the negative feminists who were always feeling sorry for themselves and saying "Poor us", she ventured. 'We were like, "Hey, we can do it!" It was about girls having fun, and fuck that sitting-around-and-being-cute.' On the negative side, 'We were so angry, we couldn't even get it together to buy equipment,' she told *NME*. 'We'd end up shouting "Fuck you!" before storming out of the shop. We thought everyone had an attitude problem when really we had the biggest attitude problem of them all.'

Most thirteen-year-olds are the definitive handful: add to it Björk's stubborn resilience, and a temperament once described as, 'you're so drunk, you don't have to drink,' and sparks would fly. Confrontations with her mother led to Björk spending more time with her father, but Hildur still maintained her hands-off approach when it came to Spit And Snot. 'I could never look at them as punks,' she says. 'They were all educated and very deep-thinking young people, so it was more like an art piece, or a "happening". Punk in Iceland was not a heavy thing. But they had a lot of things to say, being against politicians and ordinary life. You could say they saw the tasteless things in life. No, I was more worried that, as a teenager, she had too much work on her hands.'

Gudmundur had his reservations. He felt that punk had intrinsic connections with drugs, and was afraid Björk's muse could lead her into temptation. 'But after a short time, we realized that she was so strong and stubborn, and she would talk about people who got into that stuff, that they were stagnating, and she didn't want to join them. Most people thought she was on drugs because of how she dressed and behaved but I knew her more sensible side. I was never surprised by whatever Björk did. She was very free, and it was easy for her to take decisions and do it, and make them come true,' he laughs. 'She was the kind of person you trusted.'

The trust Björk was given, with a house key round her neck at five, extended to her drive to forage further afield. Introduced to camping when her stepfather's band would play outside Reykjavíc, she bought a tent and a sleeping bag, and started going on periodic walkabout in the countryside, whenever she got the chance. Her first major purchase, though, was very cool: with the money earnt from the *Björk* album she bought a piano, on which she could compose her first real songs, building up a stockpile even then. The first to be aired publicly, however, was tied in with the saddest of events. When she was fourteen, in the same year that Hildur and Sævar separated, her grandmother Godrun died, very unexpectedly (she choked on a piece of meat while in Bulgaria). At her funeral, Björk sang a song she wrote about her death, composed on the piano, which she played on the church organ. 'It was the first thing I was really proud of,' she recalled. Now it was her turn to wear her grandmother's clothes. 'Not like a greed thing, but more an emotional sympathy thing,' she explained.

Knowing Björk's musical inquisitiveness and roving mind, punk's limited palate of chords and expression was never going to capture her attention for long; anyway, was a band named Spit And Snot, consisting of four young Tank Girls, ever destined to last long? At fourteen, she went completely against the grain and, with Ásgeir Sæmundsson and Thorvaldur Thorvaldsson, formed Exodus, an extraordinary leap into the realm of jazz-rock fusion and tricky time signatures, mirroring the more dazzling manoeuvres of the jazz music she had started imbibing. Exodus was not just an album by reggae icon (and punk icon) Bob Marley, but a statement of moving away, of leaving home. Jazz's mixture of intuition and technique, heart and head, imagination and scientific application, was a challenge that Björk relished, and a sign that she was willing to push herself beyond her known capabilities. 'Exodus were very experimental for a young group like that,' Jakob Magnússon felt. 'They were all pretty strong individuals during that time.'

She had been particularly inspired by a TV showing of Ella Fitzgerald singing at the Montreaux Jazz Festival. 'I was fifteen, she was sixty, with white hair, but she had exactly the same, greatest sense of humour. She's always testing people. I guess her singing was an influence on me but not in a direct sense, more in the sense that you shouldn't take melodies too literally. It's a bit irrelevant what a melody is like in a song: the point is more the mood, and the emotions, and it doesn't matter if you forget the lyrics. You can still sing the song. You can do whatever you want to do.'

Björk was adamant that she should improve her musicality, and not solely pursue her singing. Looking back, she saw that she never had any specific singers as role models. 'Instruments influenced me more than singers, like brass and stuff,' she explained. 'You might start puking when I say it but I never had the ambition to be a singer, I always wanted to make good music. It's like learning shorthand writing. It's not so much that you are into it, but it makes it easier to write anything. That's why I sing.'

In order to keep pushing the musical envelope, she abandoned the flute and spent time learning to read music and play piano. She also wanted to learn the saxophone, to add more textual geography to Exodus' minimalist landscape. The problem, naturally, wasn't ability but money, though Ásgeir contacted Jakob Magnússon, who, by chance, owned a saxophone that he had put in for repair in Copenhagen. He said that the band could have it if they organized collection but by the time they tracked it down, the shop had unfortunately sold it on.

Exodus only left behind a garage-recorded cassette and one TV appearance; her next collaboration, JAM 80, lasted only one gig, and nobody even remembers what they sounded like. The experimentation didn't stop there; another short-lived collaboration had Björk on drums and a best friend playing a miked-up popcorn machine. 'We weren't even trying to be funny,' Björk stresses. 'And my friend organized to record my grandfather snoring, and that was supposed to be our loop, our rhythm to do a song to.' Even then, conventional instrumentation to Björk was a cage, a limit on what could – and should – be expressed.

Björk saw her way to the end of music school: she became its only pupil to study all the way through, from age five to fifteen. Not that a classical education could offer her much, or the lessons learnt in Exodus either, as Björk chose to return to the more contained world of punk pop, as part of Tappi Tíkarrass (which translates expressively as 'Cork The Bitch's Arse'), who mirrored the shrill, dynamic punk-pop practised by British bands like X-Ray Spex and The Rezillos, although Tappi had a more serrated, thrashier take on the music.

Guitarist Eythor Arnalds picks up the story. 'My band played a gig with Exodus and we decided we had to steal her, which we did, by persuading her that we were much more fun. Tappi Tíkarrass was a group based on friendship, fun, creativity and having picnics on the roof. They were very creative times, but we were different to the punks because we almost looked like hippies. Punk leather jackets became clichés very fast.'

Eythor was a bit of a science boffin so he and Björk had something to bond over. He thought her smart and unique, and though he saw her as 'living in her own world,' he also valued her contributions 'as a group person'. The original plan was to improvise the music alongside the words, 'but not the "let's be the fastest guitar players in the world" approach, as guitar solos were out,' he stresses. While Björk was babysitting in France for a month, 'we decided to start something really freaky, so we created lots of songs, not typical of pop, with semi-automatic writing. The father of our bass player said the music, "fitted like a cork in a bitch's arse," which is an expression from Western Iceland, for something that fits very well together, so that became the name of the band.'

Tappi's existence was based around rehearsals: they'd try and write one song at every gathering, while lyrics also followed this semi-automatic line. 'They were really surrealistic, more individualistic, never down to earth like punk rock words,' says Arnalds. 'We would take phrases from David Coverdale [stereotypical heavy metal vocalist, eighties vintage] and translate them into Icelandic, which would sound really funny . . . whatever came our way. One lyric was written with words we saw riding on a bus. That kind of thing.'

Bragi Ólafsson, bassist of Purrkur Pillnikk, who would share rehearsal space with Tappi Tíkarrass, and one of Iceland's leading young poets and future co-member of The Sugarcubes, thought Tappi's lyrics and persona was, 'very silly, but in a negative way. It's good to be silly but

I thought they were being pretentious, and I saw Björk as others still see her today, acting younger than she actually is.'

Björk was never afraid to be emotional, or confrontational, but Tappi's surrealistic silliness was more like a smokescreen. Icelandic punk was never going to be socio-political but the Icelandic nature's ingrained self-sufficiency and thick skin to protect against life's hardships meant that the introspective confessional style of lyric-writing was never going to be Iceland's way or so it seemed. To reveal yourself and provoke peer pressure – it could be disapproval, cynicism or downright sneering – was too intense a risk for even Björk and her rebel friends.

According to Dora Wonder, vocalist and saxophonist of the manic, fantastic Reptile, 'The Icelandic approach is, don't reveal much in emotions, have little time for sentimentality. If you start looking inside yourself and try and find a reason why you're doing what you're doing, then you get scared, that all the people see you, and what you're like. If you are suddenly so open, you forget to protect yourself. People say things to you, it knocks you out, you get so sensitive. You go to a party and have a certain wall around you or people can just walk into you and mess things up.'

Björk agreed. 'I wrote love songs when I was thirteen; now they're very funny to read. But I would never work on words and show them to people. Probably because they would laugh, and I don't want them to. You're very self-conscious. You don't give anybody a place where they can come from the back and stab you. that's very common here.' A policy of 'don't ask, don't tell' then . . . 'In Iceland, we definitely are not allowed to wash dirty linen in public', Björk continued. 'You deal with those feelings yourself. It is only in a state of crisis you ask for assistance. And that is, very much, who I am.'

Who was Björk writing love songs to? She admitted that, at fourteen, she thought boys, 'were shit. Only good for being in bands with. You can't talk to them, especially as a teenager, they were so limited. You can't get properly drunk with them, like, all the way drunk. I thought one of the most horrible things was to get a boyfriend, as all my girlfriends had just lost the plot when they got one.'

She happily owned up to typically teenage experiments with her own sex, 'but found out very quickly that I was hetero, though I like feminine boys, with long, delicate fingers.' Virginity was surrendered when she was fifteen: 'I had a huge red skirt on and big boots – quite punky, I have to say it – and I went on a mission with this boy. We actually went to his friend's house. It was dark, and I remember thinking I wasn't sure if that was it or not. But I thought it was ever so exciting.'

By then, Tappi may not have scored any proper chart hits but their mini-album debut *Bitid Fast í Vitid* (roughly *Bite Hard In Your Mind*), and full-length album *Miranda* had both cut a noticeable swathe through Icelandic punk culture, with their strident poppiness and softer vulnerability. The band played numerous live shows in Reykjavík, but also ventured outside the capital, to the far north and Iceland's second biggest town Akureyri and – weather permitting – further afield to play some coastal fishery towns. They even popped up in a film, *Nýtt Líf* (meaning *New Life*): two boys leave Reykjavík to escape money troubles, and end up working in the fisheries of the Westmann Islands. They attend a dance, and there are Tappi Tíkarrass, merrily flailing away.

'Tappi Tíkarrass live were really wonderful,' enthuses Árni Matthíasson, who was soon to become a music journalist (for the national newspaper *Morgunbladid*) and close confidante of Björk's through her numerous musical incarnations. 'Björk projected an enormous amount of energy, even though she was a very private person, and didn't enjoy the limelight like you see a lot of stars do. She might have been dyeing her hair and dressing outrageously but her statement wasn't really saying "Look at me". She disliked being a music *personality* instead of being a musician.'

The Icelandic new wave was as full of distinct personalities as it was emerging musicians, and reputations spread overseas. Two prominent bands Tappi would often play alongside were Purrkur Pillnikk and Þeyr ('Purrkur' meant 'someone who likes to sleep'; Pillnikk was an Argentinian chess player. Þeyr –the Þ is pronounced th – is roughly, 'the warm wind that comes down and melts the snow'). The brittle, wiry Purrkur had been formed, in part, by Bragi Ólafsson and vocalist/trumpeter Einar Örn Benediktsson. Einar Örn had once managed Bubbi Morthens (he had wanted the singer to drop the politics and rock'n'roll some!) and subsequently co-founded Gramme Records, Iceland's first independent record label, shop and distributor. Ironically, Icelandic rock was finally singing in its own language, but opportunities were still severely limited, especially for the kind of uncompromising art-rock direction that Icelandic punk had taken (a by-product of the country's literary tradition), so both bands felt the need to embrace a broader, more sympathetic audience.

'We would only get a hundred people to our shows,' says Einar Örn, 'so we established contact with people abroad just to know we weren't insane. We'd get people on our backs when we went to discos, saying, "You might be heavily into drugs, you seem so weird. Why don't you grow up?"'

Peyr were another kettle of fish altogether. They had occult leanings, and though they maintained that the band stood against Nazism and Fascism there was much ambivalence in their adoption of the harsh posturing of Nazi culture, the dressing up in long black leather coats and military caps (one single sleeve cover, of an armbanded William Reich, was banned in the UK). But they couldn't have been too serious as resolutely anti-fascist British bands like Manchester's punk-poet laureates The Fall and anarcho-punk collective Crass would play with Peyr (and Purrkur Pillnikk) in the UK and Iceland.

Peyr even recorded several tracks with members of the oppressive punk goths Killing Joke, after leading Joker Jaz Coleman (followed by guitarist Geordie), having abandoned both the UK and his band because of what he believed was the impending apocalypse, turned up in Reykjavík, attracted by Iceland's occult reputation and ley-line energy. Coleman thought he had discovered kindred spirits in Peyr – it was alleged that the band was keen to construct a device which operated outside the range of human hearing to establish psychic links with audiences but Coleman riled almost everyone he met. 'It's unbelievable how one man can upset so many people,' Björk recalled, and he was effectively chased out of the country (though Peyr bassist Birgir Morgensen joined the Joke for a while).

Despite the presence of better known bands like Purrkur Pillnikk and Peyr, both of which had carved out reputations overseas, Tappi Tíkarrass appeared in the 1982 documentary film *Rokk í Reykjavík*, or *Rock in Reykjavík*, which documented the city's fecund scene but also controversially discussed youth issues like glue sniffing and drugs, problems that Icelandic society rarely confronted in a public forum. Despite the greater pull of other names, Björk became the film's visual symbol and its cover star. 'She looked so magical and theatrical,' recalls Jakob Magnússon, 'a little girl in a yellow dress, with a yellow tin drum and a progressive punk band behind her.' Years earlier, Björk had seen German filmmaker Volker Schonorff's *The Tin Drum*, released in1978, which she still cites today as her favourite film. Based on the Gunter Grass novel, the film is quintessentially 'Björkian' in feel and image. A runaway hides under a peasant woman's skirts, and conceives the hero's mother, Oskar, the drummer-boy hero of the story, responds to parental sins and domestic angst at the dawn of Nazi rule with a refusal to grow up, and so he remains roughy eight years old. His favourite tin drum, and his potentially glass-shattering scream, are his 'weapons'. 'I could relate it to myself,' she later claimed scarily . . . Years later, Björk saw the film's lead, David Bennent, and admitted it was the only time in her life that she had been starstruck enough to run up to someone in the street and say hello, but the moment passed.

Like their peers, Tappi made it to the UK, in spring 1983. It was Björk's first time in a big city; the band stayed in West London with a psychotherapist friend of her mother's. 'We were these four punks from Iceland, and I think after four days, we did her head in,' Björk told *Sky*. 'I walked out of the house, and was walking and walking, trying to walk out of the city because you can do that in Iceland. I ended up finding some dreadful cemetery, very depressing. I kept washing, like, three times a day, because I could feel the dirt on my skin. It was touching bricks and it felt like it was all grease. I got so claustrophobic, and got obsessed with oxygen, I couldn't breath. I was trying to touch the buildings, and scrape off the grease, and try and get in touch with things. It sounds really funny now but believe me, it wasn't funny at the time: I completely couldn't handle it. This whole city felt so grey with nothing interesting. We went out to the studio to record every day and I ended up crying myself to sleep every night for two weeks.'

Back in her own backyard, Björk was being more industrious. One show ended with the band not getting paid, so she sued those responsible, and won. It was more a principle thing – 'I wanted my musicians to get paid,' she claimed. The hardline approach extended to the predicament of the pop-star personality; when people would ask Tappi for autographs, the band would tell them to fuck off, and infer that they should get a life.

Tappi didn't need to maintain this stand-offishness because at their most popular, Eythor decided to finish the band. 'I wanted to study the cello. I was fed up with the hassle of working with wires and other peoples' compromises. The life-expectancy of a pop group, or of anything interesting, is five years. But when you're young and can think about what you can do, it's more fun to split. To quote a furure Björk collaborator Tricky, "every negative has a positive".'

Not that Björk minded. 'I was just about to get bored with my band because I had already tried everything I could do,' she explained, and was able to view the split positively by seizing the opportunity to adopt new alliances and musical languages. In fact, she had already started. For money, and probably the hell of it, she played keyboards and sang with bar-room covers band Cactus, enduring two summer seasons entertaining Iceland's drinking communities in the south. For more musical satisfaction, she had sung with free-form rock-jazz duo Stigrim in an attempt to get into the *Guinness Book Of Records* for the longest continuous live performance (nearly 100 bands took part, over several weeks, each playing up to twelve hours), and performed backing vocal and drumming duties for the equally progressive Rokka Rokka Drum.

The latter was an occasional excuse for various Reykjavík band alumni to play shows in the capital's bustling café and art gallery scene. Alternating on guitar and bass were the boisterous Einar Melax and the quieter, unassuming Thór Eldon – both were members of Fan Houtens Koko (a Dutch brand of cocoa, of all things to name your band after), an Icelandic version of electronic pop deviants like Cabaret Voltaire and D.A.F. Eldon had embraced music ever since 1981 when he decided to buy a guitar instead of skis ('and it's been downhill from there') but he was already a published poet, and a founder member of Medusa, Iceland's first surrealist poet collective, which represented the literary version of punk's counter-cultural stance. 'The whole punk scene was always poets,' Björk revealed in the *Post* book. 'Between the bands, they would stand there and scream. It wasn't delicate.'

By the time Rokka Rokka Drum was going, Thór had become Björk's first true love. The pair met at a birthday party in late 1982; Björk noticed that he had a white shirt on, with a piece of another shirt sewn on to it in green thread. 'I fell hopelessly, hilariously in love at sixteen,' she told *The Face*. 'Literally, I kept asking my friends, "What is it? What is it?" because it had never happened before.' She'd watched her mother drift in and out of relationships, and then seen her friends, 'forget all their plans and sort of drift off into a black hole because of it,' so there was good reason to be wary. 'So when it got me,' she said, 'there was no mercy. I moved into his house the same evening.' Well, in a manner of speaking. As Hildur confirms, Björk split her time between home and Thór's apartment, which he shared with his sister, but she never officially moved in.

Björk was also entranced by Fan Houtens Koko/Rokka Rokka Drum's vocalist, Sigurjón B. Sigurdsson, better known as Sjón. He was also the unofficial head of Medusa, and soon to become one of Björk's closest friends and influences. In the *Post* book, which he edited, Sjón recollected Björk at Mensa, a popular Reykjavíc café hangout. In an earlier interview, he claimed that they first encountered each other when Sjón arrived at her Reykjavíc flat to meet his friend. 'She sat me down for tea, and a few minutes later, my friend came out of her bedroom, and it was a little embarassing because he was all covered in blue leopard spots. What happened was she had woken up before him and had just a little fun with him while he was sleeping, decorating him this way.' The friend was obviously Thór.

On first sight, Sjón thought Björk was incredibly small. In *Post*, he said, 'I thought, "Oh my God, Thór, you've picked a baby!" Even though there was only three years' difference in our ages, I thought that Björk was much younger.' The pair were drawn together by their diametrically opposing viewpoints on the nature of art: Sjón was the intellectual, siding with thinkers like André Breton, and Björk the 'instinctivist' believing more in her heart and artists like Miró and Frida Kahlo. 'When I got really drunk, say four in the morning, I'd go round to see Sjón and he'd say, "Not that girl again," and I'd start saying, "Yes, but you can't do art with the head, art isn't concepts and ideas, it has to be impulses."'

The Forum for discussion, the inspired opinions, the madcap both-ends-burning personalities . . . Björk felt totally at home among the Medusa mob, who were free-thinking adults rather than the typical teenagers of the past, who reflected her passions more than anyone else she had previously known or worked with.

'For me,' she said, 'what he [Sjón] was screaming on stage had much more to do with what I later started to do with music. Just the philosophy and energy and complete lust to have freedom. To sacrifice anything for freedom.'

Nothing supported Björk's ideal for living more than the experience of reading French surrealist George Bataille's classic erotic 1917 novel *Story Of The Eye*. Björk had been attending Menntaskólinn í Hamrahlíd, a pre-university college in Reykjavíc renowned for its artistic activities (Einar Örn and Bragi Ólafsson attended too, while Thór and Sjón studied at a similar institution) but when Hildur rented a friend's house in Selfoss (an hour east of Reykjavíc) for a year in September 1984, Thór and Björk moved with her, and studied at a local college. During the Easter break, Björk worked at a fish factory, from seven in the morning till seven at night, cutting fish and pulling out worms with tweezers. Feeling isolated from the rest of the staff who were more than likely to remain there for the rest of their lives, she was lonely – 'all hairy and wet on the inside, not saying anything, double double shy,' as she put it, when Thór gave her Bataille's book to read. 'Everyone's got a book that changed their life,' she said. 'It was one of those books that proved to me I was not insane.'

It seems typical for Björk that a book of surrealist vision, anarchic intent and sexual excess should prove to have a calming effect on her. The story is simple: a teenage boy and girl discover a mutually intense sexual relationship, and go to numerous extremes to satisfy and extend that tension, a pursuit involving eggs, a bull's testicle, a girl in a wardrobe, suicide and ultimately murder. Or as Björk put it to *Dazed & Confused*, 'It's basically a couple that go on a mission against morality and against perceived ways of behaviour and basically take it to the extreme and show that if you want to do it, you should. Well, that's implying it a bit. I mean, you've only got one life and if you don't do today what you want to do, you've lost the battle. I suppose it's a little book that teaches you how to grow up but keep that childlike approach.'

Story Of The Eye, she argued, was not to be taken literally, but represented the mind's free-thinking capacity. 'With that sort of freedom, you can play games with your mind and feel quite healthy about it. It was very good for a seventeen-year-old to read that book.'

A seventeen-year-old, who, ten years earlier, had wantonly desired to eat bananas for three days, or wear a duvet to school. 'If you feel like a train is running through your head, it is,' she argued. 'And if you feel like putting eggs inside your bottom, you should. There's so much freedom in the world, that you can pick anything you want and put it in your butt.'

How true. Not that Björk was driven this far in order to make her point – she settled at publishing a little book through Medusa, with handpainted pictures: 'At the time, I thought it was rubbish but I realized later that it was actually, ahem, about my life.' Constraint, however, was always going to be an issue, an antidote to the main purpose of being alive. The struggle for freedom was often born out of entrapment; before moving to Selfoss, she sought financial security by working at Iceland's Coca-Cola bottling plant, checking for cleanliness. The job bored her to bits, and she would fall asleep during working hours, but she knew it was a temporary concession. In 1992, The Sugarcubes were invited to a Coca-Cola party, where she met contemporaries of hers still stuck at the plant. 'They were still saying, "I'll be out of here by September,"' she recalled, clearly haunted.

By working and saving, Björk was able to move out of her mother's house for the summer. She found a flat with two girlfriends, one a local poet, the other a German friend. 'My biggest virtue, and my biggest fault was that I feel that I'm always missing something,' she claimed. 'Basically, what it comes down to is life's too good. It's an optimistic complaint.' Typically, there was an almost religious drive to her mission. 'We do have certain duties to experience,' she told *Details.* 'We can't just be born with all these presents around us like the sun in the sky and earth underneath. If we don't do anything and just sit back, well, then we deserve to be bored.'

In a 1987 interview, Björk claimed to have been so independent that she left home when she was fourteen, 'because I got the feeling that time was running out, that there were all these things happening out there, and you're missing them. You want to rent a flat and cook really bad meals. I had to come home a year later when I was broke.' But Hildur, who should know, disputes that version, and says that when Björk did find a flat, she returned home after three months in order to attend college. A case of Björk embellishing the truth again.

Either way, Björk has a low boredom threshold, and was never going to settle for any complacent status quo. She had plans to be an astronomer, and even thought of attending farm school, 'but she was always too busy with music,' Hildur confirmed. When she embarked on a new band in 1983, one which was to venture much further afield, in mind, body and spirit, the status quo would never get to go home again. The head and heart were going to sea in a beautiful pea-green boat . . .

The Sorcerer's Apprentices

'There's definitely a stage you go through where you say "Fuck The System" nine hundred times but then you realize that there are things which can be more effective. Like saying, "Fuck Logic," for example.'

The Icelandic band scene needed orchestrators as much as it needed bands, and Asmundur 'Asi' Jonsson was arguably the one man to fuel the musical eruption. Besides co-founding Gramme with Einar Örn, Asi had DJed on Icelandic state radio, helping promote the Icelandic new wave. When his stint came to an end, he wanted to exit with a celebration, and so invited those who he considered the scene's cutting-edge components to play live on his last show – Einar Örn and keyboardist Einar Melax from Purrkur Pillnikk, guitarist Gulli Óttarson, drummer Sigtryggur 'Siggi' Baldursson and bassist Birgir Morgensen from Peyr and Björk.

According to Asi Jonsson, Purrkur Pillnikk and Peyr had both burnt out after an intense period of activity, but their members were hungry to do things. As for Björk, 'she had tired of performing with Tappi because it didn't fulfil her musical interests.'

After two weeks of writing and rehearsals, the collaborators played the radio session, under the name Kukl – meaning 'sorcery' in Medieval Icelandic, or 'practioner of witchcraft'. They were so fired up by the experience that they decided to make the group permanent. Both Hildur and Gudmundur were disappointed that Tappi had come to an end but Asi Jonsson knew it was the best thing for Björk: her personality, voice, performance and urgent need to find new musical directions had always made her greater than the music around her, but she was finally first among equals.

Equals they were, but Kukl's driving musical force proved to be Gulli Óttarsson, who played under the pseudonym 'Godchrist': 'Gul' meant 'God' in Icelandic but Bragi Ólafsson pointed out that he, 'had grand ideas about himself and what he was doing. He was a very nice person but a mad cat who looked at himself as a bit of a god.'

And Godchrist saw Björk the angel, and saw that she was good . . . 'When I first saw her play in Exodus,' Gulli Óttarsson recalls, 'I fell totally in love with her musically. She could turn any accompaniment into music just by laying her voice over it. When she opens her mouth, the music comes to life. We (Peyr) had Exodus support us, and tried to drag her to all our concerts, so it was very logical to have her in Kukl. The band was instant nirvana, and working with Björk was constant goose-bumps, just totally on fire. She interpreted my dreams into lyrics.'

Siggi too 'got the goose-bumps' when he met Björk. 'She always looked much younger than she is – she has this time machine built in somewhere! But what an amazing performer. The first time I saw her, I thought, "shit, I have to play with her someday"'.

Kukl had a similarly gothic (in the true sense of the world) vibrancy and jarring, metallic resonances as Siouxsie & The Banshees' debut album *The Scream*, but its influences were otherwise unrecognizable. Asked to describe their sound, Björk came up with, 'Hardcore existential punk jazz . . . energy music.'

One of Kukl's closest friends and influences was Hilmar Örn Hilmarsson, who was president of Iceland's Alester Crowley Society – Crowley being a renowned British occultist. Hilmarsson had been a major influence on Peyr too, but Gulli Ótarsson was more of a dabbler than active practitioner, though his interests give some clue as to Kukl's dark energy. The rest of the band weren't such believers; Björk, for example, was more fascinated with the pagan aspects of Icelandic culture. Einar Örn claims he was more interested in the physics of sound frequencies that boarder on occult practice than the properties of white magic – that was Hilmarsson's area.

The group's own view of their aims was set out in a booklet included in their first album: 'They depict The Marriage Of Heaven and Hell: The Union

Of Opposites, Cold Claustrophobic Winters with the Agoric Midsummer Sun of the Summer Months. Snow fused with Vulcanic Activity: A Cold and Calm Outside covering Catastrophic Aliveness that may tear the ground from under your feet.' Anything you guys say . . .

Listening to the two Kukl albums today, that intensity is still very much present, driven by their collective volcanic youth, the resentment and anger they felt towards Icelandic society, the drive to create something lasting out of it all. 'They were rebelling against everything that was happening in Icelandic music,' ventures Bragi Ólaffson. 'They were very different to everyone else, and they were a good band, but they were only young, most of them about twenty, and when you're twenty, you want to look wiser than you are.'

In Árni Matthíasson's mind, 'Kukl were so committed, so serious, it was like a matter of life and death, so it was hard for an outsider to get involved. Björk, as ever, was introspective, very much looking inward when she was performing, and finding things to shout out about, and not trying to project as a pop star would, or to perform for the audience. She would sing with her back to the audience a lot of the time.'

Jakob Magnússon thought them, 'a dangerous looking bunch.' He singles out Gulli, 'a manic guitarist, a genius, who, when he started playing, would go into a trance, into another world. He was just mesmeric to watch.' To Gulli's occult interests, add Björk's ice-and-fire vocals, like a siren with a grudge, Einar's pranksterish prowling and vocal growling and the music's ominous, dark-carnival tension. For Asi Jonsson, 'Kukl didn't lead the scene in Iceland: they were more spending time in their own isolated corner, but musically, they have always been *the* most important Icelandic band for me.'

Derek Birkett, who became The Sugarcubes' and Björk's record label manager and subsequently her manager, was then a member of anarcho-punk activists Flux Of Pink Indians. All three bands toured together in the UK; he deemed Kukl, 'brilliant. The chemistry between Einar and Björk was incredible – for a long time, I thought they were lovers, it was that powerful. The rhythm section were incredibly groundbreaking too, as only groups like Pere Ubu and The Fall were playing those rhythms and structures.'

Kukl was where Björk got the chance to express herself as we know her today – gutteral screams, feral growls, siren-sweet enchantment. 'In Tappi Tíkarrass, Björk might have been serious but she looked like she was having fun, fooling around,' her father notes. 'With Kukl, you realized that she was going to go her own way, and go all the way, and that nothing would stop her. People in Iceland also started to realize that she was going far, as they started going abroad more. There was something big going on here.'

Through their association with Crass, Kukl had secured UK/European releases for their two albums on Crass's eponymous record label. Both albums were recorded at Southern Studios in London, which Crass co-owned: first was *The Eye* (in tribute to surrealist master Bataille) in January

1984 and *Holidays In Europe (The Naughty Naught)* later that year, although it took a year between recording and being released in 1985. By all accounts, the band never captured their devastating live performances on vinyl, and the production on both reflects the limited budgets and time, but they are extraordinary records, invested with a raw, gothically dark, unnerving atmosphere, with buried melodies creeping up through the fog. The hairs on the back of your neck will never be the same . . .

The lyrics helped to portray a world of disturbance and primal fear. Kukl were unlikely to translate David Coverdale lyrics for the hell of it; instead, they were as political as Icelandic punk was to get, not by lamenting social policies but by, in part, stressing how Iceland's ancient, pagan religions had been perverted into Christian forms of authoritarian control (although Björk, like most Icelanders, had had a confirmation service at fourteen, not for religious reasons but so she could hold a party and receive presents). This intent wasn't exactly crystal-clear to outsiders, with a collective, concerted surrealist bent too ingrained to submit to rhetoric, aside from some prose on the sleeve of *The Eye* under the heading 'Let us get rid of the bomb.' Take '*I know the power/pointing up/raised fist/exploding penis*' on 'The Spire', or '*dismembered/hugging shadows . . . play with me . . . enjoy and caress*' on 'Dismembered'. '*On the other side of a big river/lies her own body . . . Anna is not here . . . sinking deeper*' on 'Anna', was just plain intense.

'We did not talk much about what Björk and I were doing,' Einar recalls. 'When we started working together, we were still feeling each other out, not consciously walking towards the same goal, as we did not know what each other's capacity was to contribute. Which was the beauty of it, as we could be amazed by the discovery of what we were doing. By understanding it, we felt we would destroy it. So we would never discuss what we were writing – things just happened, and we'd visualize it, give it a picture and then fill it up. That might feel unreal to people who are not used to pop music with vague ideas, but something that is left to the mercy of the listener to decide what the song is about, it's the opposite of indoctrination.'

Years later, Björk and Einar denied the 'surrealist' tag – for what good are labels? 'We might not be clear in our lyrics,' Einar argued, 'because we don't sing socio-political songs. So sometimes it looks like we're being surrealistic, but we look at ourselves as being over-realistic in our lyrics.'

'To me, it's not even that,' Björk shrugged. 'We're just realists, that's all. Surrealism is simply about doing exactly what you want to do, and don't compare yourself with what has been done before. If you want a lobster on a telephone, you don't bother, you just do it. People think surrealism is just being weird, because you can wake up in the morning and you can drink a cup of tea and have toast with butter and that might be very surrealist, because you're doing exactly what you want to do. That's it – do what thou wilt. Sorry, I sound like Aleister Crowley. But that's all.'

For Björk, Kukl was an intensely political act because standing up for individuality, against conformity, was the most political act you could make.

'I think I can do much more in changing the world, saving the planet and all that shit, by just not using much the same usual jargon about saving the world', she claimed. 'Not using very much paper and throwing it away, all that stuff . . . it should be a very personal thing. The minute I stand back and tell somebody else what to do, that's not individualism, that's something else. If you would say this planet is not being cared for, then you can say that people are not taking care of individuality. They're driving over things and fucking things up. It's exactly the same thing, standing up and telling people what to do. Even things like "stop cutting the rainforest".'

Another piece of prose on the album was titled, 'Open the window and let the spirit fly free'. *'Our task is reality. Our aim is reality. From reality we draw our breath. From our wishes we get our will. We need all our wishes to become true. So they will become true we need to act. We need to eliminate those who try their best to stop our wishes becoming true. Those who try to close the window into our faces. Open the window and let our souls fly free.'* To its members, Kukl was a form of musical terrorism, created to overcome apathy and constraint, to embrace the unknown, to take chances.

Adopting punk's independent/do-it-yourself ethic – a whole political manifesto in itself – Kukl would design their own sleeves, posters too, which they'd stick up around town, hitchhiking around if necessary, and distribute their own records as well as produce them, on their own label. 'We were like, "Fuck the system"', Björk explained. 'And it's the same today. I still want to be responsible for everything and know it's mine and that it's on my own terms and done in a human way and that it's not full of things I don't know about and that people get treated with respect.'

Strange as it may seem, Kukl's anti-establishment anarchy wasn't intended to pamper mainstream Iceland's affections. Lack of respect was a two-way deal; although they had some recognition in the media, it was otherwise a blanket denial of their attitude and uncategorizable noise. 'We'd go on television and the nation would hate us,' Björk said in *Post*. 'But we just had to do it. It was necessity. Otherwise we would die! Obviously I'm exaggerating but that's the atmosphere I was brought up in. You have to push it to the limit. It's an urge.'

It was a fair deal: Kukl didn't like the concept of success, and success didn't like Kukl. 'We were regarded in Iceland as a mindless noise but the most interesting band and the spearhead of progressive,' says Einar. 'They recognized us as brave but they didn't like the music. Nobody bought the records.'

The band naturally sought more empathic audiences abroad, and they would record a lot in English to help communicate. A prime objective, as Gulli saw it, 'was to break frontiers and put Icelandic music on the map,' and to this end, Kukl played innumerable times in Europe (including six shows in Berlin) and the UK. They would play dates with The Fall and Crass or go it alone. Together with Flux, Chumbawumba and D&V, Kukl joined a benefit tour in support of the British Miners' strike of 1984.

'It wasn't like we shared the same political opinions as Crass, but they saw us play and offered us a deal,' Björk recalled. 'It was more like we had our own political statements which they respected. We stood outside the system, but the Icelandic system, not the English one, so I couldn't relate to Margaret Thatcher. We hadn't been suppressed so much by the system as the English have; it was very hard for Icelandic people who were still a bit in the Middle Ages then. I was totally fascinated by Crass's vision but with all respect to them, they were too puritanical for my taste. It starts off really beautiful and positive but ends up sitting in the corner, going like, "I don't want to partake of anything because it's all polluted". It's not such a healthy attitude to life.'

The tour apparently had a very healthy, positive atmosphere; the bands would play, camp out in someone's garden, and then move on to the next show, bonding all the while. 'Being a benefit, Kukl paid for everything themselves,' says Flux member Tim Kelly. 'As I remember, they had a much nicer van than we did, and better gear too!'

On the tour, Kelly's memory of Björk, 'was that she was Miss Average. Which sounds dreadful, but she just looked ordinary, though cute as well, and small, but then she'd go on stage and belt it out. It was Gulli who was on the trip of acting weird, thinking it was cool. He was the type of person that impresses you as a teenager, but when you're twenty-one, no way. Einar Melax was seriously into his alcohol, a wild guy, but he really was like that.'

These were dazed, impoverished days and nights. (They'd always drive the transit van themselves, making mammoth journeys across the mainland, eating sugarcubes at motorway service stations for energy when the food money ran out, even sneaking out and siphoning petrol from other cars in order to reach the next gig. One show in Norway was only reached after three days' driving from Hamburg; Björk was the navigator and so couldn't sleep. They arrived and were told they would get pizzas after playing the gig, 'on I don't know what energy,' she laughed. 'And afterwards they'd kind of forgotten about the pizzas so we didn't get any!' *Holidays In Europe* indeed.

The album title had an undertow of truth as well as irony. Asi Jonsson, working just as hard behind the scenes, twice went on tour with Kukl, where he noticed a serious attitude but room to have fun. The availability of cheap, often free, alcohol ensured that was possible. That said, read-the-riot-act celebrations were not always condusive to maintaining order, and tensions rose and fell accordingly.

Asi Jonsson noticed that Björk only rarely participated in that side of tour life. 'She would often spend time with people she knew in the places they played. You could say she was more serious about things than the others. When it came to recordings, she stood out front and really took care of her parts, and didn't stop until she was pleased.'

A year into Kukl's lifetime, she decided to take singing lessons. But a visit to a famous European teacher proved disastrous, and she never tried again. 'I was very shy, and it had taken me a long time to dare to ask her. And she said, sort of arrogantly, "You can't even speak. You talk like a chicken. How can you expect you can sing?" And then she spent the whole winter teaching me how to talk, and I was waiting for her to ask me to sing, but she never did.'

Consistent drinking would have impaired the Björk tonsils; cigarettes were avoided for the same reason. Neither was she ever sold on the myriad influences of drugs, though she confessed to taking acid once, when she was twenty. The incident reportedly involved the wearing of a carpet, an echo of her duvet-donning as a child, but she ultimately disowned the experience, 'because it isolates you and I hate things which do that to you. I prefer things which make you communicate. I think I was born a bit on drugs, really . . .'

Fresh air was her drug of choice: in *Arena* magazine, she talked of her fear of loss of oxygen, recalling a day when, at the age of five, she was accidentally locked inside an accordion box, an incident that developed into a phobia of sorts (her brother Arnar would tease her by flicking a scarf over her face, 'which would freak me out'). She preferred the oxygen-driven instruments too, like the flute, other brass instruments and pipe organs. 'People who are brought up in cities come to Iceland and get dizzy,' she said. 'They are ODing on oxygen. I am so obsessed with it that I get a deeper kick out of singing than other people; it is like a celebration of oxygen.'

Björk would always make the most of her space. She would still go walkabout, hitchhiking into the Icelandic and Scandinavian wilderness, usually alone, with tent and sleeping bag, where she could sing with unfettered glee and celebrate her independence. 'It was fantastic, waking up and coming out of the tent into an unspoilt landscape, singing and shouting and whatever you want. Freedom, total freedom. I enjoyed myself, I took care of myself: it seemed perfect.'

Árni Benediktsson, Einar Örn's brother, remembers Björk visiting him when he was working as a sheep farmer in North-east Iceland. 'She was just visiting farms, just helping out, bringing the hay in, that kind of thing. Not many twenty-year-old girls would do that. It amazed me that she, such an innocent person . . . no, wipe that out . . . it amazed me how *strong* she was to be travelling around, just looking at life. That was my first impression of her, and it still stays very strong in my mind.'

When she was seventeen, Björk decided to have a tattoo on her left arm. She chose a 1,000-year-old rune compass, 'so that I always know where I'm going. It means I will never got lost in fog, and I never have. Me and my friend went to the only tattoo parlour in Iceland and we both had the same thing done. It was a bit of a ritual experience.' She later had a second tattoo, 'a tiny spidery design behind the ear which is a symbol I made for Kukl.'

The compass wasn't infallible; Asi Jonsson remembers how Björk got lost in East Berlin, on one of her walkabouts, and then took the wrong train. 'She wasn't always thinking about what was happening,' Asi says. 'She can forget about her surroundings and go her own way.'

'In her own world,' was a favourite description applied to Björk by numerous compadres, but band life, communal experience and the process of wisdom slowly chipped away at her introversion. 'It only dawned on me that you need to deal with other people when I was about eighteen,' she claimed. 'I suddenly thought, "Fuckin' 'ell, this is too easy: the real challenge of life is learning how to communicate with your fellow human beings." And now . . . now I would describe the relationship I have with my friends as: they save my life every day . . . as I do theirs.'

After Kukl's first European trip, Björk was faced with a decision that would threaten her independence, but offer her permanent community. After returning from Seifoss, Björk and Thór had split up but Hildur confirms that the separation only lasted a month, and then it was only a matter of months more before Björk discovered that she was pregnant. Typically, the novelty and surprise were an instant thrill – 'I was just so happy – I was hilarious when the doctor told me,' she recalled. 'I ran out into the fields like Julie Andrews or something.' When she'd calmed down, doubts crept in, and she even went so far as to schedule an abortion, but either she decided that Icelandic women were duty-bound to conceive or that this was an experience not be missed, and she didn't bother to show up on the day. 'I thought about it but with things like that, you don't use logic, you follow your intuition,' was her conclusion.

Not that a little hitch like a pregnancy was going to stop her contribution to Kukl: 'She always had a theory, that children shouldn't change anything,' says Siggi. The travels continued, as did the confrontational nature of their performances. In Hamburg, with Björk seven months pregnant, a male member of the audience walked to the stage front and told the band to fuck off, to which Einar responded by beating him up right at the start of the set, and then singing the same three words for the rest of it.

In Berlin, Einar himself took the brunt of the pain. 'I nearly killed myself live on stage there. I put a mike cord around my neck and tied it up to a bar and started swinging and then I managed to loosen it and almost fainted. I was lying onstage unconscious, and when I woke up, I discovered the bassist playing, standing on my stomach. People thought I was pretending playing dead.'

The tensions even caused eruptions between friends. In Montpéllier, Björk remembered, 'a huge argument with Einar. He said music was a bogus reason to communicate with the world. I said music was the most precious, sincere thing in the world.'

With Margaret Thatcher in her prime, the Falklands war won and nuclear policies in place, there were plenty of causes for activists like Crass, who found themselves selling tens of thousands of records. By comparison, a bunch of foreboding and compelling Icelandic jazz-punk drama-warriors were doomed to make tiny frictions, although mainland Europe was more in tune with the band than the UK. Back in Iceland, Kukl were busy making enemies, primarily the Icelandic media, who would happily bait them. Even though Björk was working in a nursery for two-year-olds (the same nursery she had attended as a baby), when she appeared on stage with her hand bandaged after a minor accident, the rumour was that she was hiding a drug addiction.

A more serious affront was created when Kukl appeared on TV. Feeling ripe with health, a shaven-eyebrowed, heavily pregnant Björk wore a dirty, torn maternity dress, exposing her healthy rotundness. 'Apparently the combination was too much for some viewers, who called the TV station to complain,' she recalled. 'One woman had a heart attack while she was watching, and sued me.' The basic premise of her case was, that it was ugly to be pregnant. 'The woman didn't die . . . She was like seventy-nine. I shouldn't really say this, but if she was ashamed, she's got problems.'

Björk's scorn for the Icelandic mainstream was quickly turning her into a cause célèbre. At an outdoor festival, she took the *Story Of The Eye*'s aesthetic of free expression to literal conclusions. As Gulli Óttarsson recalls, 'There was a crowd of drunks, calling out for her to play a new pop song, or a greatest hit, or a dance song. She was very proud just to play her own music, so to make her statement, she jumped off stage, went to the centre of the dancefloor, and went to the toilet on the spot.' We're not even talking 'number ones' here. 'It demonstrates that she speaks out very frankly.'

As Björk once said, going to the toilet was as natural to her as singing. Not that anyone expected her to demonstrate a normally private function so publicly.

Like a volcano, such a continual level of pressure finally has to give. The catalyst appeared to be Gulli Óttarsson's drinking, which, in the Icelandic way, was 'all the way', but violent with it, while Einar Melax was another dedicated soak. The explosion took place the day that Kukl were to support Einsturzende Neubaten in Iceland. Einar was then living in London, where he was taking a BA (Hons) degree in Media Studies at the Polytechnic of Central London, but as he had done once before, he was going to 'sing' down the telephone. But Gulli never showed up for rehearsals, and when he did turn up, he was blind drunk. Siggi decided that this was the end, and Kukl never played again.

Jakob Magnússon: 'I remember thinking that this band is never going to survive for long. The audience reaction was not that great, and they all seemed fed up and disillusioned when I met them in Europe. They blamed Gulli for being too heavy and serious and out there, the dark element, even though he was the most fantastic element of it.'

Gulli admitted to being under pressure. Aside from starting a family, he'd also started his own electronics and computers business, which quickly took off. 'Kukl was an unprofitable concession, and it has got very difficult for me to live that life, being abroad for months. So we finished.'

'We split, just like that,' Björk recalled. 'Like an explosion, chaos.'

Einar: 'It became too heavy, too serious. We couldn't compose songs.'

Björk: 'You couldn't breathe in such an atmosphere. It was like fucking therapy. Became ridiculous after a while. But I was crying for days. Much more upset than I've been over any boyfriend.'

Reykajvík was far too small for Kukl's disbanding members to avoid each other, but there was no resentment between them to begin with, just an acknowledgement that they had gone all the way, and that was enough. Though Gulli had a personality best appreciated from a distance, Björk carried on recording with him. 'In Kukl, she enjoyed the experimental, shrieking stream of consciousness stuff that Gulli is very good at,' says Árni Matthíasson. 'He had a lot of musical talent.'

Gulli and Björk would both contribute to Megas albums but their own work was given the name The Elgar Sisters, named after the classical British composer. Gulli mostly wrote the music and Björk the vocal melodies and words, which they would test out in small clubs and cafés as a duo, though Thór co-wrote and played with them when they recorded. While Björk worked in Gramme's record shop during the day, the Elgar Sisters recorded eleven songs for an album. But the project was put on hold to await the next major development for Björk. After Kukl's sour majesty, life was about to become very sweet . . .

Today's A Birthday

'Music has got nothing to do with style. It's a question of sincerity.'

Björk and Thór had left Selfoss and returned to Reykjavík, where, on 8 June 1986, Björk gave birth to Sindri (the name was that of the dwarf blacksmith in Norse legend who made weapons for the gods, including Thor's hammer, and means 'when two hot irons meet', but also stands for 'sparkle around the sun'). They had managed to buy a tiny apartment, with help from both their fathers, and a government loan, and even got married. Under Icelandic law, from the age of sixteen to twenty-five, 25 per cent of your wages are put aside until you are twenty-five, or if you get married, so you can buy a house. In this case, the marriage was to enable Thór to buy some contact lens (he had published a couple of acclaimed poetry books but this wasn't a house-buying profession). 'It wasn't a big deal,' Bjork told *Details*. 'It's common in Iceland to get married at sixteen, to own a house, have two babies, and a leather sofa when you're twenty. I was considered quite late.'

How ironic that Bjork's domestic scenario was not dissimilar to her parents' hippie-bohemian idyll, with a young baby in tow and an apartment that provided a meeting place for the musicians of the day. The close friendships between the Reykjavík mob soon led to a plan of action, formulated by Thór and Einar, for an organization that would subvert the serious nature of their previous efforts, and simultaneously subvert the attitudes of the Icelandic mainstream, who considered their previous efforts to be in 'bad taste'. What would they call the company? Bad Taste Limited, or, should you wish, *Smekkleysa SM SF.*

Article One of the new organization was the climactic, '*World domination or die,*' but the claim, like the exercise itself, was a goodnatured attempt at making a point. The true *raison d'être* of Bad Taste Limited was based on Picasso's aphorism, 'The worst enemy of creativity is good taste.'

'We added, "saving money," to that,' Einar laughs. 'Actually, we were just trying to alter people's perceptions of who is calling the shots on what is good taste.'

The concept of 'bad taste' fell neatly into the world of confrontational politics – if we can't succeed by being good, then we'll have to be bad. And in a culture where you shouldn't confess to weaknesses, or wash dirty linen in public, then it was easier to be sarcastic or cynical, and deflect sensitivity. As Bjork says, 'That's the reason why we find bad things so funny, because we come from behind, and look at things like the Eurovision Song Contest, and laugh at it.'

After Kukl's claustrophobic exactitude, Bad Taste was a necessary holiday, and its loose gang of members started having frolicsome fun again. 'We were reacting against all this punk dressing down and being socially correct,' Björk stated. 'We wore pink and formed this organization . . . Einar drove a huge, impractical convertible and everyone hated us still. It was a magical time.'

Where there's magic in Iceland, you can be sure realism is jostling in there for attention. A baby is a magical gift; it then needs feeding, its nappy changing, and its restless soul entertaining. Jakob Magnússon remembers bumping into Björk and Sindri, queuing in a shop. 'She had a bottle of shampoo in her hand, and when it was her turn, the man asked her what she wanted and she replied that she wanted to change it. When he asked what sort of shampoo she wanted, she said, "A bottle of milk for my baby". It shows you being a progressive musician in Iceland was tough for survival.'

Tougher still when the Icelandic media remains hostile. Press-fed rumours spread that Björk was neglecting Sindri, that she gave him drugs to stop him crying. But she wasn't the type to let it affect her: years of adverse reactions, she reckoned, had made her immune.

Perhaps if people had seen her first acting role (soon after Sindri was born) in *The Juniper Tree*, which was never given an Icelandic release (it was recently released in America on Rhino Home Video), then judgement would have been more considered. Then again, if they judged

Björk by the part she played, they might have tortured her all the more. In this medieval saga, she plays Margit, who goes on the run with her sister Katla after their mother is burned at the stake for heresy. Katla meets a young widower Johann and casts a romantic spell on him; meanwhile, the dead mother's spirit contacts Margit and gives her a magic amulet that ultimately helps Johann overcome the seductive spell. Definitely a Björkian fable.

Bad Taste Limited's plans – they were almost dreams – were to give free rein to their collective pursuits. They started by forming a publishing company – both Bragi and Thór were able to publish limited edition copies of their poetry – but in their dreams, they saw a poetry book shop, an art gallery, a café, a radio station and a record label. As Kukl were imploding, so Gramme went bankrupt, and without a record label, that cherished independence was out of bounds.

'People that wanted to do something were fed up that nothing was happening in this town because of money,' Björk told the *Scotsman*. 'So we started to get together, to assist each other. If one wanted to put out a book, we would all go over to his place, type it, glue it; and if someone wanted to do a record, everyone would help him. And then on weekends, we'd get really drunk and silly because it was really exciting and going very well.'

While the practicalities of such ambitions were being talked up, the Bad Taste members decided to have some fun by inaugurating an award scheme whereby the company would honour those who it felt were pioneers in bad taste. The first diploma went to the head of the Icelandic TV arts department, 'for his incredible indulgence with public money and his own bad taste,' Einar explained. 'All he did was give jobs to his friends and relatives, and make bad spaghetti viking films. The next man refused to receive the award because he thought he wasn't in bad taste . . . but that's a matter of taste!'

Another art-prank was the creation of a commemorative postcard to send up the forthcoming 'superpower' *detente* between Ronald Reagan and Mikhail Gorbachev – an occasion worth pricking for all its inflated pomposity. Graphic designer and ex Purrkurr Pillnikk member Fridrick Erlingsson painted the card, a tacky watercolour of the two 'generals' superimposed over a map of Iceland and the national flag, with the words, '1986 Peace Meeting Reykjavík Iceland 10 – 12 Oct.' in English and Icelandic.

'We made one exactly like one we would hate to see,' Björk beamed, but it was the postcard that everyone seemed to love. Four other postcards were published but the Bad Taste effort was easily the most popular – 5,000 copies were sold in less than a week. Had Iceland decided that 'bad taste' was good taste, or, full of contempt for the Americans (and possibly the Russians), that the event was already in bad taste? Or was it that people couldn't tell the difference between 'good' and 'bad', which was Bad Taste's point precisely? It didn't matter; they had struck a vein of notoriety, and spread the virus. 'People were looking for a company called Bad Taste and nobody knew who we were,' says Einar. 'It was good PR stuff.'

The money was subsequently used to publish poetry books by Thór, Einar and Bragi, with some left aside to invest in recordings by various members, in order to play at a Bad Taste party – 'But only as a joke,' Björk maintained. After Kukl, 'serious' rock music seemed pointless, and hadn't punk – and Kukl – failed in forcing the majority of Icelandic youth to open the windows, and let their spirits fly free? In the words of Reptile vocalist /violinist Magga Stína, and one of Björk's best friends, 'Everybody wants to change their society but nobody wants to take part in changing it. If you have a government like we have here, it doesn't matter if we're on the left or the right side, they have the same opinions, really.'

Because of that manic Icelandic approach, punk had just been a passing phase anyway. 'Typical of Iceland,' Björk snorted, 'everybody was in a rock band around 1981, and then everybody suddenly became actors, and there were lots of amateur theatres, and then people went off to become poets. There wasn't a café in Iceland that didn't have a poet programme every night. Then everybody went into the media. Before 1987, there was one radio and TV station, then there were four radio and two TV stations.'

All things considered, a 'bad taste' pop group seemed in the best possible bad taste. 'It's so hard to do good,' laughs Dora Wonder, whose Reptile combo became fellow Bad Taste signings. 'It's so seldom that you drop on good things. But bad is so easy, you find so many things that are bad. It's so funny how bad things can be.'

The members of this new venture consisted of Björk, Siggi Baldursson, Einar Örn and Einar Melax from Kukl, with Thór Eldon, Bragi Ólafsson (who was living in Spain, writing poetry when he got the call from Einar Örn to join) and Purrkur Pillnikk's old guitarist Fridrik Erlingson, who had remained good friends with Bragi and Einar Örn. After hundreds of ideas had been jettisoned, they decided on the name Sykurmolar, or The Sugarcubes, which was originally Einar Melax's suggestion. 'He was pretty drunk and said, "Do you always have to have these names?"' Einar Örn recalls. 'Why don't you call yourself The Sugarcubes? It was the silliest name we could think of.'

After rehearsals in July, the first show was played at a small festival in August, though they appeared under the name Pukl. The band drove into the tent in Einar's Cadillac, which was known as The Dragon. What united these people, Björk said, wasn't just a love of music, radicalism, bad taste and the joy of something musically irresponsible, but of good old-fashioned extremity. 'We are extreme people; we love eating chocolate and we love getting drunk,' she enthused. 'We were the kind of people who liked running on roofs and driving cars onstage and doing little scandals to shock the nation.'

It also amused her to think of two poets on guitar and bass, and Einar chanting madly over the top of this pop confection. 'I just sang,' said

Björk, 'and put lyrics on it. I wasn't saying, "Look, there's no way *that* guitar is going to go *there*," though all the other stuff I did *was* like that. Every little detail had to be right.'

Sykurmolar/The Sugarcubes dated their official conception at 2.50 p.m., 8 June 1986, the time that Sindri was börn. The band made its official debut on the first weekend of September, on a bill topped by Studmenn. Due to overwork brought on by continuing success, Jakob Magnússon had hired Einar Örn as a *de facto* manager. 'I remember the newspaper printing a picture of Einar with "punk manages Studmenn", like a news item!' he laughs. 'The fact of the matter is, he's an extremely efficient guy.'

Einar was responsible for promoting the show, held in a 6,000-capacity sports hall, a sizeable event for Reykjavík. Fridrik Erlingsson designed the poster, which Björk plastered all over town while pushing Sindri around in a pram, but the timing of the concert clashed with another musical event, and a worried Einar started advertising on radio. 'He went a little over the top,' Jakob Magnússon recalls. 'It was a good turnout in the end, though not our normal sold-out extravaganza.'

The Sugarcubes were due to appear after Leoncie, who claimed to be an Indian princess with a PhD earned in England but who had married an Icelander and orchestrated a singing-stripping style of act. Her arrogance and ruthlessness were legendary, and the organizers put her on the bill as a joke. Leoncie was having trouble in her rehearsals, and so took her playback cassette home before the show, where she promptly botched up the re-recording. Once on stage, wearing huge gold platform shoes, Leoncie's backing tape began, as usual, with the apparently romping, 'My Icelandic He Man', but when the song was done, it appeared again on the tape, and Leoncie was forced to repeat herself. With numerous acts on the bill, that was her lot, and she came off stage, kicking and screaming, sure she had been sabotaged, the audience none the wiser.

In this congenial atmosphere, The Sugarcubes scrambled on stage. Entrepreneurial as ever, Einar Orn had made a deal with the sugar manufacturer Dansukker, to get free advertising in return for a quantity of sugarcubes, which he and Björk would gleefully throw at/into the audience . According to Jakob Magnússon, 'The band played hard pop music, which didn't seem too different to Kukl, so the crowd didn't respond that favourably, and started throwing the sugarcubes back.' Thus the career of Iceland's most famous international band export began, in a hail of disapproval and sweeteners . . .

Afterwards, when Jakob Magnússon checked the books, the advertising bills and construction costs (a specially designed stage hadn't been accounted for) meant there was no money left for anyone. Einar suggested that, because of his role in over-promoting the show, Sykurmolar wouldn't ask for money, but would accept some free studio time instead, at Studmenn's studio Syrland, situated in a converted boat-building hut. 'I gave them fifty hours of studio time, they got the keys and started doing work,' says Jakob. 'I visited them there, and recall Sindri crawling around on the floor, and the band just jamming, making music in the most charming, relaxed way. And they came up with "Birthday"'.'

'Birthday' ('Ammæli' in Icelandic, this being the child's version of the adult 'Aimæli'), The Sugarcubes' debut single, came about by the band's usual process of starting with bass and drum rhythms, which the guitarists or the vocalists would then add to. 'Everybody contributed to the songs,' says Bragi. In this case, the bassist remembers, the song's haunting atmosphere was the result of shaping the music to echo Björk's delicate, definitively surreal saga of a five-year-old girl.

Together with 'Köttur' ('Kat'), 'Ammæli' was released on seven-inch under the title 'Einn Moli Á Mann' (meaning 'One Cube Per Head'), on 21 November 1986, Björk's twentieth birthday. The band printed up 500 copies, and had no great ambitions for the single beyond its own creation, which was fortunate, because it sold just 299 copies. According to Árni Matthíasson, Icelandic radio had found the track too spaced out and preferred the poppier energy of 'Cat'. 'Everyone hated "Birthday" at first,' Siggi recalled. 'They thought it was the weirdest motherfucker they'd heard.'

It didn't bother the band a bit. Its members intended the single as a side project, a basic diversion. 'We're not paying ourselves in the group,' Einar announced. 'We're professional hobbyists.'

The members were all furiously busy with other ventures and jobs. Einar, fresh from obtaining his degree in Media Studies at the Polytechnic of Central London, was living back in Reykjavík and teaching media communications, with one poetry book, the delicately titled *Shitheap*, to his credit. Thór was working with problem teenagers at a youth club while writing poetry (choose between *Death Poems*, *23 Dogs* and *Drink Some Petrol Darling*). Likewise Bragi, a newspaper paste-up artist by day and writer of *Six Leaf Daisy Murdered By A Cow* by choice. Siggi was a newspaper researcher; Fridrik was a graphic designer and fledgling writer; Björk had Sindri, a part-time job selling books and diversions into experimental and film music. She had also taken another, smaller, acting role, playing a troubled young girl in a TV production of a Matthias Johannesen play. 'She was decent but acting isn't really her forte,' says Árni Matthíasson.

Professional hobbyists they remained until The Sugarcubes released 'Birthday' in the UK, on the new One Little Indian label. Like Kukl, Flux Of Pink Indians had recorded for the Crass label, until Crass helped them set up their own label Spiderleg, releasing albums by Subhumans, Epileptics, D&V and their own records *The Strive To Survive Causing Least Suffering Possible* and *The Fucking Cunts Treat Us Like Pricks*. When Spiderleg fell out with its co-owner John Loder, they needed a new label to release their *Uncarved Block* album, which they set up with help from Midlands-based distributor Nine Mile. Thus One Little Indian was börn, and The Very Things, D&V and The Sugarcubes became Flux's first labelmates.

Derek Birkett had been friends with the Gramme boys after meeting Einar Örn while he was in Purrkur Pillnikk, while Flux and Kukl had built up a camaraderie on the Miners' Strike tour. Birkett had always wanted to work further with both Einar and Björk, so of course One Little Indian wanted to work with The Sugarcubes when Einar phoned up to tell him about the band. Despite the free studio time and Einar selling his car, the band ran out of money, so they released 'Birthday' in Iceland first, before the label went in search of finance. They approached Rough Trade, the UK's largest independent distributors, 'who we told that The Sugarcubes were going to be huge, and we needed finance to facilitate it' says Tim Kelly, 'only to be told by them that we had to be joking, because no Icelandic band had ever made it, and that we should put money towards The Very Things if anyone. There was real prejudice to overcome.'

They found a backer in Brian Bonnar, who headed up the cassette manufacturer Mayking, who gave them money for recording, an office and the chance to make One Little Indian a professional concern, with two staff (one being Tim Kelly). Derek Birkett was working as a tape operator at London studio Berry St, where he was able to procure some dead time for the band. He also roped in Ray Shulman, once of seventies progressives Gentle Giant, and now a highly skilled producer of TV commercials, to co-produce The Sugarcubes' album sessions with him.

After the track was remixed, One Little Indian released 'Birthday' in the UK in September 1987. Tim Kelly remembers that *NME* were as prejudiced against the band as Rough Trade had been – 'the paper felt that Iceland didn't have bands as such' – but a copy eventually found its way to *Melody Maker* staff writer Chris Roberts, who immediately made it Single Of The Week.

'Single Of The Week' status wasn't a guarantee of sales or success but Roberts' enthusiasm was so total, his use of adjectives so wildly intoxicated, that you felt compelled to hear the track. This was many peoples' first exposure to Björk's extraordinary vivid tones and range, with its quixotic array of ethereal dreaminess and impish shrieks. Her child-like demeanour and wiser adult nature were both clearly audible, and the effect was stunning. Allied to an uncanny, elliptical rhythm, the music's aquatic swirl and Einar's off-kilter, druggy trumpet, the band clearly had something much greater than 'bad taste' pop; it was a song that appeared to *reinvent* pop, even by the standards of the UK's post-punk swell. A creative rebirth had followed the sixties-pop-influenced cul-de-sac that formed in the wake of the sensational Smiths, spearheaded by the likes of My Bloody Valentine, AR Kane, Throwing Muses and Young Gods, but even in this company, 'Birthday' was utterly unique. It came from . . . *out there.*

As did the words. Erotic, enticing, disturbing, surreal, and quite brilliant . . . what bewitchment *was* this? From the top, then: *'She lives in this house over there, has her world outside it, grapples the earth with her fingers and her mouth – she's five years old, threads worms on a string, keeps spiders in her pockets, collects fly-wings in a jar, scrubs horse-flies and pinches them on a line. She's got one friend, he lives next door, they listen to the weather, he knows how many freckles he's got, she scratches his beard, she's painting huge books, glues them together, they saw a big raven, it glided down the sky, she touched it. Today's a birthday – they're sucking cigars. He got a chain of flowers, sows a bird in her knickers, they're sucking cigars, lie in the bathtub, chain of flowers.'*

How much of the singer was captured in her words? The child who collects insects and who glues paper together?

The praise from the British media spread. Even the national newspaper, *The Independent*, was driven to praise the track's 'truly unsettling phrases, brittle-boned moans that suggest a psyche on a knife edge.' The Sugarcubes knew little of the accumulating fuss, so when Einar got off the ferry in Reykjavík, he had no idea that the TV cameras present on the jetty were there for him. He was subsequently set upon by a TV crew, and asked what it felt like being number one in the UK? Einar had to explain that Single Of The Week wasn't the same thing as being number one, but in Icelandic terms – typically hypocritical of a small nation – The Sugarcubes were famous abroad and thus worthy of attention.

'Icelandic journalists, they are always very cautious and say that we have artistic merit, so they never say that we are bad,' Einar sneered. 'They say we *are* and nothing else. So how they will treat us now is to say, "Oh we told you so."'

Einar and Björk flew to London to do the first Sugarcubes interviews. It was this writer's fortune to be first in the appointment book; the three of us sat down in the office of the monthly *Underground* magazine, a title devoted to the world's newly flourishing alternative music network. The initial impression of Björk had come from The Sugarcubes' first publicity shoot, on a beach with a fish-eye shot of the singer cradling an ornamental frog she had found there, looking about fourteen years old, with hairslides. In the flesh, she might still have appeared child-like but strong with it. Einar had a similar quality, with malevolently twinkling eyes and a quintessential jester's grin that spelt out as much danger as friendliness. He wore a scorpion-encased bolo tie he had bought that day, and a Batman belt. The beast to Björk's beauty. Yes, they were immediately different. Fascinating. You couldn't help be as mesmerized as you had been by "Birthday".

The duo were happy to talk about Iceland, then admitted that they had agreed between themselves *not* to talk about the country because it would be too predictable. They talked about the Icelandic mentality, about Kukl, about how their name had no drug connotations (in the sixties, acid was often adminstered in sugarcubes). They reinforced the act of being, 'professional at being amateurs. Our main objective is to entertain ourselves, and play what we want to play, to play pop music and disgust ourselves. We looked at each other and said, "Can we play this – it's such a cliché?" And we said, "Fuck it, because we're The Sugarcubes, we're a pop band, a living cliché."'

Björk: 'I guess it's a lot about being opposite to Kukl. It had finished because it was so serious you don't breathe, so The Sugarcubes is to enjoy ourselves, and do exactly what we want to do. In the bands before, we were becoming quite snobbish because we were worried about being "pure" and "intelligent" and things like that. Now, just have fun. It doesn't matter how stupid we look.'

Einar: 'If you're an independent band in Britain, what do you sound like? Crass or Discharge, who say, "Fuck it". But where are they now? We have a big time mentality on a small time level. We're mainstream – it's Rick Astley, Tiffany and Bros who are offbeat!'

What about the offbeat 'Birthday'? Björk was forthcoming with details. 'It's a story about a love affair between a five-year-old girl, a secret, and a man who lives next door. The song's called "Birthday" because it's his fiftieth birthday, but not many people can figure that out of the lyrics 'cos it's more about the atmosphere around it and how they touch. It's a tasteless pop song – not even that. A pop song – very unusual.'

Einar: 'The story is the reminiscence of an older lady, who remembers when she was a kid, and all the old men aroused her erotically without going in the full sexual intercourse way. It's distorted pictures of memories.'

Björk admitted that the words took time to capture. 'I was always changing my mind about what the lyrics should be about. I had the atmosphere right from the start but not the facts. It finally ended up concentrating on this experience I remembered having as a little girl, among many other girls' experiences. It's like huge men, about fifty or so, affect little girls very erotically but nothing happens . . . nothing is done, just this very strong feeling. I picked on this subject to show that anything can affect you erotically: material, a tree, anything.'

Einar: 'Is that surreal? To me, conventional love songs are a lot weirder.'

Conventional love songs usually spoke of platitudes. 'Surreal' pop songs like 'Birthday', however, spoke of 'reality', as the mind's true experiences cannot truly be explained away in a sentence. Fractured, half-remembered memories were much closer to the truth. Not that Björk or Einar even listened to conventional love songs, except if they were eligible for the Eurovision Song Contest. Björk admitted that she hadn't bought a record for years, until discovering America's decibel-threatening metal extremists Swans. 'I haven't listened to anything else for the last six months,' she said in her imperfect English. 'We don't listen to music much as a group. We're always reading and we talk a lot about books. If one reads it, everyone in the band reads it. We don't treat music as God, like so many people do. As we don't approach it like that, music is not everything in the world, we also listen to people talking, whatever. We approach music in the same way – as a fraction out of life put to music.'

Knowing Björk today, that seemed like a pose. Music, as she had once argued to Einar, was, 'the most precious, sincere thing in the world.' Einar felt differently, however, and he talked of how the praise they'd received for 'Birthday' meant that they now viewed the song as a cliché. It was almost as if Einar saw it as his duty to sabotage the idea of 'pop perfection'. 'I blatantly try to destroy the song by blowing a trumpet so loud that it suffocates the rest of the band and people cannot hear it,' he said, proudly. 'I think it's funny if people start liking the song then one of us destroys the whole mood of it by going wild with a trumpet.'

After all, the point wasn't so much the music, but the fun, escapism, the *crack,* revelling in the ridiculousness of pop music. 'The Sugarcubes are more about just enjoying life, just simple things, you know,' Björk told *Sounds*. 'That's why they think we are sexy, because we sort of allow ourselves to have a cup of tea and just enjoy it. Go to a supermarket and enjoy picking the right stuff, watching TV and getting drunk . . . even though it is completely stupid, it is fun.

'We also want success. I would be lying if I said we didn't. We all understand what money can do for you but we also know what it *can't.* We will probably be getting a lot of "success", and we'll probably be getting some money and we won't refuse that. We just try to enjoy it while it lasts.'

You could say the same for relationships. By the time The Sugarcubes were operational, Björk and Thór had decided to split up. On the outside, Björk the Wild and Thór the Reserved had been an attraction of opposites, with Björk appreciating Thór's intellectual artistry and Thór appreciating her unfettered energy. But their youthful naivety when first meeting, an unexpected baby and a premature marriage, plus – so Árni Matthíasson thought – the struggle to survive with badly paid day jobs, saw them drift apart.

Not only did they remain cordial towards each other, they agreed to work with each other in the same band. Bad Taste was life-and-death material after all, while they would be seeing each other regularly because of Sindri. 'We're still friends,' she told *Details* in 1993. 'In Iceland, you grow up knowing you cannot run away because you're going to meet the people you know every single day of your life. It's considered silly if you couldn't deal with meeting your ex-husband. You would have to move to another country and become a monk. It's all a question of guts.'

It was a matter of months before Björk was dating Óskar Jónasson, a graduate of London's National Film And Television school, and the director of The Sugarcubes' earliest videos. Thór later started dating Magga Örnolfsdó ttir, Reptile's keyboard player, which eased the tension between the new divorcees. Sindri was still a common bond, and they kept the baby around. 'I was really lucky,' Björk later admitted. 'He was able to travel with me until he started school, whereas I had to watch my friends put their children into day care for eight hours a day. The Sugarcubes' working situation was such that I could take him to a rehearsal and if he was crying, we would just stop.'

It turned into a time of fluctuation and change for all. After the band's initial rehearsals and debut show, Einar Melax found that he didn't share the same commitment and left them to it. Then, one show later, Fridrik Erlingsson decided not to pursue the pop career that The Sugarcubes were being offered. 'The idea of touring and adulation didn't appeal to him,' says Árni Matthíasson. 'He wanted to step back from fame.' Despite his graphic design training and musical interests, Erlingsson was more committed to writing, a vocation he was to successfully take to national celebrity levels, penning screenplays and childrens' books. Einar Melax subsequently accepted the band's invitation to rejoin, which meant The Sugarcubes had full-time keyboards (Björk had played them on the forthcoming album), leaving Thór as the sole guitarist.

Melax wasn't back on board in time for The Sugarcubes' debut UK show, so it was a quintet that supported Björk's beloved Swans at London's 3,000-capacity Town & Country Club. During their set, a boy climbed up on stage, not to stagedive, but seemingly just to touch Björk, as if he had seen an angel.

The band subsequently supported The Very Things at the much tinier London Camden Workers' Social Club. *Melody Maker* were fascinated by the two singers, starting with the observation that they were, 'dressed in what appeared to be their grandparents' curtains. The boy, Einar, and the girl, Björk, amiably wrestled for attention in a set rife with intentional disharmony. Einar, skinheaded and badly theatrical, like Steve Harley weaned on The Swans and Nick Cave, grimaced like his brain was being drilled from the inside and looked cutely smug . . . Björk, a beautiful rag doll, lived in the songs, appeared too rapt to entertain ulterior motives, mouthing little oaths and promises to herself off mike, whinnying in silent joy like a frisky Camargue colt.'

The Sugarcubes' unique, challenging perspective was bound to be dissected in full by the UK media, making conclusions that the band would feel were complimentary but also patronizing and plain wrong. At least they could always expect more understanding than from the Icelandic media but they were still amazed to be treated as exotic specimens, like insects in a jar. Even in the eighties, British society, and thus British culture, was obsessed with manners and convention, and viewed those who deviated from the norm with an ironic distance or unfavourable condescension. Was Einar an epileptic because of how he danced? Were they on drugs? Were they just a bit insane? 'I could tell everyone that I have four breasts on my back and everybody would believe me because I'm a weirdo from Iceland,' Björk told *Melody Maker*.

True, the band were exotic, and they recognized the cultural divide. 'We do reflect the way we were brought up and we think, which is different from Continental European people a hell of a lot,' Einar acknowledged. To stir things up, the band would spend portions of interviews spouting off about eating severed sheeps' heads, and scooping the eyes out with a spoon. Next to the typical Icelandic version of Western pop Einar sneered, 'everyone else is just weirdos. Us? We are *enfant terribles*.'

Björk admitted that the band were enjoying living double lives, and that, if she wasn't in The Sugarcubes, 'I would be bored to death.' But even this early, the promotional trappings that went with music-making were beginning to taint their enthusiasm. 'When we come here, we are musicians twenty-four hours a day with a strict programme of recording, interviews, concerts and stuff and we're together all the time,' said Björk, clearly weary. 'When we go back to Iceland, we can behave like normal people.'

Oh, really? It was soon the turn of UK journalists to visit Iceland, for the full Icelandic scene-setting experience, in time for The Sugarcubes' second single 'Cold Sweat'. Liz Naylor, One Little Indian's press officer, was in charge of herding a handful of writers over, and so was able to view Icelandic normality at close quarters. Though first, there was the problem of the *NME* and *Melody Maker* journalists who ended up sharing a fist fight within hours of landing. At least that seemed par for the Icelandic course . . .

'On our first night,' Liz Naylor recalls, 'the band took us all to a wedding reception, where Einar was bouncer for the night and introduced everybody. It was my first encounter with the phenomenal alcoholic intake of Icelandic culture. When I first started working with The Sugarcubes, I was very nervous. I'd heard the debut album and imagined them to be rather precious, but I think everybody just passed out that night. Björk was running around, singing these Abba songs. She wasn't at all pompous about stuff, her attitude was, "just have a fucking laugh, get drunk". She's an idiot like the rest of us, dancing on tables at 7 a.m. There was a picture of her published in *Q* where she's waving her fist towards the camera, and that's much more her than any other picture I've seen. She is very sane actually, very robust, very capable. and very amusing. She's quite a hedonist, not at all waif-like or elfin-like or anything that denotes some kind of small creature. She's just a bit of a boot boy, really.'

Björk put the confusion down to the fact that she refused to surrender her youthfulness. 'I am convinced I am exactly the same age now as I was as a child,' she told *Melody Maker*. 'There must be some kind of art, to add loads and loads of things to yourself and stay the same as the day you were born. The way I look at it, I was born the person I am, and I take all the information and experience I have, translate it, throw it away again and remain the same person. You can add things to yourself and speculate about things and still be the same. If you manage to do that, you always remain at point zero and you can see everything with open eyes. That's probably why people call me innocent.'

Normal/weird, elfin/boot boy, innocent/wise: who cares ultimately what the caricature is, as long as it sells? That was the concern of the major record companies who had contacted Derek Birkett with a view to hearing more songs and snaring these potential stars. Swamped by all the fuss in the UK, finding it hysterical on the one hand and ridiculous on the other, The Sugarcubes insisted that any record company representatives fly out to Iceland, to meet them on home turf. What the band didn't say was that they were inviting all interested parties at the same time, which meant that the A&R representatives only discovered they were not alone when everyone was sat on the Icelandic Air plane. Once they arrived, they all had to attend a meal *en masse* before being treated to a live set sung entirely in Icelandic.

The band could afford to be irreverent when excessive offers (up to £750,000, $1 million) were being made but they were serious about the idea of funding an art gallery and café, and of being funded for their pop-prank programme. If The Sugarcubes really did approach music as a fraction of life, then you could understand why they might adapt to another approach. Getting attention after all those years of being disliked, or worse, ignored, would have flattered even the most modest ego, while the thought of finance for Bad Taste's plans was too good to turn down. Most of all, it was *fun*. 'At first we didn't want to do it but then we thought that if we didn't, we might regret it,' Björk said. 'If you and your five friends had the chance to work together and travel the world, you wouldn't turn it down either, would you?'

The Sugarcubes still had to decide whether to accept major-label funding, and with it, the idea of commercial pressure and compromise, or to refuse the financial carrot and remain with One Little Indian, among friends and freedom. Offers made in lieu of discussing the band's future recordings, Siggi says, were never considered. 'Only we must be in control of our music, no one else, and I'm not even sure we are at times!'

Self-sufficiency was an Icelandic trait, so control over your destiny was ultimately the key; there was little point in realizing Bad Taste's aims at the expense of the band's. Their view of major labels was coloured once and for all by one MD who, at an aftershow party for The Cure, put his arm around Björk and led her outside for a chat – it was evident that she was 'star' quality, and overtures were made to her to go solo, which the band all found offensive. 'The major labels behaved like total idiots,' Einar told Q. 'They forget that The Sugarcubes may be daft but *we're* not idiots. And we're not young – we've survived for eight years in Iceland without a major deal.'

Derek Birkett felt that, even with the backing One Little Indian had had, the label couldn't support a band that threatened to sell as many records as The Sugarcubes. He encouraged them to keep talking, and a deal was in fact drawn up with Warner Records, including complete artistic control. As they had a final meeting, Warner's representative Malcolm Dunbar admitted that, even in the case of total control, there would be some element of compromise. For example, if the band agreed with Warner's choice of single, then the company would market it that much harder, but if they didn't, the label could let it drop.

Derek Birkett: 'The Sugarcubes as a whole basically said that they would be happier selling 100 records that they wanted to sell than one million that Warner's did. The music and friends were more important, so they stayed with One Little Indian, even though the label was more like a hobby then. When we left the meeting, I was devastated and they weren't. Einar bought me a bottle of brandy and Björk bought me a little ceramic model, where the snake pops out of a pot. We all sat in the park, having walked out of half a million quid and they don't give a shit, which was an eye opener. And it's been a bit like that ever since.'

The band did go with Warner's in America, but only because America's size prohibited as good an independent distribution system as Europe, which would mean that The Sugarcubes couldn't even sell the records they wanted to. (They chose Warner's imprint Elektra, 'because Elektra was from Greek mythology,' Einar explained. 'She killed her mother and father because they had, um, adultery going on. So it's nice.') But it was a licensing agreement through One Little Indian, which meant that Electra couldn't act independently of the UK.

The Sugarcubes thus ended the year well set up for the next. 'Birthday' may only have reached sixty-three in the UK national singles chart but it made Single Of The Year in *Melody Maker,* and they got a total of five music press front covers on the back of it. Two weeks before enjoying another snowbound Icelandic Christmas, the band returned to the UK to play a headline show at the Town & Country Club. After the last encore, Einar shouted, 'Thank you for paying your money. We don't need it!'

Life's Both Sweet And Sour

Back in Reykjavík, the media were tussling with the concept of a famous band from Iceland. As Thór observed, 'They were still having traumas over us because they want to ignore The Sugarcubes but because English culture is thrust upon them, they can't, so they pretend to have liked us all along!'

As for Iceland's intellectual mafia, 'They think we're bad, weird people, corrupting their lives,' Björk told *NME.* 'Go to England and stay there,' they think. People have always thought that of us. And now they see us refusing all these record companies' money, they think we are yuppies, like a class of people who have so much money, we don't care.'

The band hardly had sacks of cash, but neither were they liable to starve. Day jobs were surrendered as the lead-up to the new single and debut album got under way. In Iceland, they released 'Luftgitar' ('Air Guitar'), a rock parody with Johnny Triumph, a.k.a Sjón, on lead vocals. 'The theme of the song is really to liberate all the boys in the universe,' Björk explained, to which Siggi added, 'It's about boys not being able to dance.' Meanwhile, in the UK, The Sugarcubes released 'Cold Sweat', housed in the first of their primitively scrawled, childishly sweet, primary coloured sleeves.

The track – originally titled 'Hot Meat' until an (unnamed) vegetarian member reputedly objected – was the result of the band asking Björk, 'Why can't you fucking write a proper pop love song lyric?' she recalled. 'I did my best,' she thought. 'By the way, that's meat as in somebody in love. Why not? It's about somebody who's madly in love with somebody and she's going to get him. That's what these love songs are about, isn't it? . . . the song is very greedy'.

Einar: 'I think we started calling the song 'Cold Sweat' because a cold sweat is something that happens to you, and that was the working title and it got stuck'.

Björk: 'I still think "Hot Meat" is a better name for the song. But I'm totally happy with the "Cold Sweat" tackiness'.

The band were amazed to find Óskar Jonasson's video for 'Cold Sweat' banned by the British censors because of supposedly sexually suggesive shots of Einar's jewellery-encrusted bare stomach (British society once banned the sight of bare ankles) and the closing image of a crucified

Einar eating money. The offending scene was replaced, hysterically, by irrelevant shots of chimpanzees.

'Cold Sweat' was manic and feverish but a more conventional pop-rock surge than 'Birthday', though great enough to be eagerly embraced. Despite its lyrical drama – *'I tear your lungs out this side of the blackest meadows/I will make my winterdwelling and crush my bones'* – the track appealed to daytime radio, although it wasn't until March and the band's third UK single, the gorgeously sultry 'Deus', that The Sugarcubes got a UK Top 40 hit. Björk and Einar co-wrote the lyrics, a gently blasphemous, irreverent view of God. *'He wasn't white and fluffy'*, Einar burbled, *'he just had sideburns and a quiff.'* He also suggested that, *'God is a bathtub'* – a logical explanation, Einar claimed, 'because I can't imagine God without Mary. It must have happened in the bath'.

With each single, sales and press interest escalated, and with it the excitement surrounding Björk. Almost all the front covers that The Sugarcubes had secured singled out Björk, with the rest of them out of focus in the background, a trick which she soon got wise to. Of course, it wasn't her agenda that set the tone but the magazines and newspapers, almost entirely staffed and run by the male of the species. Journalists might have been well aware of the similar siren-sorcery of The Cocteau Twins' helium-toned, bush-babyfaced Liz Fraser (*NME* had even called The Sugarcubes, 'a heavy metal Cocteau Twins') and the Bronte-style, eccentric heroine Kate Bush, but Björk was something else, something more wilfully unpredictable and provocative and, it has to be said, sexual. But writers sadly avoided looking at a bigger picture, and consistently painted caricatures of Björk as an exotic variation on the fragile waif/elfin/pixie/fairy character that lived in Iceland's rockery, albeit with a gale-force voice. Examples: 'A vivacious, elf-child so much given to squealing laughter that her interludes of adult mental clarity come as a shock' (Q) and 'Björk dances with the self-contained indulgence of a child, oblivious to onlookers' (*Time Out*).

'It was how the music press used to write about women', Liz Naylor frowns at the memory. 'The thing was, Björk is an incredibly down-to-earth person. She's had to be to bring up a kid. And have you heard her laugh? It's one of the dirtiest I've ever heard.'

Björk admitted that she may have got used to being treated as 'different' in Iceland but had never before been repeatedly whittled down to a caricature, and given a sex-symbol tag by way of 'Birthday' and her 'cute' persona. 'I don't know why people would see me as a sex symbol', she said alarmedly, which meant she was either being truly naive or purposely obstructive. 'Maybe it's a question of me being easier to merchandise because I'm one instead of six.'

She later told *Sounds*, 'Of course, there are some parts of me I'm quite proud of but sometimes it confuses me because I find it very difficult to see myself from the outside. When I'm onstage, I can't even look into the eyes of the people; the only thing I can relate to is myself. I know it sounds tacky.'

Liz Naylor, however, saw both sides of the Icelandic coin. Her fondest Björkian memory is the night after a Sugarcubes show in Lisbon, Portugal, when she and Björk ended up in a strip club at 5 a.m., 'and her just being an animal, drunk and dancing lasciviously. She's a sex animal and she knows it. We once went to a country club run by two *NME* journalists, where we were two of about six people there, and she danced on her own to country records. What a fucking laugh she was to go out with and get drunk, fall over and be an asshole. She's an incorrigible flirt too, with everybody, on whatever level, which is what people find charming about her, but she also doesn't suffer fools gladly. She'd tell journalists who wanted to always interview her, "Fuck off, talk to some of the others". When *Melody Maker* came to Iceland, the photographer was told there would be no front cover unless he got Björk on her own, and Einar would get insulted, which put immense pressure on her. When you're with your mates, what does that to do you, how do you get around that?'

Björk's answer was to hide her face in photo sessions, and maintain that she could not be photographed on her own (she broke that rule only once). It was a near impossible task but she would attempt the same understandable spoiling tactics on stage. 'In the bands I was in in Iceland, I even tried to look as ugly as possible so that people would listen to the music but not look at me,' she maintained. 'With The Sugarcubes, I was always going to stand at the back of the stage.'

Media evils aside, the freedom that this new life presented The Sugarcubes in general was incontrovertible. When it came to titling their debut album, they could see the poignancy of *Life's Too Good*. The phrase was uttered by an impoverished poet friend in Reykjavík who, on being given a cup of coffee and a cigarette, exclaimed, 'Life's too good!'

'It was a statement that we could all say all the time and laugh about,' Björk told *NME*. 'It's an optimistic complaint. It's like, you go to a restaurant and there are twenty fucking dishes and you want them all and you have to pick one. It's a joke.'

'It's a complaint, because for us life *is* too good, so why waste it on human-made issues?' Einar told *Melody Maker.* 'Why not just solve human-made issues immediately, and enjoy yourself? Sure, it sounds silly, with unemployment, famine, war, disasters, space shuttles . . .'

'I like disasters!' Björk interrupted. 'It puts people in a position that they either have to live it fully or just . . . give up or something. It puts people on a . . . if the cliff is like that? Cliff-edge? I want to eat life. If I could do this, I would do it. I would like to die by being eaten by a tiger or being hit by lava from a volcano. Usually after the most disastrous periods of my life, I find out that I was really experiencing something. So it is not bad really. The point is to live everything, to eat it up.'

Life's Too Good confirmed that The Sugarcubes' music stood apart as strongly as their uplifting attitude. Like Kukl, the usual cross-referencing of influences, the cultural influences that too often stifled Western pop and rock, were noticeably absent; you just couldn't tie them down to any one era, genre or trend. Widescreen twisted goth pop, anyone? Conventional love song imagery or political rhetoric was also noticeable by its absence; this was a world of open-ended, abstract happenstance, glee, unpredictability and playfulness. Both Björk and Einar saw the lyrics as complementing the atmosphere of the songs. Consequently every track came on like some tiny, darkly imaginative screenplay, in the style of 'Birthday'. Some seemed plain obtuse ('surreal', even), like the opening 'Traitor' or 'Sick For Toys', but others fell into place when the band explained.

At least there was a lot more going on to steer any review away from the topic of sex and sensuality. 'Before, when people only knew "Birthday", Björk complained, 'it became very tiring and stupid to pick sex out and isolate that subject. I wasn't denying that Sugarcubes' music can be sexy but it's all other things as well – it's stupid, it's witty, it's lazy, it's active, aggressive. That's what we want it to be so "sexy" is hopefully one of 10,000 things.'

With a broad, expansive production totally at odds with Kukl's buried textures, ten Sugarcubes tracks twisted pop and rock into 10,000 different shapes. Take 'Delicious Demon', 'about economic values, things that have value and things that don't,' said Thór, who stated that some of the words were discovered among Egyptian hieroglyphs. Or the suicide setting of 'F**ing in Rhythm And Sorrow' (*'don't act like there's no tomorrow/life's both sweet and sour'*), or Björk's personal favourite 'Mama' (*'swinging her handbag with her back and forth so joyfully/she's drawing circles with her breasts in her jumper'*).

'Mama' is about being how unfair it is being grown and not being allowed to have a mama,' Björk said. 'We should have the same proportions. If I am a metre sixty, then I should have a mama who's three metres something. So when I need her I can still climb inside her.'

'Motorcrash' developed from an opposing theme of belonging. Björk has an image of, 'a little girl forced to nurse an older woman, which is really wrong. It's a thing she always wanted to do, but now she's being forced into that position. She takes a big woman out of the car and she's all brooding and the girl manages to take her to her room, despite the fact that the woman has a husband and children. She should go to the hospital, and the girl hides her from her parents. They go in a taxi to the woman's home and expect to receive thanks but she doesn't because the husband is a really stupid bastard who doesn't understand emotions and he just says, "Where have you been all this time?"'

A track like 'Blue Eyed Pop' was more specific. 'It's about how it is to go out on a Saturday night in Reykjavík,' said Björk. 'Not so much the sex and alcohol side but more about the fact that when you go out dancing, you are always waiting for something . . . unbelievable to happen to you. Like you're gonna have ecstasy, a star is gonna fall on your head, and you just get an ecstatic, happy orgasm, and you just dance and burst like . . . fireworks all over the place.' Like *Life Is Good*, in fact, and the nature of Björk's voice, which, high up in the sound mix, in super sensarround, was revealed in all its brilliance. Einar's buffoonery took longer to love, but to borrow the title of a Sugarcubes B-side, he was the original 'Organic Prankster' and his presence in song and on stage made a vibrant constrast with Björk's.

With the band's customary disregard for finance, they decided to release *Life's Too Good* in six different-coloured, dayglo sleeves. The reviews were unanimously positive; *Melody Maker* even went so far as to call it, 'one of the best albums I've ever heard.' *Sounds* was especially perceptive, noting an air of innocence, 'but never naivety, as children are often more perceptive than adults.'

The Sugarcubes were more modest. 'There's only one really special thing about this band,' Björk reckoned. 'It is the only one in this universe that contains us . . . the best thing about The Sugarcubes is that there is no meaning to us. There is no answer because there is no question.'

Life's Too Good was the highest UK chart entry that week, coming in at fourteen. Here they were, able to embrace new, expansive experiences, praised for playing silly pop music, and getting paid for it, and being taken seriously. Now this *was* surreal. There was also a point to be made, even if it came about by accident. While Kukl had made a stand, and tried to put Icelandic music on the map, The Sugarcubes had done it without even trying. Moreover, this positivism flew directly in the face of alternative rock's quintessential nature. The Smiths had made the definitive statement in 'complaint rock', which Kurt Cobain and Nirvana were to match (as distinctly American in their language as Morrissey and The Smiths were resolutely English in theirs) but if The Sugarcubes were not to be influential, they were provocatively original, and a vital presence. To those who would listen, they seemed to make a difference.

There was one casualty in the world-domination-or-die mission, when Einar Melax was asked to leave after the second round of UK shows, which culminated in two sold-out gigs in London, at the Astoria and Cambridge Theatres. The cause? Once again, the demon drink. Árni Matthíasson, who watched the first seventeen Sugarcubes shows, saw the situation unfolding before him. 'The punk idealism, that everybody had a right to do his thing, was very important to the members of The Sugarcubes, so it was a very tough decision to fire Einar Melax, but they had to. When they played at the Cambridge Theatre, he was totally out of his head because of drink.'

Having swept across the UK and Europe, it was now time to wake up America. Their first attempt to tour in May 1988 was thwarted by immigration problems. It was rumoured that the, 'God does not exist,' of 'Deus' was the problem but the band had made the simple mistake of applying for visas through the UK rather than Iceland, which was rectified the next time around. The Sugarcubes' US tour subsequently started in New York on 28 July.

Björk later admitted that she had been looking forward to visiting the States. 'But I also dreaded it very much because I understood that, all the time, I would have to be outgoing, and expressive about everything that happened to me and I couldn't really hide that much. That's tough.'

To compensate, there were new, appreciative audiences to seduce (they even reached prime time viewers when appearing on the legendary *Saturday Night Live* show) but more importantly, there was the intense thrill of new shocks and new sights in a new city. Björk's first experience of towering skyscrapers sent her giddy with joy. 'When I saw them, my first thought was, "look at those trolls!"' she screamed. 'Huge, tall trolls, watching me. They're gorgeous!'

Despite the inevitable warnings about a city like New York, Björk felt compelled to go walkabout. 'The minute I got here, I just fell in love with the city. I just love walking around here.' She was seemingly unconscious of any dangers that might be out there. 'Björk is more interested in New York than the city is in her,' said Einar, amused. 'People shy away from her.'

Scott Roger, the band's tour manager for the next four years of their life, confirms that, as soon as The Sugarcubes landed in another city, Björk would disappear. 'You wouldn't see her again until soundcheck, but she'd always find her own way there. Then, straight after, she'd disappear again and turn up five minutes before the show. She was always a bit separate to the rest of the group.'

His first day on the job, the occasion being a secret show at New York's legendary punk/new wave club CBGBs, was a nightmare start. Roger recalls that he had trouble even finding the band. 'Björk was sitting in a bar round the corner, having fun, and she heard me panicking, running

up and down the street. She told me, "Don't worry, it'll all be on time."
We toured everywhere, like Russia and places, and she was never late.'

Coordination and punctuality were necessary evils on tours but the
band drew the line at the record company schmoozing that greeted them.
America's over-attentive, hands-on approach was the diametric opposite
of Iceland's distanced culture, and it drove them mad. 'There were lots
of hassles on the tour,' Einar remembers, 'people trying to see to our
needs, like [puts on whiny voice] "are you OK?" . . . "have a nice day".
We couldn't understand what they were telling us.'

Björk: 'If there is a typical Icelandic characteristic, it is an arrogance. If
they like something, when they've known you for three years and are
very drunk, they'll whisper in your ear, "I like you". It is the opposite of
what people in the States do, which is run at you screaming, "I love you,
I can't believe it, are you really doing your own shopping, ohh, ohhhhh,
I love your music, jeez, I love this bag, what do you wanna do, do you
wanna sell this?" In Iceland, people go, "Huh, who do you think you are?
An artist?" [makes farting noise] I used to think of it as a weakness but
I think it's ten times better than the American way. There you just wanted
to say, "Fuck off".'

Einar: 'We went into hiding for one gig, and from then, it was brilliant.
We don't have a manager to tell us where and when to be, leading the
flock. We just have a tour manager to get us between concerts. People
in America find us strange but they've not tried to control that chaos.

They realize that this is a difficult band to work with but when we talk to other people about what we have seen, we know we are the most amicable people to work with.'

Björk had the best excuse to avoid record company duties, having Sindri along for the ride. He would sleep in the tour bus when she was on stage, after which they would return to the hotel, where he could sleep and Björk chill out and watch TV. The next morning, they would have breakfast before hunting out a laundrette to wash their clothes. 'If you ever go touring and you want some security and not to go crazy,' Björk recommended, 'take a child with you.'

The cinemascope of America gave the Icelandic media licence to print rubbish in the band's eyes. 'It's like we've been lying to them for years and suddenly they've got something which they believe is true, like our so-called success, so now they're lying about us,' Thór sighed. 'We are supposedly doing things that we don't know of.'

Björk: 'They think we ride in limousines and eat caviar and are friends of Joan Collins.' Not so, but luminaries like David Bowie and Iggy Pop would come and see them play, and photos were taken alongside the likes of Sinead O'Connor, so you could see why the Icelandic media might exaggerate a little.

When the band could forget about the negative aspects of public attention, The Sugarcubes had no difficulty in getting on with the task of living the good life. 'It's quite fun leading a double life,' Björk revealed. 'It's quite fun because they're so different. I mean, last week I was baking cakes because my kid was having a birthday party. And now I'm in America. It's really exciting, and I couldn't imagine things any better. Being in The Sugarcubes is like a holiday. It's probably like a job except for the idea that we know we can stop any time, and that's what makes it fun. The minute you get tired of this, you can go back. We've all got different reasons why we are in this band, and we all respect that each member could quit tomorrow. We're not dependent on this. We can always go to Iceland and start to work in a fish factory.'

For now, 'The Icecubes from Sugarland!' – as the band had once been introduced on the American tour – were happy pursuing their world-domination-or-die manifesto, although the touring schedule meant that there was no time to record new material. The decision was taken to re-release 'Birthday' but alongside a re-recording of the original (re-titled 'Christmas') with assistance from brothers Jim and William Reid from The Jesus & Mary Chain (the pair had supported the 'Cubes at the Cambridge Theatre show), who added their customary guitar screech.

A break allowed the band to write new songs, and when they ventured out on their second European and American tours in the autumn, and to Australia for the first time, they were able to road-test them in a way that they couldn't on the first album. With Björk and Einar out front, Sugarcubes gigs were always dynamic, inspired and messy. The duo would use luminous face paint and wrestle like kindergarten kids, ricocheting off each other like gleeful pinball dervishes, whipping out water pistols and 'shooting' the audience. Einar came in for some heavy criticism, for his gooning around and whacked-out declarations, for what writers (and probably portions of the crowd) saw as his defacing of the music's beauty, but the partnership still struck a good balance, Björk the Id versus Einar the Ego. As *Melody Maker* wrote, 'There are impunities and impugnities, wraiths and strays, sins and whims. And because they're responsible for delicious irresponsibilities, the whole escapade is like being five years old again. Only better.'

While Björk was feisty, she didn't tend to bait the audience like Einar. In Houston, he bounded on stage, hollering, 'Congratulations on Space Shuttle Challenger!' in reference to the recent air disaster, where the crew and the first public citizen on board had been killed when the craft exploded just after take-off. Typical Einar, happy to be confrontational, happy to be his own master of 'bad taste' . . . 'When I have a problem with communicating, I just lock myself up. And Einar's problem is the opposite,' Björk told *The List*. 'He gets very aggressive and he communicates too much with them.'

The band embraced the kind of post-modern madness of touring that they could only have imagined in Kukl's impoverished days, but they equally had to endure the sapping routine of adhering to a lengthy tour schedule and playing the promotional game ('Not being able to work,' Einar deadpanned, 'is a strain'). Before, if Björk hadn't felt like singing, then she simply wouldn't sing. The choice was hardly hers now, 'so I'm going to threaten myself, and I'm going to find some kind of attitude which will interest me,' she retaliated. Her plan was to take advantage of whatever mood she was in by exaggerating it. 'That way also makes it interesting because I change the songs I'm singing.'

Back on the tour bus, Björk would have Sindri for company, and her little ghettoblaster, 'and all my pockets full of tapes.' Competition for the cassette deck was intense, with wildly differing tastes conflicting; Siggi was keen on ethnic music, with Björk currently obsessed with the visionary American hip-hop rappers Public Enemy. 'I was probably the only one who was into what's going on today,' she told *Raygun*. 'The others were more into Julio Iglesias, Fellini music and classic rock. We'd always compete on tour buses, and it was horrible. People would be talking, a certain atmosphere, and I would put a tape on and see what happened. Each person was allowed to play two songs, and everyone would complain about them and say how horrible they were. We just couldn't have more different musical tastes.'

On her travels across America, Björk could experience hip-hop music at its roots for the first time, in the clubs, 'where a lot of things were happening. These are records you can't exactly pick from your house and play, you might have to go to fifty clubs and at number fifty-one, at six o'clock in the morning, there comes the most brilliant half an hour you've heard in your life, when the DJ stops worrying about pleasing people and just pleases himself. And the records he has in his hand just prove once again the theory that one plus one equals three. A lot of it can be genius. In 1988, and also 1989, they were playing a lot of live synthesizer and percussion, but what happened to that was it was so limitless, so open, that they had to categorize it very quickly, so it became very one way and clichéd, instead of taking off. I think there are so many things to do, so many options.'

At the opposite extreme, Björk found herself as possessed by Boney M, the great best/worst Euro-disco act of the seventies, a group who epitomized 'bad taste' pop. She would constantly sing their refrains and choruses from the songs, in a mini-Boney M routine, before she was given Boney M's *Greatest Hits: The '88 Remixes* as a present, which joined Abba and Chaka Khan on the bus cassette deck.

Inside the cocoon of the bus or out, organic pranksters like Björk would always manage to cause a few ripples. Outspoken as always, when she and Einar were interviewed by a DJ in LA intrigued by the numerous pregnancies and births among the band and entourage ('maybe eight or nine people,' Björk said), she enthused about 'lolloping women with big stomachs, eating and having fun and just about exploding with life,' and then told the listeners to go out and get pregnant (she got faded out). A more serious incident occurred in France when she was arrested after a policeman enquired whether Sindri had shit on the grass in the park they were enjoying. Björk, thinking that the man was either joking or just stupid, said he had, and was promptly carted off to the police station, although she was let off later that day.

An incident in Belgium proved more serious. As Siggi tells it, various 'Cubes were out clubbing after a show, when a drunken Björk got all excited at the tacky photos of the club's layout that were illuminated down the entrance hall. She jumped up at a photo, but neglected to see a German shepherd guard dog in its cage, which, startled by her sudden leap, nipped her through the bars. Björk was predictably upset and tried kicking the dog back, which the bouncers dealt with by grabbing her and throwing her out. Björk came running back at the door, and one of the bouncers opened it right in her face, half knocking her out, and splitting open her lip. She ended up having stitches and a tetanus shot. 'She has a temper, of course, though she has a good control of it,' Siggi says. 'And when it comes out, it's normally used very positively.'

Of course, when Björk told the story, she described the dog as 'going mad for the noise,' and it getting out of its box and biting her. She expected the bouncer to apologize 'but he looked at me as if I was another idiot,' and when she was thrown out, she 'just lost it. I knocked on the door, he opened it and I hit him, bit him and tore at his clothes. He picked me up by the hair, took the door, which was huge and metallic, and pressed it into my face about five times, BFFF BFFF BFFF BFFF BFFF, then threw me out. I've still got the scar.'

Siggi is the first to point out that Björk is prone to a little exaggeration. 'She likes to make up her own little history,' he laughs. 'Björk has her own agenda, her own little view of the world, and makes her life fit into that, so when she looks back and recounts things, she loves to fit them into moulds, but we all do that. This is human behaviour. She has such high principles for herself but she is human, and can't live up to them, like other people. Nobody's perfect, and she isn't either.'

Just when you think you've found a chink in Björk's seemingly sorted persona, she owned up to recognizing her failing. 'I have difficulty finding what is a lie and what is the truth. I exaggerate a lot. I'm trying to stop it. I manage to change details into the main thing, and the opposite way around. Sometimes I find myself in a world of detail . . .'

Exaggeration was part of the mad life The Sugarcubes were leading. Such escapades were born from on-the-road pressure, as days turn into weeks, weeks into months, and months on tour into tour madness, especially if your in-demand status encourages constant media attention. Audiences loved The Sugarcubes; they looked cool, talked sense, sounded unique, so everyone wanted a piece of them. The band saw the 'bad taste' aspect of their views being taken seriously (and, having egos as well as intelligence, saw also the chance to be appreciated) but by the end of 1988, they reckoned they had conducted over 400 interviews. The last of the year was the front cover feature of *Melody Maker's* Christmas issue: where the band enacted a ludicrous recreation of the Bethlehem manger – Björk was Mary cradling Einar the Baby Jesus, surrounded by the Three Wise Men. The frivolity of the photo made a stark contrast with the weariness of their quotes. Had their attitude towards the world changed since their success? 'Our attitude to hotels and restaurants has changed,' Björk replied, sourly. 'That's about it.'

How did the band now feel about being treated as weird? 'I don't know: I've stopped worrying about that,' Björk sighed. 'I think you should ask somebody else, because the moment I think I'm the most normal and obvious thing in the world, people laugh and feel uncomfortable to be around me.' With the bit between her teeth, she wasn't going to let this pass. 'Everything we said in the beginning was taken out of context,' she carrried on, clearly overreacting. 'We were made to look like people from outerspace or something. People just wouldn't believe that we work, shit and fuck and do all the normal things in life.'

Einar 'If we're disappointing other peoples' images of how to be a radical independent pop band, then that's just too bad. We're just Icelandic people having fun.'

But just exactly how much fun? Einar Melax had been replaced by Thór's girlfriend Magga Örnolfsdóttir (at Björk's suggestion too), who they stole from Reptile, but the subject of the band splitting up was even broached. 'We could explode at any moment,' Einar reckoned.

Björk: 'The other day I was round my grandmothers' and it just fell out of my mouth that, in a way, I don't believe this band will last so long. I look upon it as a short period and I will enjoy it while it lasts. These sort of things don't last long anyway, it's not their nature.'

Siggi: 'I don't think any of us has the same vision of what we are doing as opposed to where we are going.'

Einar: 'If we start thinking about what will happen tomorrow, we will never wake up.'

In a 1993 interview with *Vox*, Björk admitted that the concept of success to The Sugarcubes still felt alien; there was clearly still a lot of Kukl in their collective genes. Pop was just a laugh, an escapade, not something worth real kudos – after all, her heroes weren't singers and musicians, 'but the chemistry experimentalist in the back room in a small village you could sneak in and watch and be completely obsessed with his ideas. Or the guy who was really into making synthesizers out of old televisions. We thought they were sincere and it was almost a rule that if you were doing anything that was worth anything, you didn't get famous. I guess our attitudes in The Sugarcubes come from that. So in our heads, if we get famous, we are selling out.'

In world-weary mood, the band returned to Iceland for the Christmas holidays. They had sold 100,000 copies of *Life's too Good* in the UK and 450,000 in America, but they needed grounding. Björk's recording of a traditional Icelandic carol 'Jólakötturinn' ('The Christmas Cat') for a compilation album, was not just a hit, but a taste, or memory, of the 'unspoilt' Icelandic music scene before all the madness had begun. Life can be too rich sometimes.

A Future Woman In An Irresistible World

*I*t might have been a holiday but the band were not willing to take off much time. They had agreed to a number of European festival shows in late spring, but being desperate to make a new album and move on, they began tentative recordings the day after Christmas.

By early spring 1989, the album sessions had been completed, back at Syrland Studios and four more studios in London besides. Despite them professing not to care less, it would have been hard to ignore the pressure of expectations surrounding a follow-up to such a commercial and critically acclaimed record, with the words 'sell' and 'out' most likely ringing in their ears. Once you entered the commercial world, your motives had to be doubly secure while the outside world judged you with double the scepticism. Typically, backs to the wall, The Sugarcubes adhered to an internal manifesto. 'When we became so famous, so talked about after the first record, we said, "Fuck the world," and decided to make the most unpredictable album we could,' said Björk. 'I think we all have in common that we are addicted to shocking ourselves. We do what we like to do and we have to go one step further than that just to surprise ourselves and say "Wow! I didn't know we could do that!"'

As the band's co-lyricist and tactician, Björk had a lot to say about the band's new music direction. Her championing of Boney M and general love for pure pop (when asked by *Melody Maker* what songs she wanted to cover most, she cited Tom Jones' 1965 classic 'Delilah'), allied to Einar's championing of the ridiculous, saw a reinforcement of the 'bad taste' principle that had originally inspired them. Which meant a shift away from their first attempt, the perverse-pop of *Life's Too Good*, and towards what they saw as the pure-pop sound, in the disco image of seventies icons like Abba, Kool & The Gang and Boney M. It made sense to the team – regular live shaping of their songs meant that they had become more rhythmic, and the band wanted to reflect this progression.

'We haven't reached pure pop yet but that's where we're going,' Björk announced. 'Pop music is underestimated, it is such a pure form. It's making music for people and it has become such a dirty word. Sumptuous lines that get to people. It's a very personal thing. People have realized that in pure pop music, there are real lyrics about real things that happen. The things that Rick Astley is singing about are not real.'

But were Boney M, who specialized in tacky nursery-rhyme nonsense, any more 'real' in their pursuit of 'pure pop'? As Einar pointed out, determining what is and what isn't 'good taste' or 'bad taste' in pop, put you on, 'a very slippery intellectual slope.'

Not that that was going to stop The Sugarcubes from fulfilling their pure-pop vision. It gave them the chance to have fun, and something to cling to intellectually – to be a tacky pop group in 'bad taste', to view the art form as superficial and escapist, rather than take it seriously. After all, to be a 'serious' pop group would be a contradiction in terms. Being a pure-pop group meant some measure of revenge against the pretensions and ambitions of the music industry, to 'get them from behind,' as Björk would have it. They could also send up Iceland's vain attempts at making 'Western' pop, and sell thousands more records doing it.

'When you live in a place like Iceland, you can watch the rock and pop industry and see the funny side, but young British musicians are so serious about everything they do, because they are going to make a living out of it,' was the view of Dora Wonder. 'Here, you have to be very lucky to, if you aren't going to play MOR. So it's easy for bands like The Sugarcubes and Reptile to make a joke out of what we do. Maybe there will come a month when we take it very seriously and sometimes we do, but never too seriously.'

The Sugarcubes had seen the seriousness of Western alterno-culture close up, thought it stifling and pompous, and wanted no part of it. 'If there are some bands that we would be categorized with, it would be bands like Abba and Boney M, you know, that sort of stuff; Björk claimed. 'It's far away from what we want to be but it's still closest because to be called an indie band is even worse than being called a hippie band. Indie is a totally exhausted word.'

The band's success had meant that, while they were touring, Bad Taste could at least expand its operations. The plans for a radio station/gallery/café were still out of reach but the record label could blossom, and following *Life's Too Good*, Bad Taste released albums by harmonious punk-popsters Bless, pomp/hard rock parodists Ham (a particular favourite of Björk's, who do a slashing version of Abba's 'Voulez Vous') and the exhuberant Reptile. Not that Icelandic youth were any less bamboozled by the irreverent spirit of these adventurous bands. 'Teenagers take themselves so seriously in Iceland, and think we're absolutely stupid; Reptile drummer Totti sighed.

Dora: 'They stand, listen and say, "What are you doing?", and then you meet them on the street the day after and they point at you and say, "You were drunk yesterday." "Sorry, I don't drink," I reply. "Yes, I saw you," they say. That's their only explanation for our freaking out on stage. They thought the same about The Sugarcubes too.'

The 'Cubes were less concerned about their home audience than the job of pleasing themselves. Maybe disco pure-pop lunacy would appeal, especially if those pop paragons Benny Andersson and Björn Ulvaeus of Abba would produce the album, or even one or two Sugarcubes singles, but the Abba supremos turned down their offer. With Ray Shulman busy elsewhere, Derek Birkett was left to co-produce the album with the band.

Armed with their Boney M-anifesto, the band tried to replicate the live atmosphere of their songs but left room to experiment. On what became the album's opening track, 'Tidal Wave', Björk worked on a brass arrangement with an Icelandic avant-garde composer, which Derek Birkett then asked British saxophonist Gary Barnacle to play. 'I thought it was in the wrong key because it sounded so odd, but when we played it back with the track, it sounded great,' Barnacle recalls. Working with these Icelanders as a whole was as unlikely a session as the key of the song. 'Maybe it's the months of darkness and of daylight they have but they had an otherworldly feel to them. A very interesting bunch. And I have to say, in a way, Björk's really quite elf-like . . .'

Fine-tuning the album proved much harder than anticipated; in fact, it was a major nightmare. Replicating the 'live' version conflicted badly with the presence of a full-time keyboardist, with all the extra layers, arrangements and way too much time and freedom to experiment with. Six-way democratic decisions made the process more complicated; no one could decide on what tracks to include, and so ended up throwing them all in, and worse, no one could agree on the final mixes. When they ran out of time and had to go off on tour, tapes of individual mixes would be Fed-Expressed or personally taken over for approval (or not). The album budget subsequently soared way above its original level, to an astronomic (for Iceland and One Little Indian anyway) £150,000 ($200,000). It was a salutary lesson in what it means to be a pop band with principles. 'We just couldn't compromise internally, which was silly,' says Siggi. 'We should have postponed the album or the tour.'

When The Sugarcubes finally emerged into daylight, for a new round of interviews to coincide with the release of a new single 'Regina' and live dates in July, Björk's look was drastically different – her hair now shorn, with a side-parting, and her girlish, neo-hippie dresses replaced by man-made fabrics – plastic, latex, nylon – with streamlined sports styles and space-age dayglo colours from the skate/surf catalogue that predated the Western fashion fad by at least four years. Was this a pure pop look? Quite possibly. The vitalized anti-Levis priestess now favoured bomber jackets, leggings, trainers and brothel creepers, often in silver, looking like an innovative futuristic distillation of the glam-rock seventies. 'I'm not compatible with people who are obsessive with the past,' she confessed, naming Bragi in the process.

Scott Roger: 'She created her own fashion sense. She once bought a pair of Adidas trainers, pre-1970s style, and wanted to get four inches added on to the sole. Trying to explain that in German was tough, but we managed it, and paid £200 just to do it. It was pretty much like that all the way. She'd spend a lot of time around NASA in Texas, buying silver jackets and astronaut food.' As 'Speed Is The Key' put it, *'I'm a future woman in an irresistible world/fast and sparkling'*.

The band hit the European festival circuit without a new record release but with a whole new set. At the open-air Bizarre festival in Lorelei, Germany, they shared a bill with fast-emerging, riveting pop-noiseniks The Pixies, leaden goth-rockers The Mission and, headlining the show, implacable goth-fathers The Cure. In their mid-afternoon slot, Björk's blue glitter hair gel was a bit lost from a distance, as was leather-clad Einar's new tail-feather addition to his customary number one crop, but their combined stage presence was combustibly loud enough to communicate with the sleeping logs at the back, especially after plenty of time to hang out backstage and drink. Einar was in typically argumentative mood. After the band kicked off with an Icelandic nursery rhyme, he bellowed, 'Why are you clapping, stupid? We are not The Cure.'

The band's view of these communal rock spectacles vacillated between treating them as foolish fun and a bit tragic. Neither Einar nor Björk were motivated to 'go to the toilet' on stage to show their level of contempt for their audience, because their integrity was far less of a sacred cow these days. But if Kukl was nothing like an act, then The Sugarcubes must have felt a bit false. That said, they accepted the offer to join the horrifically titled 'Monsters Of Alternative Rock' tour across America, in support of Public Image Ltd and headliners New Order.

The internally renamed Hamsters Of Rock tour swept into New York during the heat of the summer and the city's annual New Music Seminar shindig. In its earliest days, the NMS was meant to provide a showcase and forum for independent labels and culture but each one became progressively more mainstream, as independent labels tried to show how organized they were and major labels tried to show how alternative and caring they were. 'Monsters Of Alternative Rock' might not have been a contradiction but it was at the very least an uncomfortable irony – but at least 'Alternative' was now sufficiently armed to combat the mainstream.

One of the NMS showcases was a Bad Taste label night that Asi Jonsson organized, with Reptile, Ham and Bless playing and poet Jon Gnarr bridging the gaps. The Monsters Of Alternative Rock schedule actually prevented The Sugarcubes from attending their own showcase. Surely there was something about the whole debacle – New York, 'alternative rock', record company schmoozing – that qualified for one of Bad Taste's awards? Give one to yourself! Yet Einar disagreed: he actually saw a serious purpose to their mission, displaying a sincerity not often shown to the outside world.

'No, it qualifies for letting this music be heard in America, because people didn't know that music like this existed,' he argued. 'It never gets mainstream radioplay. It's necessary to get to people, to let them know that mainstream music is not the only music in the world. We are as mainstream as Tiffany. She is regarded as good taste but who says it's good music? Bad Taste and The Sugarcubes want to challenge the good taste of the world. Who are the trendsetters of the accepted face of mainstream pop? The New Music Seminar is talking about new music – why is it getting bigger and bigger every year? Because people have started seeing that what is defined as good taste music every year isn't valid. So let's bring chaos to pop, to the mainstream.

'For American people,' he went on, 'their business has come to an end with this music, like a snake eating its own tail. Some clever guy said, "Let's tap into the alternative scene because things are happening there." Look at the audience who are coming to see the tour. I saw maybe ten to fifteen punks out of 20,000 which is very strange to see. In the UK, people dress up according to which type of music they listen to – The Cure and Mission get hippies. Why should alternative music be played to only fifty or sixty people in a club?'

For their part in the Monsters tour, The Sugarcubes were paid $95,000, and though their expenses were $94,450, T-shirt sales of $50,000 put them into profit. Money wasn't a primary concern; the band turned down an offer of $20,000 for the use of a four-second segment of 'F***ing In Rhythm And Sorrow' in a TV ad for an American clothes company (though only after demanding twice the amount!). A request to don designer ski clothes for a *Rolling Stone* photo-session was also declined. 'We'd only do it if we could alter them to our tastes,' Björk explained.

The band's underlying lack of love for the pop life was reflected not in the attempts to wrestle with what the media and tour organizers wanted, but in their reluctance to accept their prolonged absence from Iceland. 'There, we don't have a schedule and we can concentrate on other traits,' Björk lamented. 'We can rehearse and relax. We can be normal.' But hadn't she claimed that she would be 'killing herself' with boredom if she was stuck at home? In America, The Sugarcubes could afford to enjoy being abnormal, if only they were allowed to run free, and if they weren't, well, they would act a bit like petulant children.

'They weren't the easiest band to work with,' Liz Naylor recalls, 'because they were very intelligent and just rather wilful. Björk ultimately wants her own way, and if she doesn't get it, then she'd suddenly slip into an, "I don't understand" vein, and not understand English too well. She could be a complete pain in the arse sometimes. You'd tell her that there was a photo session in Paris and she'd wander off shopping. But all bands are like that, aren't they? It's just the boredom of having to do endless photo sessions and stuff. The un-fun times were dealing with TV companies which just wanted to interview her and Björk having to keep saying, "No, fuck off, you have to interview some of the others." The 1989 tour was the hardest because of trying to keep a handle on all the press. They didn't enjoy themselves that much, so they didn't socialize that much.'

On the day I met them, twenty-six floors up in Elektra's mid-town New York office, their ambivalent attitude – acting playful but bored, engaged but restless – was clear to see. Thór had temporarily gone back to Reykjavík to be with Magga, who was just about to have their first baby; they had accepted the fact that they would have to use tapes in place of keyboards on this Monsters tour. Ironically, Thór was the one who enjoyed touring the most, while the others probably wished that they could have gone home too, instead of being dropped into the middle of tour/seminar madness, over-humid American summer madness and all-round Yankee madness.

Madness seemed a good place to start. So, guys – America, insane or sane? 'Depends,' Björk shrugged, and started talking of her experience ploughing her way through amusement parks, for Sindri's sake. She was still happier to have him around than not: 'When you have a baby, it's like the purest love there is, so you don't ever, ever think about things like that. It's instinctive and reassuring to have him with you. And it means you're always trying to do something brilliant, for his sake almost more than yours.'

The result being, as Björk said, 'Sindri has probably seen more Disneylands, Seaworlds, amusement parks, museums and dinosaur exhibitions than any American kid.' In every town, she would look in the hotel booklet to see what was on for children.

Einar: 'At least we haven't had to contact the child abuse centre in town. We just go to an amusement park.'

Björk: 'We are actually getting very good at going to very American places, picking up very interesting things, ignoring as many people as possible and leaving very happy.'

New York also made her happy because the city embodied her current futurist manifesto. 'It's such a brilliant place, because it made me realize that people think cities are something that's wrong, and plastic is something that's wrong, and tin foil, that it's not natural. It's bullshit because everything that is on the earth came from earth, and earth is natural, and how can anything on earth be unnatural? It's just stupid.'

As much as she loved her home, Iceland was still heavily rooted in its past, by way of its history and procedures, and America was very much the opposite – gleaming skyscrapers, cosmopolitan people, food to match, and a huge choice. 'You can go to a petrol station and buy fruit salad,' she said, wide-eyed in wonder.

'You can buy Icelandic opal mints at a truck stop in the middle of the desert,' Siggi laughed.

'Actually, English food is the best,' Bragi interjected. 'Fish and chips. Simple and quick.'

Björk: 'Fulfilling? Yes. French fries . . . chips, chips, chips . . .'

The subject turned to compromise. 'I think that the only compromising we do is hotels,' Björk reckoned. 'Even that is not really a compromise because it's interesting, and it's a challenge as well, how to get what you want in a hotel room. To feel free in a hotel room . . . to have no limits in a hotel room. Some people may say that doing this tour with Public Image and New Order, playing in stadiums in front of twenty or fifty thousand people, is a compromise, but it wasn't. It was very challenging and exciting. We'd never done it before. We knew it was possible. The first gigs were not very good but after a while, we managed to create an atmosphere in a stadium, with sound and everything. So each gig had a different atmosphere, which I'm really proud of.'

The connection with a crowd bothered them; being the first band on, they often played to an auditorium that was only slowly filling up. 'Half of the people have their tickets and are looking for their seats and you just have to get their attention,' Björk says. 'You have to make that connection.'

Siggi: 'By making a lot of noise.'

Björk: 'I guess that's something you just have to believe in. It's the same question as what makes The Sugarcubes interesting. It's just seeing whether you like or feel something, so it doesn't matter if people are miles and miles away, it's just a question of believing you have something, and to rely upon it to get attention. I'm conscious that we exaggerate a bit of what we do.'

The band's greatest fear appeared to be lack spontaneity, of the feeling of miming to backing tapes. 'Like Boney M do,' says Einar. Which began Björk's fervent praise for their Boney style, tackiness and danceability – properties The Sugarcubes hoped to share. 'I would love to be a simple, classic, pop tacky band,' she said. Why tacky? 'To be normal . . . does that sound interesting? It's a challenge. It's easy trying to be mystic, or intelligent, but being tacky, that's tough.'

Weren't the band starting to think too hard, to be too conceptual? Surely you can only be tacky by accident? 'You're right there,' she agreed. 'That's the difficulty. You can try and be an intelligent pop band and you can get a target and work hard, and you will get there, but wanting to become tacky is almost impossible.'

Siggi: 'History always turns something tacky.'

Björk: 'But it's still a challenge.'

Einar: 'Like wearing white clothes is very tacky for me, and I feel really bad about it, but it is tacky.'

The subject moved on to clothes. Björk admitted that she was wearing a T-shirt that day, 'I think for the first time in my life, but it's because it's a very special T-shirt. It's of my lover. T-shirts, jeans and sneakers have always been the most tackiest thing . . . I puke. But I have to admit, I have got sneakers.'

After discussion of the songs on the new album, the four again reiterated that The Sugarcubes felt like a temporary concern. 'This is our job, we know it,' said Einar. 'We might spend another one or two years, make possibly another brilliant album, but we want to be rich. This is no life.'

Siggi: 'Our life is in Iceland. This is work. I see it as building an empire – world domination or death.'

Einar: 'That's my view of the situation. Work hard for a few years and build an empire. And then we can do what we want.'

Any last words? 'We might be wrong,' Einar smirked . . .

While they were in America, a new single, 'Regina', had been released in the UK, registering another Top 30 hit. The track boded well for the forthcoming album, with an elastic, muscular, swaying propulsion and soaring chorus. The subject of the track – the words written by Thór this time – was an Icelandic heroine of the band's, a housewife and local journalist who wrote a column for a national daily evening newspaper, delving into local issues. 'Like when her friend next door or some great relative has done something special,' Siggi said. 'Like . . .'

Björk: 'Jimmy Brown had a brilliant carrot harvest last week. I actually tasted them and they went to his place . . .'

Siggi: 'When beer was legalized in Iceland in March, she opened the article by saying, "I even saw children carrying cases of beer bottles into the parents' cars".'

Björk: 'The song is basically about us worshipping a lady who comes from the East of Iceland who has to crash down in the south. Like the sun. So we compare this lady Regina to the sun. She's just as brilliant as the sun. That's all you need. A worshipping lyric.'

'The line, "*lobsters and fame*", was inspired by an Abba biography, where the Swedes say, "we're only in it for the caviar and fame".

When the Monster tour was over, at the end of August, The Sugarcubes headlined the annual Reading Festival in the UK before touring the country through to October to coincide with the release of their new album. The working title had been the pun-heavy *DethZaDrag* but they settled on *Here Today, Tomorrow, Next Week*. The phrase was the property of Mr Toad of Kenneth Grahame's famous children's book *The Wind In The Willows* – 'an eccentric, selfish, crazy, a vain creature,' to whom the band likened themselves.

'*The poetry of motion! The real way to travel! The only way to travel! Here today – in next week tomorrow! Villages skipped, towns and cities jumped – always somebody else's horizon!' (The Wind in the Willows.)*

Like *Life's Too Good*, it was another phrase that amused the band. They were inspired to use it after a trip to the former Soviet Union. 'One of the things you do most there is wait,' said Siggi. 'And then you wait a little more, and then you're asked to wait. It's one of the places that you wish for things to happen quickly and efficiently. So *"Here Today, Tomorrow, Next Week"*, is like, "let's get it on, things are happening fast".

Björk: 'I think it's about worshipping the next minute, what's about to come.'

Siggi: 'An obsession with "future"'

Einar: 'Mr Toad gets into a car and says, "here today . . . tomorrow next week!" and flies off! And for us, or at least for me, people have said, "The Sugarcubes are one-hit wonders, here today, gone tomorrow," but we're not. We are, and we're going to be.'

And you thought that Sugarcubes types were impervious to criticism. You could accuse them of being oversensitive as there was little proof that the band were treated as one-hit wonders, but those who had heard the new album were adamant that nothing was approaching the uncanny magnificence of 'Birthday'. The pure-pop ethic (which started with the gatefold sleeve photo recreating a Boney M cover, down to the all-white costumes) meant a loss of the first album's darker extremes, and a surfeit of bouncier dynamics, shinier surfaces and bubblegum-brash melodies – this was less like Kukl and more like the B-52s. In retrospect, there were numerous gorgeous moments – specifically 'Regina', 'Pump', 'Water' and 'Planet' – while 'Speed Is The Key', 'Nail', 'The Bee', 'Dear Plastic' and 'A Day Called Zero' vibrated with sassy energy and moments of glory. But there was too much clutter, too many confusing ideas, especially over thirteen tracks, and a soggy production to boot.

Back to the wall, Björk made the bizarre charge that the music press had something to do with the album's disappointment. 'We'll never manage another "Birthday", she indignantly claimed, 'because our work could never have the same air of mystery about it now, the mystical thing that journalists painted it to be! The answer lay closer to home – the intellectual pursuit of pop tackiness had partly robbed them of the intuitive process that shaped their more original creations.

A less biased Árni Matthíasson thinks that a lot of the problem lay in the early departure of Fridrik Erlingsson. 'For me, a lot of The Sugarcubes' spirit went out when he left, because he was a melodic, intelligent musician, with a gift for pop melodies. Though everyone left their preconceptions at the door, and nobody came up with finished tunes, they just jammed, I think a song like "Birthday" was down to him. Look at the music after his departure. *Life's Too Good* sounds like a Greatest Hits collection, as every song is something special. I'd heard all these songs live over and over and they sounded much worse when they recorded them!

Like the music, *Here Today . . .*'s lyrics could throw up flashes of brilliance – the environmentally prompted day of judgement in 'A Day Called Zero', say – but were dominated by an engineered wackiness. 'Plastic' reflected Björk's love of man-made fibre (*'be proud, don't imitate anything'*), 'Dream TV' was Einar's real-life recollection of dreaming of last week's TV; 'Nail' reviewed the problems with communicating (*'I like them but I hit them/they scream and run away even though I say I'm sorry/I like meeting people'*); 'The Bee' was a party game gone wild; 'Eat The Menu' was the thrill of too much choice, American-style (*'limousines, oranges, stars, moons, submarines, jeeps, glaciers, cars, caterpillars, even grapes'*).

But this was life as The Sugarcubes led it – the strategies, the lunacy, the frivolity of touring life and bad taste role playing.

The British critics, smitten by the debut album's gutteral energy and ethereal swirl, came down on *Here Today . . .*'s reinforced organic prankstering like a ton of bricks. The arrival of Acid House in 1988 was creating a new, vibrant dance scene, Ecstasy was *de rigeur,* and The Sugarcubes' take on dance dynamics seemed flat and dated by comparison. In the light of the rock revisionism going down, the band's humorous positivism was seem as trivial and unwarranted. *NME* wrote of *Here Today . . .* as being, ' too damn pesky-menace-in-your-face.' *Melody Maker,* their inititial champions, hated, 'the banal materiality of things, flying in the face of the massive abstraction suggested by Björk's voice,' before floating the incredible suggestion that humour had no place in rock music.

'Another *Life's Too Good* was the last thing we needed,' Einar retaliated in *Melody Maker.* 'We didn't want any references to that album at all. I don't even think the album was very good . . . it's so fucking sloppy.'

Derek Birkett confirms that when *Here Today . . .* was originally mixed, 'it was incredibly commercial, but the band said it didn't represent them live, and so got their monitor man to remix the album. They didn't want artificial dynamics, even though they knew it would be more commercially successful that way. They were adamant that they would rather sell ten records on their own terms than ten million on any other. That sounds like bollocks but it was true for that bunch.'

If The Sugarcubes had been amazed at the British music press's initial superlative hyperbole, what did they make of putdowns as equally heated? A live review in *Melody Maker*'s Christmas issue showed what vindictiveness awaited them, calling the band 'a contrived charade. What grates is their smugness, Björk's ever-so-pat gobbing-by-numbers, Einar's deluded belief that we really care how he doesn't give a fuck, and The Sugarcubes' self-satisfied masquerade as some kind of extra-terrestrial visitation come to shake up dull old Planet Pop. They come from *Iceland*, for fuck's sake, they don't need to try to be different . . . Björk's the loser in all this, of course. She is constantly stifled, snowed under or shouted down by Einar's brutish semantics or the band's bully-boy thrash.'

Only *City Limits* saw strength in Einar's role – 'the way it valuably shatters the group's harmonious elements and re-orders them according to a principle of heterogeneity that is The Sugarcubes' abiding strength.' Otherwise it was constant descriptions of court jestering, the writer of lyrics like, *'Oh Johnny teeth and gums in my life/moon and sun in my life/lobster and shrimp in my life/I don't really like lobster'* ('Regina'), the disperser of Björk's magic spell, the voice like a wounded hyena. To which Björk retorted, 'Don't forget there are six Sugarcubes, not two! Some people don't know fuck.'

It's probably true to say that, anticipating criticism, the band overcompensated for the suggestion that they should downplay Einar's role, and so spread him all over the album. Einar, the other members argued, was the true spirit of the band, the creative spine, the catalyst, without whom they wouldn't be inspired to greater heights. The music press were romantics to a tee – to say humour has no place in rock music was a ludicrous notion – while Einar was the original anarchist. 'The more dangerous he is, the more beautiful he becomes and the more we love him,' said Thór.

Ultimately, the band were interested in what they wanted more than what any critic or consumer wanted. 'Your perception of what we are has nothing to do with us,' Einar told *Hot Press*. How could it be any other way? 'Of course we wanted to do something different,' said Björk. 'I can't imagine any band that wants to repeat itself. But we're basically obsessed with doing exciting things.'

Who knew whether people would be playing Sugarcubes records tomorrow, let alone next week? But here today, in 1989, the band still stood out – brashly exciting, richly imaginative, full of ice and fire.

Some of that spirit was captured by a live video *Live Zabor* (more bad punning) that followed the album. Besides the live clips, each member faced the camera for their own little cameo – in hers, Björk compared circuit boards to 'little houses'. The band had originally planned a live album for the loss-making price of 99p/$1.50, much to One Little Indian's exasperation. They settled for releasing a series of box sets – on 7 inch and 12 inch single and on CD – comprising the video's fourteen live tracks plus twenty-one other tracks from albums, singles and B-sides (which were then deleted) at similarly knockdown prices.

Derek Birkett: 'I have to say the band are fucking impossible to deal with. I love what they are doing but they are the only band I've ever worked with for whom the band isn't the priority. That's why they all went off and got jobs after the second album. We operate a profit-share but when they made money they'd blow it in ridiculous ways. Like, last year, when they brought out a poetry book which cost £8 to buy and £18 to produce.'

In order to keep up the momentum, the band's tour schedule was punishing, but they maintained their disco-fever energy. Björk continued to do her bee dance, Einar his mad-puppet dangling, and both of them their verbal and physical *pas de deux*. Between autumn and winter, they visited the former Yugoslavia and the Soviet Union then the UK, on to America and South America, then Australia and New Zealand, and finally Japan.

Despite the routine, there were numerous escapades that the band would look back on fondly. Bragi was especially smitten with the memory of Björk in Lithuania: faced with unspent roubles that they thought would have to be thrown out of the window, she came up with the brainwave of investing in Russian synthesizers, 'which were absolutely useless but it was a brilliant idea.' The Soviet tour was one of the band's favourite memories; away from the usual critical/jaded Western audiences, they could relax. As Bragi notes, 'Although Björk likes to drink, she usually doesn't get very drunk, but this one time in Lithuania, she got hilariously drunk. She stormed into the hotel bar where all the rest of us were sitting. We couldn't believe our eyes. She started dancing around the bar, and

I remember her taking down the big TV screen which was elevated from the floor, up near the ceiling, and putting it on the floor. The bartenders threw her out. But the funniest thing about Björk is to see her holding a cigarette. She looks at smoking as a very stupid occupation. That's my fondest recollection.'

Less fond was the general realization that, in each territory, the band weren't selling as many copies of *Here Today . . .* as they had *Life's Too Good*, though the shows were always well attended and audiences were stirred by the band's aggressive gleam and especially Björk's dynamism. According to Dietrich Eggbert, head of marketing for the band's German licensees Rough Trade Germany, 'the second album got some quite bad reviews in Germany, the same as in Britain, but because they didn't tour the first album that much, there were still a lot of people who had never seen them play before. I noticed that the older songs were accepted better than the new ones, and that the songs based around Björk rather than Einar went down bwtter. Peolpe were always into Björk and didn't accept Einar as a second singer.

Under pressure, the band's morale would dip. Their press officer Liz Naylor was the closest at hand to see all the fluctuations and tensions. She regarded The Sugarcubes as a family, like a bunch of very old friends can be: 'the relationships are so established, and you fall out with each other, but they're always there as part of your life,' she says. And like a bunch of old friends, the band would stick together, even more so when Einar was under attack.

'They were really close culturally, and whenever there was a row or a disagreement, they'd start speaking in Icelandic, so any problems they had were kept very much to themselves,' Naylor noticed. 'But they would row. People forget that Thór is quite obnoxious, and I always found him very aloof, Siggi and Bragi are easy going but pretty strong people, while Björk and Thór were a very unlikely coupling but it was hard to get an insight on that particular set-up. Overall, they were difficult to be around, quite cliquey, and quite obnoxious. Obviously they were very intelligent. Einar would play at being obnoxious but I think he was anyway, and nobody would challenge him because they were this little unit, with the constant feeling that you were an outsider, and they just tolerated you.'

Naylor regarded the *Here Today . . .* tour of the UK as the lowpoint, 'with everyone saying it was a crap album and how they should get rid of Einar. Plus they had very grandiose ideas, like having an inflated 30 foot lobster on stage, and most nights it wouldn't inflate properly. Everything they did seemed difficult, and no one was having what you'd call a nice time. One Little Indian was wanting to push them up another level, with money spent on advertising and everyone booked into nice hotels, but they were an expensive band to run, as they were always popping over to Iceland and stuff. It was too premature, because the second album wasn't good enough to break them in a chart mainstream way.'

In the UK, some dates were cancelled when Björk contracted flu and lost her voice, but she quickly recovered and the band fulfilled their commitments. A moment of whimsy took place when, on 9 December, Einar and Bragi announced that they had got married in Copenhagen just months after Denmark had legalized same sex marriages. Over dinner, the pair realized that they had been friends for more than ten years without arguing once, and thought that this constituted the perfect marriage. Thanks to the new law, they also realized that they could make this official. The press release concocted that night (including the news that Thór was best man and Siggi maid of honour) was only a joke, but one that the One Little Indian press office took at face value, as did a slew of newspapers.

In spite of the success of their prank, the band returned to Iceland more fed up than elated. Instead of world domination, it looked as if death was a more certain option. They couldn't even bask in the light of escalating success this time. Manic global touring and the release of the superb 'Planet' as another single (most notable for its swirling strings and Björk's wide-eyed exhilaration: *'The universe is so big, I feel dizzy when I think about it/Long ago it was so small I could have kept it underneath my little skirt'*) didn't help *Here Today . . .* sell anything like *Life's Too Good* worldwide. The debut sold a million worldwide; its successor sold but 200,000.

Back in Iceland, the band had time to contemplate their navels. Siggi admitted that media criticisms of both the record and Einar's involvement had got to them: 'We were going through a heavy period, when Magga was away having a baby, and the press slagging us off personally was funny, an accident to us but when people rip you apart for whatever reason, then the joke becomes a bit sick.'

Typically, Einar was more confrontational. 'Analysing music is like paralysing music,' he sneered. 'We try to give them a new perspective on what we are like as people but they always put it to our music, and boil it down to, "Einar is a complete bastard, he should be hung and quartered", "Björk is a sex goddess". But I'm not bothered, because I will be rich and famous and they will still be working for the shit corporation who don't care about individuals, who will be unemployed when the next trend comes around. On our Australian tour, we got great reviews and sold out the whole tour, but *NME* managed to find a bad review. I just feel sorry for these people.'

Not that the band were crying too much: on the proceeds of fame, they'd all bought flats or houses – Björk's was an old, converted blacksmith's shop, overlooking the fishing boats in the harbour, which she soon filled with paraphernalia – model boats, a stuffed iguana, a framed picture of Boney M. But it was clearly time to stop the world and get off. Time, too, to get back on solid ground, to re-establish original intentions. As Bragi said, 'We were all full of energy for the first two years but it changed very fast after the first album because we started getting money and got lazy and too occupied in spending that.'

The tiredness and laziness had been accelerated by over-touring. 'We would do two and half months in Europe, then a month in the UK, and it wore us out,' said Siggi. 'We hadn't realized that this wasn't our piece of cake, and we weren't playing well because of it. It does more damage in the end. We plan another record but how and when is a different matter. It has to be a shitcracker, otherwise it's down the drain.'

This Wasn't Supposed To Happen

'I've got a lot of courage but I've also got a lot of fear.
You should allow yourself to be scared. It's one of the prime
emotions. You might also almost enjoy it . . . if you ignore these
things, you miss so much.'

The Sugarcubes were burnt out and needed a big break, not necessarily from each other but from the band itself. It would hardly be stylish for any band member to idle time away in their newish comfort, so 1990 proved to be an industriously Icelandic-manic start to their decade.

Bad Taste itself had suffered for its owners' prolonged absences. Sugarcubes' sales had bolstered the coffers, allowing them to release a label compilation *World Domination Or Death*, debut albums from Reptile (*Fame And Fossils*) and Bless (*Gums*) and various poetry books, while the label had also partially funded Óskar Jónasson's debut movie *SSL 25* (a simple plot involving Viking squadrons, specialist terrorist bomb squads, three brothers and two girlfriends), the soundtrack coming from Björk and Siggi (on just synths and percussion). But the cost of, and energy consumed in, organizing the band, plus meagre public interest in other Bad Taste releases, put a limit on what could be supported. The decision to make the next Bad Taste signing the middle-aged TV celebrity Rosa reflected the collective's continuing preference for content over commerce; the project (which Björk was to co-produce with Sigurjón from Ham) never materialized anyway, and Bad Taste only released one album in the next two years.

At least the album was a number one in Iceland, and went on to secure platinum status. It was Björk, typically enough, who came to the rescue with an album she had itching to make since she had done some scat singing with a jazz trio in 1987. In just two days, she completed an album of Icelandic jazz/swing and Western pop standards from the Forties and Fifties (such as 'Oh Mein Papa', a 1953 hit for Eddie Calvert), plus equally sterling English versions of Leiber and Stoller's 'Ruby Baby' and Oscar Hammerstein's 'I Can't Help Loving That Man'. The backing came from the veteran be-bop ensemble the Gudmundar Ingólfsson Trio, led by the pianist of the same name, Iceland's only professional jazz musician until he died a year after the album was made. The album was named after its opening track, *Gling-gló*, Iceland's version of a bell's ring, as in 'ding dong'.

Björk: 'It was the opposite of The Sugarcubes' second album. We'd fallen into the trap of spending two months on each song, whereas I have always been an obsessive fan of spontaneous music, and behaviour. So I did that album in two days, which was so much fun.'

She met the trio when they were both guests on the radio programme *Good Friends Meeting*. Gudmundur Steingrímsson, who played drums on the album (after a career spanning nearly fifty years, he is affectionately nicknamed 'Papa Jazz'), picks up the story: 'Another time, we were asked to play whatever we wanted, so I asked the presenter, "Do you mind that we have a singer too? I know a girl that is fabulous and can also improvise blues and jazz". Asi at Bad Taste noticed we were rehearsing, so we ended up making an album. Björk was just like a lamb, so soft and nice to work with. I've listened to her since she was very young, I was born in 1929, and I immediately thought, this is different to what's going on. She was unique. People disliked her because she was such a . . . *nature child*. They said she was pretending but I always said, "That is Björk." There is no pollution there, just pure Björk.

'She wanted to sing these old Icelandic tunes that older singers had made famous. The pianist, bassist and I went wild, we did the whole thing live, no double takes. The song she sings with just the piano is just one take. She is as good as the old singers, but very different. She changed the musical style, with more improvisation. She made it lighter. I think she is brilliant, whatever she sings, jazz and pop. Even at my age, you can tell what she does and how she sings is from the heart, and that's what counts.'

The record wasn't just fun; it was a hit in Iceland too, selling more copies than *Here Today...* and going on to platinum status, as her last solo album had done thirteen years earlier. Björk and the trio played live too, including a prestigious show at the Icelandic Opera House. Árni Matthíasson: 'Gudmundar was a drunkard and sometimes he couldn't play, or when he did, he would veer off sometimes into any direction and his band would have to follow. But when he played with Björk, he was sober. It was a big deal to him. And to her too. There were live tapes that could have been released as an album but when he died of cancer in 1992, Björk said, "No way. Never again"'.

The other Sugarcubes were finding plenty to occupy themselves with. Despite his pleasant but not over-trained voice, Siggi pursued his love of cabaret crooning, under the name Bogomil Font & The Millionaires, playing a series of live shows and later releasing an album of Latin/Mambo standards (in 1993) that also went platinum and contributed to saving Bad Taste's financial arse again. Various Icelandic band scenesters contributed to the part-time, party-time Hljómsveit Konráds B, a.k.a. The Jazz Band Of Conrad B, a big band of up to fifteen players formed by Bragi that played Icelandic versions of British and American standards, but the point being that everyone played instruments they weren't familiar with – Björk was on clarinet, Magga on accordion, Bragi on drums, Einar on trumpet (!). Siggi and Magga also formed a cabaret duo, Caviar, and played the local club circuit.

Such pastimes gave the band members the chance of, as Einar said, 'putting together my reality sense. Pay my bills.' Though it wasn't always that simple for Einar himself. His work as a club bouncer failed because he was too small, but the window opened to host a chat-style radio show and he became a media celebrity instead. Bragi kept writing poetry, and together with Siggi, edited a book of poetry for Bad Taste. He also worked a flea market pitch with Magga, who moonlighted as a bartender between family duties. Like Bragi, Thór wrote and published more poetry books, and sold two cars and some amplifiers to help support the new family. This was a time of industry, of avoiding the thought of a third album and more gruelling tours, and restoring the original balance.

Dora Wonder: 'For the first time in a long time, I saw The Sugarcubes enjoying themselves, when they played in the garden at this café in Reykjavík, with the audience *here*, not just twenty miles away and security guards. You always need a break in this business.'

Even Björk felt more settled about the situation, with time to reflect on what had happened to her and the band. She enthused about the fact that, even though the Gramme record shop had closed down, Bad Taste people were working in record distribution, 'so they're in charge of what music comes in from abroad, so at least you can buy some proper music in Iceland. That was always our main target, our ambition, to change Iceland, or Reykjavík basically. That's the world we've been fighting since we were born. And we've made progress. All this thing about The Sugarcubes being "weird". It seems now that people are beginning to take us as we are, they've got a similar idea of us to what we have, our sense of humour, that it's all a bit of a joke.'

For the sake of her sanity, Björk had been reacquainting herself with Reykjavík: 'I just love that place, very hard, you know. Going to the bakery. Getting pissed. Getting jobs.' One job was working in a friend's antique shop over Christmas: 'I became really interested and got to know a lot of things about Reykjavík that I didn't have a clue about.' She would go out dancing in the city centre, or in a little disco by the harbour, 'full of sailors and hard drinkers. If you give the DJ enough drinks, he'll leave and you can bring your own records.' She was being rejuvenated.

Of all The Sugarcubes, Björk had the drive and the vocal/instrumental range to throw herself into all kinds of musical manifestations. Plans to form Scud, a speed metal outfit, with members of Ham, remained grounded (unlike the Scud missiles), as did a planned collaboration with Sinead O'Connor ('We talked of doing a duet a while ago, but it was enough of a thrill to just have met her,' Björk said) but projects got off the ground more often than not. Besides *Gling-gló*, she contributed to an album by industrial experimentalists Current 93 (led by an old British friend David Tibet) alongside Einar, Thór, Siggi, Gulli and Sjón (Johnny Triumph), sung backing vocals on Bless's album, and sung on two tracks for Óskar Jónasson's first film, *Sódóma Reykavík* (retitled *Remote Control* outside Iceland), based around Iceland's club scene – a local fifties standard 'O Borg Mín Borg' with The KK Band and a techno track 'Takk' ('Thanks') with DJ Pórhallur. All this as well as playing the organ.

It was in such a club that she met an Englishman, Simon Fisher. He was the first musician Björk had met who improvised music on computers, and the pair ended up sketching ideas together in London. Björk's patience in accepting the guitar-bass-drums framework of The Sugarcubes was wearing thin, while the life's-too-good aspect of being paid to travel the world was no longer a compensation. The first flowering of ambitions beyond the band emerged when a February press release announced that a Björk-related collaboration was ready for release. Her accomplices were UK techno radicals 808 State, whose gleaming, complex instrumentals epitomized the British dance scene's exhilarating advances.

On her 1989 walkabouts, Björk had continued to search out clubs, tracking down the cutting edge of dance – 'treasure hunting' as she put it. It led her away from hip-hop territory and into the steely new world of Detroit techno, Chicago's Acid House and the vivid response from (primarily) the British. 'A lot of people don't like dance music,' she told *NME*. 'They find it too strange, but I love it because it's so fresh and new, so strong and so . . . romantic. It's the only pop music that is truly modern. What I also like is that anyone can have a go. It's very much like the atmosphere around punk. With music like this, anything can happen . . . It's so innocent!'

It seemed clear enough that if Björk was to forge her own style, it would be propelled by dance music. 'Usually the most intimate relationship I have is with the percussion people, the drummers,' she said in *Post*. 'The ingredients, the core of what I have been doing for ten years, was a sort of prolonged conversation with Siggi. That was the structure. That's what turned me on. That's the real thing. But at that point, I was freaking out because I could not only feel that he was becoming predictable to me, but also the other way round. I knew what he would do and he knew what I would do. The erotic, sex thing goes out of it and it's not, whooosh, one plus one equals three anymore. It's just one plus one equals two.'

The UK's nascent techno scene was a source of joy, and 808 State were, 'one of the very few bands with direction today, that aren't just following everyone else,' she reckoned. 'There was this core of rhythms that I could identify with very deeply. One day I decided to be brave and phone them up. I just introduced myself as an Icelandic girl who wanted to sing on their records.'

Founder member of 808 Graham Massey confirms Björk's story: 'She didn't say who she was — "a composer from Iceland," is how she put it, although I had an idea. She was listening to our *90* album and was looking for help on the drum programming side.' Björk agreed: 'I can do all the musical stuff, and all the bleeps and bits and sounds and noise and lyrics, but beats have always been my weak point.'

Björk asked her mother to babysit Sindri and she flew over to meet 808 State, on the set of the infamous Friday late night TV show *The Word*. Their musical empathy was a sign of personal connections. 'There was no period of getting to know each other, we were straight in there,' Massey said in *Post*.

By the time she called Graham Massey, Björk had already started turning her fantasy into reality. 'I'd been making songs since I was small: little stories about people,' she confessed. 'In my head, they had harps, but in reality, it was banging spoons on tables and clapping your hands – the kind of sounds you can make in your house. It was my own private thing, it kept me going. There was no intention of conquering the world with it. Then, about ten years ago, I realized I wasn't a teenager anymore: it's now or never! You have to do it now or you'll die and no one will know except you!'

In 1990, Björk had demoed two of her own songs, 'Aeroplane' and 'Anchor Song', singing in Icelandic over three Icelandic brass players (saxophone, trombone and trumpet). She had given the tape to Graham Massey to inspire him to come up with some rhythms, and planned a second meeting. The night before she was to return home to spend her birthday with Sindri, Graham Massey called out of the blue.

'Something stuck in my head after our conversation,' says Massey, 'and I phoned that night to see if she'd do something for our album. We caught her just as she was off to the airport, and she had to make her mind up there and then. So she postponed her flight back to Iceland and came up to Manchester the next day, and did two tracks in as many days. We've worked with lots of people, but in this case, it was definitely a case of musical empathy. She's not just a singer but very much a writer, which is something people might overlook.'

On arrival at 808 State's studio in the Manchester suburb of Cheadle, it was raining hard but Björk put on her coat and traipsed outside, with an 808 demo on her headphones, to get vocal and lyrical inspiration. An hour later, she returned with a bag of fruit and they proceeded to complete two tracks, 'Ooops' and 'Q-Mart', both of which ended up on 808 State's 1991 album *Ex:El* (Bernard Sumner from New Order was the album's second guest vocalist).

Graham Massey says it was an experience he was unlikely to forget. 'I've never seen anybody quite so physical as when Björk records,' he told *NME*. 'It's not just a matter of loading the song into the microphone, there's a lot of jumping about, as she is on stage, and if you isolate the microphone, you can hear footstamping noise.'

'Ooops' was originally titled 'Grab The Rays' but ended up employing Björk's first utterance on the track. Freed of The Sugarcubes, what was she going to write about? *'Dog, I won you . . .'* was an intriguing start . . . In a *Melody Maker* feature, Massey's bandmate Martin Price reckoned 'Ooops' was written about, 'her attitude towards men, about being owned. She understands men and writes about them in her own way, but I don't think blokes can recognize what she's going on about most of the time. It's great, though, 'cos you can read your own personal things into it.'

Björk disagreed, adding, obtusely, 'I consciously made a certain relationship into a love affair once but the song is not about a love affair.'

In the same interview, Björk mapped out her likes and loves. These included, 'extreme' people, harmoniums, wind instruments and computers, cooking for Sindri, her boyfriend Óskar, the World Saxophone Quintet, NWA (Niggers With Attitude), Public Enemy and 808 State. She also made the point that she saw the act of singing and art in general as part of everyday life, and not something above all else. Music was still a fraction of life. 'You shouldn't sit around all day thinking that you're not doing important things, like washing the dishes or brushing your teeth or having a walk or going to the cinema and then – tadaa! – suddenly you're on stage at a concert and you're doing a super-important thing,' she argued. 'I think that's the wrong attitude. It's a question of doing things with equal importance.'

'Ooops' was subsequently released as a single. The video was directed by Óskar Jónasson in Iceland, during which time 808 played a show in Reykjavík, 'one of my favourites', Graham Massey remembers. Months later, Björk joined 808 State on stage at Manchester's voluminous G-Mex Hall, where the throbbing audience were suddenly stilled by her appearance. The experience wasn't one Björk was likely to forget. 'The most fun things I do are the ones that take all of you, that are very difficult,' she vouched. 'And this show was very difficult, but very enjoyable.'

In March of 1991, she admitted to *Melody Maker* that she had been working on her own material with Graham Massey. 'I can't really describe this new music that I am doing. It's probably going to be unlike anything people over here have ever heard, I'm not sure you can imagine what it will be like. But I can tell you one thing – it's going to be pretty personal . . . the music and the words are about private sorts of things.'

But Björk's private and personal life was going to have to wait awhile; after a layoff of a year, The Sugarcubes had reconvened to make another album. Björk was against the idea but the band were under contract to deliver a third. 'We also felt a big pressure on us to do the album,' says Bragi. 'It was a mixture of guilt and the need for money, which we didn't have enough of at the time. We had never got used to having so much money and we had gone into debt.'

They had taken ages to come up with songs; as Einar confirmed: 'We all had other obligations, and rehearsing and writing songs were the least of our worries, even if they should have been the biggest.' But they slowly got organized, and after rehearsals, Bragi would take the tapes home and recommend which parts they should work on. The band had clearly acknowledged that the methodology behind *Here Today...* was not worth repeating because they agreed to record in rural seclusion, and to have an outside producer, 'as a bouncing board,' says Siggi. With a little prodding from Elektra, no doubt, as Siggi reckoned they would have turned down *Here Today...* if it hadn't been a licensing agreement. They eventually settled on Bearsville, upstate in New York Country, and on Paul Fox. Fox was no household name but an assured technician whose credits on XTC's *Oranges And Lemons* and Robyn Hitchcock's *Perspex Island* meant that he had an understanding of modern yet idiosyncratic guitar-pop. They would come to nickname Fox 'The Whip'. 'We have to work twelve hours a day sometimes,' Björk told *Rolling Stone*. 'There's been so much hard work involved in this, we can't believe it. I've had different kinds of jobs and I like to sweat but I've never worked so hard making music.'

Björk wanted to encourage her own commitment and effort by taking dance tapes into rehearsals, hoping that the other 'Cubes would listen, but to no avail. 'She said, "We have to do something new, we have to move in another direction",' said Árni Matthíasson. 'There weren't any real arguments but there was a lot of tension because they didn't want to listen.'

One of the songs Björk had offered was the vocal melody of 'Human Behaviour' (then titled 'Murder For Two'), which subsequently became her debut single but was rejected by The Sugarcubes because they couldn't find the right music to go with it. Björk said that she would never bring finished songs to the table. 'In The Sugarcubes, it was never like that. Bragi would never have brought a three page poem to us to use, it would have been ridiculous. It's like, would you go to your grandma's place and discuss your sex life? It wasn't the place for it. We would never discuss music. That would be the bottom of the pit.'

Instead, she took time out to play her demos to Paul Fox. 'She was carrying all this music around in her head, that didn't fit into the Sugarcubes' musical sphere,' he says. 'She played me tapes of brass pieces she'd written so I could already see her heading in a different direction. We had a brief discussion relating to the Sugarcubes record and she realized that it would benefit her solo career, which I think it did in that "Hit" was a big hit single for them later on, and gave the band and her a lot of exposure. There was tension in the studio, but it was the usual kind, the tension that surrounds a family, but family business always gets taken care of. As always, Björk gave all of herself to the situation.'

Bragi admitted that it was clear that Björk had very different musical ideas. 'She could no longer pretend to be interested in the music we were making, conventional rock'n'roll music, with guitars: it was a minor miracle that we finished the album. The tension had become unbearable, musically and personally too. There was always a delicate relationship between Björk and Thór . . .'

Siggi put the decline in 'the creative spunk of the band' down to the internal problems between members, mentioning Björk and Thór again.

'When we formed, we were this clique of people, with Björk and Thór married, but when they broke up, they decided to work together and give this thing a shot, and I think they did a very honourable job. But they started out on this trip with an extra few pounds of baggage, and ultimately that wore them down. Listen to Thór's new band Unun, then check out Björk's two solo records, and they're pretty different. I also know that Björk was very tired of having to work with another singer. She'd been singing with Einar for almost nine years and definitely needed to do her own stuff on her own. I'm more surprised that The Sugarcubes lasted as long as it did.'

In Björk's mind, the album had been driven by, 'six different ideas of how to make a record.' At the same time, Björk worked on her own stuff, with help from Paul Fox's wife Franne Golde, a singer-songwriter in her own right (though of an R&B persuasion), who also assisted with grammatical and literary translations of lyrics. 'She did most of the work anyway, she knew exactly what she wanted to say,' says Golde. 'I just made the flow better in English, like, 'is it *"she"* or *"I"*? I don't know exactly how she goes about it but her lyrical approach was very raw, emotional and honest, and said exactly what's going on in her head. She turned everything into a positive, for herself, and to grow from.'

The sessions completed, the team moved on to LA to mix the album. Björk, in her lengthy stretches of time outside the studio, was always thinking of going treasure hunting, except that this time she turned up more than she probably bargained for . . .

On a musical tip, she was to embark on a collaboration that would have significant ramifications for her solo plans. Björk esentially went missing for several days, and was later found to have been recording with eighty-year-old harpist Corky Hale. 'I've always been quite obsessed by harp music, not the angelic stuff but the contemporary, twentieth century harp music, which is very challenging. Paul Fox told me he knew of this woman who played jazz on the harp, which is music I'd had in my head for many years, so he introduced us. I wanted to have a voice and harp alone, and quite twisted, stretching chords, and I prepared some notes for her, and visited her, and fell for her character.'

Hale was a jazz institution, a figure who had carved out her own niche, and played with singers as diverse and seminal as Billie Holiday and Frank Sinatra. 'She's a tough little cookie who talks, like rude, Mafia language, and lives right at the top of a skyscraper in Chicago, and goes there in a tracksuit, and watches the city and plays harp on her balcony, really really sweating when she does it, really hardcore harp,' Björk enthused madly. 'I don't want to tell people what to do, I want them to come into it, to do what they think is right. But she comes from a different generation, she wanted the notes and the chords and the time signatures, nine chords a second, sort of jazzy or whatever. I realized that my own songs were a bit too much of a generation gap, just the way we work, so we ended up meeting in the middle. I'm a big fan of the songs that Chet Baker has sung, he really is one of the best singers of this century, so we went into a studio one very hot night in LA, recorded for three hours all his jazz standards we could think of, that we both knew, like 'My Funny

Valentine'. 'Like Someone In Love' and 'I Fall In Love So Easily', eight songs in all, which I just sung one take of each.

'I didn't think she quite knew what to make of me because her music was so moving, I kept bursting into tears. But that's why I love working with people – it's my favourite thing because they bring out so many different parts of you . . . she's more being in character than trying to be a woman, and that's what stands in the way for a lot of women all the time: they can't be themselves, they have to be women. Guys can be all sorts of things: they can be scruffy, fat and thin, funny and serious, intellectual and silly – all those things. And women can't. It is changing, and that's to do with her. I'm not saying it's only her, but she's allowed to be a character.'

Had she ever wanted to change sex for an hour, a day, a week? 'No, I never wanted to be male. It's much more fun being a woman. Harder, but more fun.'

As she was about to discover. On a more recreational trip, Björk was also looking for some spontaneous fun. A friend suggested she go to Disneyland, and naturally Sindri pushed her into agreeing. Among the group of Mickey-maniacs congregated that day was 27-year-old Dominic Thrupp, or DomT to give him his DJ mantle. Dom had been half of Bristol's 2 Bad DJ crew alongside Ed Sergeant; the duo made waves in Bristol clubs like Moon and Dug Out, building up a friendly rivalry with the Wild Bunch sound system that gave Massive Attack, Tricky and producer Nellee Hooper to the world.

'The Wild Bunch were more creative and unusual whereas we catered for the party people. We just played serious fun music,' Dom told Bristol's *Venue* magazine. In the late eighties, 2 Bad drifted apart after Ed moved to San Francisco, with Dom shifting to London, picking up a residency at London's Wag Club, then moving to LA, working on the house scene. At Disneyland, 'I just thought, who's this wild and wonderful Icelandic girl?' he told *Mixmag*. 'She's like she is. She doesn't put on a show for anyone.' He would invite her to parties he was DJ-ing at, and they would party on the LA club scene, and drive around looking for *more* parties.

Like 2 Bad, Björk and Óskar Jónasson had also drifted apart. Óskar had spent a lot of time in London studying film, then busy making them back in Iceland; Björk was here, there and everywhere, so time and distance weren't on their side. Björk said she wasn't looking to set up any replacement, although she was still seeing Óskar when she met Dom. Even though there wasn't the instant 'KOW! POW!' that she was used to when meeting a man, Dom had a delicate strength and level-headedness that appealed to Björk; she was smitten with his ability, 'to know exactly what is going on, to know what everybody is feeling,' as an (uncredited) friend of hers told *Select*. 'And she finds that interesting and rare, especially in a man.'

Björk herself told *Select* that she never thought she would go out with someone as sane, as romantic as Dom; before, she would fight and scream maniacally, just in order to make her relationships work. But there was enough feeling there for her to admit that, when The Sugarcubes returned to Iceland with a completed album, she couldn't concentrate, or even eat. 'It was a bit of a cliché.' As she sung in 'Hit', *'this is not supposed to happen . . .'*

A full twenty-two months after 'Planet', in November 1991, 'Hit' became the first single from the new sessions. The song was about the giddy, nervous exhilaration of falling in love, and the sleeve featured an obviously excited sperm wriggling through a beehive (Björk's lucky charm is a silver sperm). Björk tells the story, honestly and vividly, with no surrealist intent: *'I lie in my bed/totally still/my eyes wide open/I'm in rapture/You've put a seed inside me/and while you're away/it's growing silently/starts in my stomach/embraces my insides/and about to reach my heart.'*

The track was a thrilling return to form too – lithely rhythmic, Eastern-flavoured synth parts, and even Einar's part seamlessly fitted alongside Björk's excitable melody. 'Hit' subsequently became The Sugarcubes' biggest ever UK hit; it almost reached the Top 20. *Melody Maker* were dishing out compliments again: 'quite marvellously alive, exultant and, have mercy, *sexy*,' the reviewer frothed.

Sexy sperm wriggling their way towards life also decorated the new album *Stick Around For Joy* which followed in February 1992 – a good two and a half years after its predecessor. There were doubters like Árni Matthíasson who thought it the worst of their three albums because of its predictability but that aside, the album often wriggled with the same heady vitality as 'Hit', mixing some of the gnarlier verve of *Life's Too Good* with the pop vitality of *Here Today...* while Paul Fox's production gave the band the raw, live setting they had wanted. If there is ever to be a hypothetical Sugarcubes 'Best Of', then 'Hit', 'I'm Hungry', 'Walkabout', 'Hetero Scum' and 'Vitamin' (almost all contained in the second half of the album) should make it, while the instrumental closer 'Chihuahua' sounded like a band having nothing but fun, totally contrary to the tensions that existed when making the record.

The album could have been called *'We're So Happy, We Could Spring!'*, *'Plethora'*, *'Spleen'* or *'Skilmadinkadinkadink'*. Instead, the band chose another on-tour favourite phrase, which Siggi had muttered during a band poker game on the Japanese leg of their last tour, where each member had a nickname (Björk's was Skull Girl). 'The Japanese think the most posh thing in the world is to be American, and therefore like to speak what they think is American,' Björk said. 'The guy at the Japanese record company bought me a Coke, and said, "Have a Coke and a smile" . . . They take all these phrases like "Stick Around For Joy" and "Enjoy A Refreshing Time" and "Can't Beat The Feeling" . . . they were just so charming. We decided to give all our new songs Japanese/American titles and call the album *Stick Around For Joy*.'

Given Björk's obvious lack of joy, how much insight did the album give into where her head was at? After all the mental screenplays and observations of the previous two albums, she maintained a clear-headed, direct view, as 'Hit' suggested. But if 'Hit' looked at love as joy, 'Lease Called Love' was a savage depiction of love's entrapment: *'you love him/you want to make him happy/he loves you/he wants to humiliate you/he's a bastard/you should leave him/paranoid manipulator/to hell with him!'*

'Walkabout' linked the joy of the Icelandic countryside and the body as landscape; the piquantly titled 'Hetero Scum' was inspired by comments by militant lesbians about how the straight population would be punished for homophobia in the future; but like 'Hit', it was 'I'm Hungry' that gave the truest picture: *'I'm made up and know that this is the day I am leaving/I'm going alone with no map/I need room and need space/I have to try something that hasn't been done before/I want to go to places where I don't know what it's like/listen, I'm hungry, thirsty for surprises/ready for experience/have to get what I need right now.'*

Einar's response was equally revealing: *'Am I on my way out?/lying in the grass I allow myself to feel/am I growing further/I want to go on/am I dreaming?'*

The Sugarcubes played a bizarre one-off show at the French Embassy in Reykjavik, when French president François Mitterrand, on an official visit to Iceland, requested to hear them. The press dutifully reported this but there was another story at the time that Björk has been cautioned for stealing a policeman's helmet during a drunken champagne rampage through the capital. Though you wouldn't put this kind of behaviour past her, no one today can corroborate the story – though both her mother and Siggi remember a similar incident in her teenage years. Missions accomplished, she flew back to LA to be with Dom. Love was still the proverbial mystery: why *had* she fallen for this laid-back Englishman?

'I actually asked my ex-husband about it,' she told *Details* two years later. 'And he said, "It's just chemistry. You can't explain it. It just works." Like if you've got tea, you can't put both milk and lemon in it. You don't put chocolate on pizzas. Actually, I once made a chocolate pizza with licorice.'

A January interview in *NME* proved that The Sugarcubes had not put their well-publicized bugbears to rest – their relationship with the UK music press, their depiction as loopy foreigners, and criticism of Einar The Loud. Yet there were concessions. 'I always thought the Sugarcubes were very real but other people thought that something about us was weird and wacky,' Einar began. 'We don't like that . . . but we were a bit daft at times.'

'The English music press were so bored with themselves, their bands, their scene,' Björk continued, putting the blame back in the court of the press. 'They just wanted so hard for something extremely unusual to pick them up like a drug and throw them up in the air and they would be there for ever. And they wanted us to fill that position . . . We're not into being a drug for people, we're not in the service biz, we're doing this for ourselves.'

On Einar's 'shouty' singing, Björk thought the reactions were, 'just an attitude problem. Who makes the rules anyway? Einar's target has never been anything except being Einar and that's what he's about . . . , we have always been about just six individuals and, if there's any manifesto, it's individualism. People just don't get it. Because we can't be categorized, because we're not like anybody else.'

Einar: 'Like you can't say that Björk's singing style is somewhere between Sinead O'Connor and Kate Bush.'

Björk: 'It's like saying that chocolate is somewhere between a biscuit and coffee, because it's coloured brown and it's kind of solid. Where does that take you? A digestion problem, right?'

In March, they released 'Walkabout' as the new single (backed by a live version of The Carpenters' 'Top Of The World') before heading off for more globe-circumnavigating tours. Sindri was still mostly in tow – now nearly six, he had grown up in the company of British and American road crews, the exclamations, 'high five!', 'fuck off!' and 'rock'n'roll!' were second nature to him. With a nanny included in the road crew, Björk still had the freedom to go walkabout. 'Towards the end of The Sugarcubes, when she had started working on her own project, she would often just disappear,' Siggi observes. 'Like in Berlin, she'd be alone in some crazy Turkish bar full of Turkish men, fooling around on her own. But she was always very cool: she was never afraid of getting drugged or mugged or raped, to the point of making you uneasy, but she somehow got away with it. No, she's not much of a herd animal.'

In August, 'Vitamin' was also released as a single and then 'Birthday' followed yet again, both releases coming with a multitude of remixes.

Siggi admits that the band – Björk apart – saw the remix ideology as more of a marketing device 'and nothing to do with our songs,' but in October, One Little Indian released *It's It*, a whole album of Sugarcubes remixes by club/DJ figures like Justin Robertson, Tony Humphries and Graham Massey that were either specially commissioned for the project or had already been released as B-sides. It didn't seem to have much to do with the band themselves, who were then attached to U2's stadium tour of America, as much of a rock institution as you could get, and in retrospect the album signalled the end of the creative line. Although there had been nothing verbalized, says Siggi, everyone was aware that the tour would be their swansong. Playing pop meant that the band could no longer surprise themselves, making their only *raison d'être* the funding of Bad Taste, and they had seen the company falter in their absence, so there was no point in continuing.

Supporting U2 around America was a wonderfully inflated, 'bad taste' move for any unintentional pop band, and a suitable climax. A final, headlining date at The Limelight club in New York, on 17 November, proved to be their last show. Having been pelted with sugarcubes at their first show, their last was decorated by a couple of transvestites, nothing too fancy. Björk wore a fur-lined pink velour minidress, Einar got the audience to sing along to The Beatles' 'Ob-La-Di, Ob-La-Da'; they left the stage to their unofficial manifesto 'Blue Eyed Pop', and returned for just the one encore, the self-descriptive 'Delicious Demon'. As they walked off, Einar bellowed, 'Thank you, we were The Sugarcubes!' . . .

There's no place like home: Björk clutches a bunch of Icelandic dandelions on her return to Iceland, 1994. (Borg Sveinsdóttir)

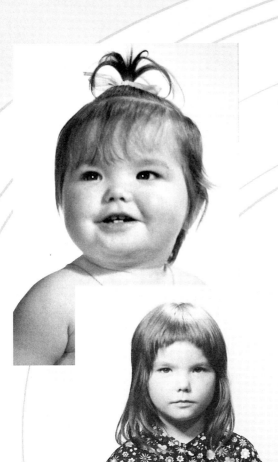

Björk's first attempt at hair styling. (Hildur Hauksdóttir)
(Left)

Devoted: Björk joins music school, aged six. (Hildur Hauksdóttir)
(Middle below)

Fifteen-year-old Björk and her tin drum on the cover of the 1981 compilation Rokk í Reykjavík (Rock Over Reykjavík).
(Below)

Upprunaleg tónlist úr kvikmyndinni
ROKK Í REYKJAVÍK

ÞEYR EGÓ
BARAFLOKKURINN FRIÐRYK
GRÝLURNAR BODIES
PURRKUR PILLNIKK
SJÁLFSFRÓUN ÞURSAR
TAPPI TÍKARRASS
MOGO HOMO SPILAFÍFL
VONBRIGÐI START
JONEE JONEE
FRÆBBBLARNIR Q4U
BRUNI B.B.
SVEINBJÖRN BEINTEINSSON

1981–1982

Let's get unconscious: Björk scat-sings with jazz trio Gudmundar Ingolfssonar at the Hotel Borg in Reykjavík, 1987. (Borg Sveinsdóttir) (Above)

Black moods, black dress: Kukl face the camera, 1984. Left to right: Siggi, Birgir, Gulli, Einar Örn, Björk, Einar Melax. (Morganbladid) (Below)

Life can be sour: Björk reacts against being singled out, 1988. (Bjørg Sveinsdóttir) (Right)

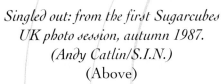

Singled out: from the first Sugarcubes UK photo session, autumn 1987. (Andy Catlin/S.I.N.) (Above)

Beauty and the Beast: Björk and Einar in 1987. (Timothy White/Retna) (Above)
Björk with Sindri, aged two, Iceland 1988. (Kevin Cummins/Retna) (Left)

Re-make, re-model: the new six piece Sugarcubes and Björk's new space-age sportster style, in Reykjavík harbour, 1989. Left to right: Thór, Magga, Bragi, Björk, Siggi, Einar. (Joe Dilworth/S.I.N.)
(Right)

Life is sweet: the photo that made The Sugarcubes' first NME cover. (Tin Jarvis/Retna)
(Left)

Björk settles by the water, in Little Venice, London, 1993.
(Lenquette/ All Action Pictures) (Above)

Violently unhappy: Björk squares off with journalist Julie Kaufman in Bangkok airport, February 1996.
(Right)

Moving on: Björk with Graham Massey of 808 State, on stage in Manchester, 1991. (Ian T. Tilton) (Below)

Paparazzi pop: Björk and Tricky get trailed in London, 1995.
(Big Pictures) (Above)

Party mood, white dress: Björk takes to the stage with help from designer Hussein Chalayan. (Neils van Iperen/Retna) (Right)

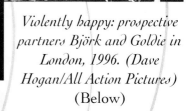

Violently happy: prospective partners Björk and Goldie in London, 1996. (Dave Hogan/All Action Pictures) (Below)

Björk in her Little Venice kitchen, deciding which of her favourite records she'll eat for lunch. (Chris Taylor/Retna) (Below)

Plate section created by D Ramadan

Just don't call me Pixieface . . . (Phil Nicholls/S.I.N.)

Melody Maker reported that the band flew back to Iceland the next day, and that Björk would be releasing her debut album *Björk's Affairs* at the beginning of 1993.

'Some of us had known each other since we were nine,' Björk said. 'We loved and respected each other so much, it became difficult to assert your own viewpoint – it was a bit like a marriage. We became afraid of stepping on each other, which is why I had to change partners.'

'I always saw The Sugarcubes as a party band, a piss take,' she reminisced. 'They were about us getting hilariously drunk and simply having this permission to travel around the world because some foreigner liked us and decided that we were brilliant. We worked together for social reasons, and always had a good time together, whether or not we were stuck in a boring German suburb eating cold hamburgers, and the music was always secondary. So we didn't have this big ambition, musically, and to be brilliant. I don't want to sound like I'm dissing them but it wasn't serious music for me. I used to look around and think, "these people should be writing novels, not doing bass solos in Texas." We held out against the majors for two years but in the end, we gave in. I was very ambiguous but I felt I couldn't let the others down. And as the group went on, I felt that I had to do my own thing.'

As Björk said, The Sugarcubes never even planned their collective life more than two months ahead, they acted on a whim, which the usual career-conscious band would never have dared do. There was no one in control, no one had any control over them. No one cared about being a pop star. 'It's like if you get really into gardening, go to gardening school, get really good at it, then someone notices you have a great sense of how to put gel in your hair. So you're travelling the world, putting gel in peoples' hair, and you don't exactly dislike it, but it isn't what you planned. So you find yourself among all these hairdressers, and you think, "this is fun, but can I have my garden back, please?"'

Would anyone see this particular combination of delicious demons again? 'I haven't a clue,' she confessed. 'Remember, we got together a lot earlier than The Sugarcubes. We're still doing a lot of other things that we always felt were far more important than The Sugarcubes, which took over because of all the attention. A lot of our things are starting to work in Iceland now. I don't know if it's because we've hammered it in over the last twenty years, with our books and bands and whatever. I don't know if it's because people finally understand us, or that we are old and acceptable!'

Björk could hardly escape the irony that, out of all the musical ventures she had been involved in, the guitar-bass-drums and escapist mentality of The Sugarcubes had been the one taken the most seriously. If she had anything to do with it, that was going to change.

Sugarfree

'*Through the unknown, we'll find the new.*'
(Baudelaire)

You could say that Björk was fond of the odd metaphor or two. Here are a couple more. She was a proud parent of The Sugarcubes but she knew it wasn't her baby. 'All I did was add the melodies and write the lyrics, and then watch how the music came out. It was like going to someone else's house for a party. You have a great time, have a few drinks and a laugh, but at the end of the day it's not your home. You're a guest.' It was time to go home.

The Sugarcubes might not have been her musical passion but every experience was necessary schooling for Björk to get closer to establishing her independence. Music school had given her the discipline to hone her instincts and nurture her talent. Spit And Snot, Tappi Tíkarrass and

Kukl gave her insight into communal, collaborative creation and the struggle to survive. The Sugarcubes provided the strength needed to combat the music industry, and the experience of how other bands function, working with demands and expectations, with session musicians, and even what you could reasonably ask for from hotels.

'In The Sugarcubes, I could be in the background and watch a lot of things go on,' she admitted. 'Sometimes you're learning and sometimes you've learnt enough, so that you can use what you've learnt, and it took me a long time to develop, ages to grow up, so about two years ago, I became a grown up. Well, not a grown up, but I was in charge. I've been very lucky.'

The tensions involved in leaving a group are not dissipated so easily. You are part of a collective good, and a collective ego – without it, self-esteem and insecurity are threatened. Am I good enough alone? What *are* my strengths? It seemed obvious to anyone who had been originally bewitched, bothered and bewildered by Björk, that she could maintain a solo career. Björk herself had reservations. Besides the fact that she had never truly worked solo before, having never been in charge, she felt guilty severing ties with The Sugarcubes and paranoid that people would assume she was adopting the arrogant role of the now solo, 'pop star.'

'One of the reasons it took me all these years to make a solo album was because I thought it was so selfish and egotistical,' she reasoned.

'But finally I knew that I had to do an album which had my face on the front and where I wrote all the songs. Something I could sit down with at seventy and be proud of.

'Although I did a solo album when I was eleven, it seemed the easy way out, a bit of a sell-out, but it must have been in my head from that day that this was something I wanted. I always thought it was more challenging in a situation when you're learning, when you're working with other people as different to you as possible, and you learn from them, you have to make it work. It's easy, living on your own, with your own dirty and scruffy toothbrush, very easy and very boring, and if you don't like something, you can just throw it out. But when I started doing it, it didn't feel so selfish. I did this album for my songs, and the way I did it, I sacrificed myself for the songs, and they would get any instruments they deserved, any work they deserved, any pain and happiness, any singing they deserved, so I tried to forget about myself. Like a plumber would do brilliant work, a very unselfish piece of work, so in a way, it's a lot easier than being in The Sugarcubes.'

Where and how to record this fabled solo album were the only decisions she need take. Having been away for extended tourathons, Björk was only too happy to base herself in Iceland; she could be housewife, mother, daughter and friend there better than anywhere, near her beloved water and wilderness, 'a world both isolated but also open to modern influences. I like those extremes.' She even attempted to set up an office in Reykjavík, but Björk and her little fax weren't going to overcome the country's limitations. This was the first, and most painful, sacrifice to make, because she knew enough of the advantages of the West to realize that, if she was to move forward, she had to move away.

Björk considered Paris, LA and New York but realized that, even though she had never enjoyed London on her numerous visits, it was the only really plausible choice. First, One Little Indian was based there, offering familiarity and that sacred independence. Second, Björk may have had her own cosmopolitan infusion of ideas but London had a cross-current of ethnic and musical cultures second to none, including its cutting-edge dance scene. Third, Sindri had to be considered. Now nearly seven, he needed a settled school education, and English was already his second language. Besides, Dom was English, so they could all settle in London together without visa problems.

'I was feeling guilty because I was being handed everything on a silver plate,' Björk admitted. 'I had a very easy life in Iceland, then I started getting into reading biographies of authors and composers and thinking about all the sacrifices they had made to do what they believe in. I had been thinking about these songs for years, since I was a little kid, they were like a diary for me, and I knew that I might submerse this creative impulse for ever. But I realized that at least once in your life you have to go out of your way and do what you're best at. I had to share the songs and take the risks that come with that, or I'd have felt guilty for the rest of my life. And to do this properly I had to move to London. I looked around me and thought of all the good things that had given me the greatest joy in life. It might be incredibly good wine that's just perfect or the right music where you can tell that the artist has gone all the way, done anything to create a perfect song. I had to have a go at least once before I die and see if I could do the same thing.'

After almost eighteen months of transatlantic dalliances, Björk and Dom finally moved together under one roof. They initially settled in the North-west London suburb Belsize Park, to be near the huge, open greenery of Hampstead Heath and the adjoining Primrose Hill, with the best view over London. 'That was the only way I could bear it, if I had a view,' Björk maintained.

Sindri appeared to have no problems settling down. He was already showing signs of inheriting Björk and Thór's intelligent genes. Just as Hildur had noted baby Björk getting goose bumps at the sound of music, so Björk saw that baby Sindri would get them when he heard a certain phrase, and as he grew up, words and precision were his tools. He would plough through encyclopedias, searching for knowledge; an early fascination with dinosaurs – his drawings of which were the only decorations Björk had time to put up in their new home – expanded into cosmology, and more encyclopedias. 'He is more into his brain, if you can say that, more into books, like his father Thór,' says grandmother Hildur. 'He likes music but he is not completely in love with it like Björk was. But he knows everything about things, and is always telling you them, which is a bit tiring at times! But he is very easy to chat to, and loves being around people.'

With Sindri sorted, the luxuries Björk promised herself to make life easier were free airline tickets for friends to visit, and an unlimited phone bill. Yet the transition wasn't easy; she was used to being homesick, but a landlocked London wasn't her ideal environment. The thought of living there made her tense, and she admitted driving Dom a little mad: 'I would be saying, "Why are the taps on the bath-tub that shape?" . . .' The process of moving itself hadn't bothered her; she had got over the stage of missing her belongings, the days when she would carry 'all sorts of stupid stuff around with me in boxes. It took me a long time to learn but I gave up. I just realized that the best thing to have, when you go somewhere, is what you're wearing. One book and you're laughing. Especially when you're trying to move from one country to another, you have to start again. All that stuff makes you too concerned about the past.'

The musical present soon occupied her mind, and reinforced just why she had had to move, to get access to the studio equipment necessary for the diverse album she had in mind. 'If I'd done my album in Iceland, it would have been a religious act because I would have had to learn to be an engineer myself, and build the studio myself. Respect to the people there but I need certain tools and it's all here in London. My album will sell, if I'm lucky, five hundred copies in Iceland as it isn't big enough, but here, I can hire the best saxophone players in the world, and my record company will pay them. It's such a luxury being here because you can see anything you want: if you're into this music, you can buy the record. Maybe, in Iceland, it made the whole thing more exciting, but if you wanted some album of, say, Russian gypsy music or acid jazz, you'd have to call people abroad, send money, go on some sort of a trip but over here, you just buy it and bring it home.'

Not to mention the availability of good, cheap Indian food – the price of a chicken korma in Iceland was £25. If only there wasn't so much pollution, which she claimed stuck to her skin . . . That said, in the *Vessel* video, she even admitted having overcome the grease and the lack of oxygen, and had even got addicted to cities – she was a future woman, after all.

Even so, the conservative, traditional side to British culture felt like an alien world to her. 'People here are good at keeping all the good bits hidden,' she had decided. 'The humour, the warmth and the beautiful bits are all locked in closets, just like the English themselves. They're so civilized and can't lose it unless they've done three E's or something. And they don't think they look good if they're sweating. Me and my friends do everything all the way – we cook like that, we make music like that, we have babies like that.'

As Björk would know, every insular, island culture has its self-protection, even if the UK had less excuse than Iceland. Instead of feeling at home with the natives, she found herself feeling at one with other immigrants, especially the Indian population. 'Even though I always felt quite misunderstood in Iceland, that's basically what I am. So when I'm in London, I'm a visitor here. I call myself an immigrant housewife. I hang out with the Indians in Southall and go to Thai takeaways. The Indian culture is a beautiful one and, for me personally, it's a taste thing. It's much more interesting than the British. I think it's some sort of support, or sympathy, I felt like I belonged there, and was very happy there. They come from somewhere else, and they're very proud of their culture. It's not like they're going to sacrifice that for fish'n'chips and hooliganism, or if you want the other extreme, some sort of Victorian dandyism. It's not like they disrespect that, but it's more like, "this is what I am and I can still live here."'

Homesickness led Björk to resettle nearer water and boats. In the end, she decided to buy a house instead of renting, the final destination being just off Little Venice, on the cusp of the city's inner city border and its leafier West London suburbs, in a former ballet school, on three floors. Once settled, Björk had to negotiate the 'how' of making her record. Believing that, 'the only right that labels have is to pay the bills,' financial independence was as crucial to her plans as artistic independence, though Derek Birkett thought she should have the best of all possible worlds, and so sign to a major label with himself retained as manager. A deal was put on the table but Björk eventually elected to stay at One Little Indian, to retain all aspects of control and licensing to non-UK and Icelandic territories.

After all, Björk was being so independent about the making of her album that she didn't even tell Derek Birkett about it until she had five demos finished (including the Corky Hale recording and the two Icelandic brass arrangements). Birkett remembers being bamboozled by the diversity of the material at this stage, but Björk was adamant that she knew what she wanted. 'I said, "Listen Derek, I want to do an album, but it's not going to be what you think it's going to be, because I am in no mood to please anyone, and it's not going to be your chanteuse, easy-to-sell album".'

Birkett had previously heard material that Björk had recorded in LA with Franne Gold, 'which I thought were the most commercial things she'd ever written,' and was disappointed she wasn't going to follow it through. But he trusted her enough to put money behind her, 'which was very surprising to me. I thought he'd want me to do hit songs, go commercial.'

Birkett admits that he did want Björk to follow the least resistant path to gold discs, yet when she played him a demo of 'Violently Happy', he hated it, 'and I still do, actually! But I told her she could do whatever she wanted, because that's the way I work.'

Being solo didn't mean total solipsism or autonomy. Having worked with Corky Hale and 808 State, Björk saw collaborations as being the most natural way of working. If music was on a par with sex, better to make love than to masturbate. 'I could easily have done an album on my own ages ago and done everything myself but that's not really an ambition for me. The real kick I get out of making music is working with people and preferably in a one-to-one situation. It's almost a musical love affair when you meet the person who can complete your creation and vice versa, you complete theirs.'

Her working method was flexible, 'but it seems to be my role usually to become the other musical half of the person I am working with. I've never really had a problem with my ego or anything – I don't really mind what it takes to make a song, whether it takes for me to just wave a teaspoon or whether I have to do nearly everything and the other person is just there.'

The mother of all Björk's collaborations was her work with Nellee Hooper. Dom knew of the Bristol-based man, who had left The Wild Bunch to work with Jazzy B of Soul II Soul down in London. The pair worked on the collective's hugely influential debut album *Club Classics Volume 1*, where a slinky backdrop of funk, soul and hip-hop motifs shone a torch for the mainstream dance industry. After working on Soul II Soul's follow-up, Hooper was equally lauded for his input on Sinead O'Connor's million-selling Prince cover 'Nothing Compares To U'. Dom thought Nellee and Björk should meet each other.

'I didn't have any intention to have any producer, I thought things would happen by themselves,' she confessed. 'But then I got to know Nellee accidentally, and we started going out to clubs together, and after six months, we were just calling each other all the time, with brilliant ideas, and it took off. He was as sick and tired of where he was coming from as I was of guitars and concerts and being in a band, and he wanted to try something completely different.'

'I was still in LA at the time so I wasn't there when they met but I could tell from phone calls I'd get from each of them that there was a big buzz going on between them,' Dom recalls. 'That doesn't often easily happen without much effort but their ideas obviously gelled, as you can tell by the album that followed. They both realized there was a wide range of music that they could both relate to.'

Björk was initially more taken with Nellee than his music; she knew of Soul II Soul from hearing them on the radio. 'I thought it was brilliant but it wasn't exactly what I had in mind, it was about ten times too sophisticated and tasteful, too "good taste" for my liking. But our work together had nothing to do with where we were both coming from: we had different backgrounds, and in a way, that worked, that was what jammed us to each other. He had complete faith in me and believed in all those quirky faculties that were in my head. He seemed to be very sensually into my ideas and it seemed he would arrange my songs with me from the point of my lyrics, not from a musical history vibe. So I didn't let him loose on the album, I would criticize every footstep he took, but he seemed to have an open mind like myself.'

The original plan was to have a different producer with a different treatment for each track, which then changed to Nellee producing a couple, as would Graham Massey. But Björk ultimately felt so comfortable with Nellee that she asked him to produce the whole album. 'When Graham and I met in 1990,' she told *Dazed & Confused*, 'we were really sparking big time off each other, and for a few years, we sent each other tapes.

But when I started doing the album with Nellee, it just became very obvious that it would end up as a very musical affair between me and Nellee. I talked to Graham and decided to kep the other songs because they were just too different.'

Like Massey, Nellee was a brilliant technician and master of beats, but he had much more conflicting tastes which, as Björk was fond of saying, could make, one and one equal three. Her particular poison was hardcore or industrial techno, 'hard beats with an experimental edge,' while Nellee mined a softer-focused sophistication, producing a balance between force and subtlety, between mesmeric trance and mellow lushness. Her long-standing 'marriage' to The Sugarcubes was one of convenience but this relationship was true musical love, and ideas intuitively flowed. 'With me and Nellee, it was very intimate,' Björk admitted. 'Even though I wrote all the songs, it's hard for me to take full credit for them because we were so dependent on each other. It was great, you forgot about eating, you didn't have to go to the cinema. We got lost in music!'

She had never collaborated with Nellee's type before; besides 808 State, she was only truly used to Icelanders, and his British sensibility, tastes and methods were another kind of tension altogether. Most of all, Björk found herself influenced by the effect of his high standards.

'When you go to his house, he knows where to get the best brandy in Europe, he's got the best cheese. He'll have a record that could only be bought from some record store in Texas in 1953. Everything is the best.

And so, in a way, when he is working with you, you feel immediately quite special. And it's a turn on in a way but in another way, you become an object – you are not a human person any more but an interesting object in his collection. But because he has such high standards when I was working with Nellee, I would write five times better lyrics and five times better melodies and five times better everything – because he was so hard to please, you see? And then at the end of the day, you look at the song and he didn't do anything. I did everything but it happened like that just because he was there.' Björk subsequently wrote 'Big Time Sensuality' about their liaision: *'I can sense it/something important is about to happen/it's coming up . . . we just met/and I know I'm a bit too intimate/but something huge is coming up/and we're both included . . .'*

The admiration was obviously mutual. 'It's probably her energy I got into the most,' Nellee Hooper admits. 'She would arrive, really buzzing from an idea, and we'd literally dive into it, and in a couple of hours, would have something resembling the final product, and the rest would be fine details, which we could spend a week on.

'The sound of her voice and all its ethereal qualities are well documented by now. What I like about Björk is the way she never writes a lyric that actually rhymes. I'm used to working with more soul or rap-oriented people, and most soul and rap tracks rhyme, whereas Björk works in a language that isn't Icelandic or English but more of a North Sea gibberish. It's a specific language with a certain melodic sound she only uses when she writes. It sounds like words but if you ask her, it doesn't mean anything, and then later, she translates it into either Icelandic or English. If you read her lyrics, they are as poetic as the way she sings. It's such an original approach to songwriting, just working from melody. She's really out there on her own.'

Nellee saw Björk as coming from the classic songwriting stable, combining lyrical and musical melodies, working from an overall picture of the song, starting with voice and keyboards. He approached music by starting with the fine details, 'and building up from there, layering textures of sound, creating overall concepts and atmospheres, which she liked. She doesn't pay attention to the smaller details, which I would add. Björk also liked the way I didn't take her too literally. She'd say, "I want this track to sound like 'Scheherazade'", and I'd play a Quincy Jones loop from an old film score, and she'd say, "That's exactly what I meant". I'd fish out something from the groove-oriented end of the spectrum: if I hadn't, I wouldn't have brought anything to the party.'

The working relationship meant that Björk saw the divisions between producer and singer/songwriter break down. 'With Nellee, I become less a singer/songwriter, I almost became this kind of naive person who brings him a big bag full of songs which he then sort of completes, sometimes doing almost nothing, sometimes replacing half of it. I wrote all the songs, but some changed a lot in the studio, just in the arrangements. It was all collaborative. I'm interested in the ingredients of songs. I'm not really into sophisticated surfaces, whereas Nellee is very much a stylist, a stylish character who likes things to look immaculate.

Stylists often don't actually create things, but they are the ones who pick things and put them together brilliantly, which is just as important.'

The first step had been to style the sound. Nellee brought along his trusty programmer Marius De Vries, and then got Bruce Smith from Bristol's late-seventies punk-funk innovators The Pop Group in to play some drums. Björk also knew a thing or two about styling: she asked fellow One Little Indian signing and Shamen vocalist Jhelisa Anderson to sing soul-deep backing vocals, Indian percussionist Talvin Singh to play tabla and arrange strings for a brand new track 'Venus As A Boy', and Gary Barnacle to play sax on 'The Anchor Song' alongside Oliver Lake of American jazzateers The World Saxophone Quartet, one of her favourite ensembles. 'Björk sung live as we put our saxes down,' says Gary Barnacle. 'All we had to guide us was a drum loop, which is a very unusual way to record in these multi-track days. We also had no chords or instruments to pitch against, to make sure we were in tune, so we had to hope that we were in pitch with each other. We played until the vocal and saxes went together. She didn't like the idea of patching things up: she wanted it to be spontaneous.

'Music is this paintbox for her: she has great ideas but doesn't know what the notes or chords are, but gets the right people in to recreate what she hears in her head. It's particularly refreshing as people can get jaded with the mechanics of writing, recording and promotion, but she had the same enthusiasm as when she started, which puts everybody in a positive frame of mind when you're recording.'

Though Gary Barnacle talks about Björk not knowing the chords, Graham Massey thinks that: 'She always plays down her musicality, because she is obviously trained at music, but she hides it under a blanket, as if she doesn't want to tread on anyone's toes. She did some string arranging on her second album and you have to have a big musical knowledge to do that.'

Wind, brass and string instruments were always going to figure in Björk's solo plans, to the exclusion of traditional sounds like the guitar. There was a guitar employed on the album, though for decorative purposes only, not that anyone outside the studio would notice. 'My ideal band would be an open-minded group that wouldn't let anything get in the way of creating something new,' she said. 'They could use saxophones, teaspoons, drum machines or anything to communicate a whole concept, whether it be a house track, experimental music, pop, or just a nursery rhyme.'

Through the second half of 1992, all those elements, and more – synths, violins, unidentifiable Björkian noises – were scooped up and fed into the Nellee/Björk machine. Out the other end came a staggering array of styled sounds, scouring dance's wide diaspora, different 'world' musics, from Nordic to Indian, with pop, jazz and classical motifs. She hoped to incorporate the real modern beats, like those made by machines and cars and elevators and roadwork and people shouting and dogs barking – 'that's what daily life sounds like, when you close your eyes and listen.' She also wanted to feed off the world of film soundtracks, 'because they capture lots of different moods. It allows human feelings to exist, the music allows you to be unpredictable whereas pop music today is so clinical and sterile. There's so much bad pop music around because people don't believe in magic any more.'

There was no obvious meeting point for such disparate music – just Björk, whose understanding of each idiom and capacity for experimentation made for a unique, quintessentially nineties recording.

Nellee was so excited by the work in progress that he would rush home in order to play tracks. Naturally, as on any adventure or experiment, there was a down side, and Nellee admits that it wasn't a simple joy-fest. 'There were tears of course, from both sides, and arguments, but that's how you make a good record,' he reckons. 'We'd argue about the process of writing because it was so exciting, and to be involved in that amount of excitement but not have any extreme emotions was impossible. Emotionally, I still haven't recovered from the goose bumps. Even when we were sketching the guide vocal, I'd have them from the neck down, and they don't really go away.'

The team mostly shifted between seven studios in London, but tended toward working more sociable hours than the usual through-the-night sessions. 'Every night,' Nellee recalls, 'we went out after recording, to a different club. Every morning was a hangover, and every evening was a party, just to hear new music all the time, so there were a lot of good times. But the last thing Björk wanted to talk about was music when she went out. She could be quite rude to people who asked her about it.'

Having secured the music, Björk faced her first solo interview, in a February edition of the *Sunday Times*. She spoke of modest ambitions: 'In Iceland, The Sugarcubes are thought of as stubborn punks who refuse to grow up. We're well known and respected, but we're not popular. I'd like to achieve that position abroad. To get my little thing in the corner and get enough money to make another album. That would be perfect.'

The first track to publicly emerge was 'One Day', as part of the April 1993 issue of the monthly CD magazine, *Volume*. Editor Robin Gibson recalls that the track was received, 'with no particular amount of excitement, possibly because it was one of the more conventional tracks on the album.'

Two months later, that was to drastically change as the first solo Björk single, the much more idiosyncratic 'Human Behaviour' was taken to heart. It was a great opening gambit; minimalist, quixotic dance music without the usual regimented structures. Just hear the layered percussive intro – a mix of taut African and Asian rhythms with a neo-military shuffle over the tundra, derived from a Quincy Jones-produced sample from 'Go Down Dying' by Brazilian artist Antonio Carlos Jobim, and modified by Hooper & Co. The B-side, 'Atlantic', was a curio too; part Caribbean reggae, part smooch soul – hardly the techno-animal anyone was expecting.

The inspiration behind 'Human Behaviour' said it all: *'there's definitely no logic to human behaviour.'* No logic to Björk then, but what a return:

'you ever get close to a human and human behaviour/be ready to be confused . . . they're terribly moody, then all of a sudden turn happy, but oh, to get involved in the exhange of human emotions is ever so satisfying.' It sounded like a child's motto, or at least an outsider's unofficial manifesto, her voice charged with wonder, telling you that, *'a compass wouldn't help at all.'*

Björk saw it as a meditation on humanity's weirdness: 'I was singing about all those strange, complicated adults I saw every day,' she said. In the *Sunday Times*, she introduced the notion that the song dealt with, 'my very complex family. My son has eight grandmothers and eight grandfathers and it's all about the love and the complications of that', she concluded with typical exaggeration.

'Human Behaviour' was quickly followed by a second CD and 12 inch vinyl version, containing remixes by some of her favourite dance/club activists – in this case, East London dance/rock fusioneers Underworld and Dutch DJ Speedy J, who both took a techno angle, boyfriend Dom T, whose tastes were more house-y, and The Bassheads who vacillated between the two. Björk saw remixes as part of the equation. 'There are many sides to the same story,' she claimed.

Björk was also able to tell a story with visual magic. She chose French animator Michel Gondry to direct the video to 'Human Behaviour'; Björk had seen his showreel and loved the disarming/charming fairytale-FX skills he had employed for the promo videos of his own pop group

Oui Oui. 'It was the first time someone had appreciated the work I had done on my own terms, without compromises,' he said in *Post*. 'Björk understood that while the images and the animation can look childish or sweet on the surface, they can operate on another level.'

Her instructions were simple: 'a bear and textures like handmade wood and leaves and earth, and I want it to seem like animation' (the absence of direct 'human' behaviour was probably the point). Gondry's version looked like a surrealist take on Goldilocks And The Three Bears, with a chase sequence echoing the dreamy, nocturnal atmosphere of the impressionist movie thriller *Night Of The Hunter*, where a miniature Björk is joined by a multitude of fluffy, giant animals – a moth, a hedgehog and, of course, the bear, who, in this ecologically correct version, beats up the human hunter: 'I guess it was the teddy's job to avenge in the name of all animals,' she suggested.

If the single and video were a brilliant introduction to Björkworld, then the complete debut album *Debut* was a ravishing diverse statement, Björk as many continents. Ten songs, a multitude of styles, fusions, tensions: *'be ready to be confused'* indeed. Cocktail jazz! Avant-indie! Torch-folk! Nordic techno! A verdant soundgarden. This was a work of errant imagination: playful, brash, delicate, introspective, off-kilter. Elvis Costello likened the sound of *Debut* to, 'dance music played by a jazz quartet.' Spearheaded by that sublime gale-force voice with as much sensitivity of touch, how could you fail to be totally seduced.

The album was officially Björk's third solo album, after 1977's *Björk* and 1990's *Gling-gló*, but she christened it *Debut* because she felt that the record was her proper debut, with all her own songs and ideas, the true *essence du Björk.* 'For me, it's quite a brave thing,' she told *NME.* 'It's like putting your diary out for everyone to read. Of course, I didn't put everything in, I very carefully edited it. I'm very good with the scissors . . .'

She still left enough in to tell a good story, to let everyone know that this was more about Björk's heart than her love of man-made fibre. 'Human Behaviour', which opened the album, represented her sense of wonder at her place in the wide world but the remainder was a reflection of her own human behaviour, of the inner world of Björk.

She laid no claim as a lyricist – 'I'm neither an artist nor a poet, who can create something with words that can stand up on their own on paper, that become a world of their own you can enter.' The emotion was the main point: 'I can write a song in half an hour but it might take me four weeks to write the lyrics. It is not my natural way of expressing myself. For most Icelandic people, it is easy to be witty and intellectual. For me, being brainy is a disease.'

She stressed that her words were dependent on their music to try and make the music into a world in its own right. 'Beyond that,' she sighed, 'I haven't got a lot to say.' To understand her vision, she wanted people to, 'look at the whole picture. A lot of old country songs, like "I Go To

Pieces", or jazz songs like "My Funny Valentine", or "Let's Get Lost", are very emotionally extreme. I want my songs to be real, alive. That's the only target I've got.'

Why was Björk writing lyrics, then? As *The Face* said, she was mirroring an anthropologist, like David Attenborough, who explores emotional landscapes and attempts to capture them in music. 'I walk around saying, "Listen, there's love in the air, the lights are dim, look . . ." And I try to make music from that, which excites people, which inspires them and gives them joy.'

Her lyrics might be free of egoistical self-pity and doused in life-affirming joy yet the album's emotional terrain revealed surprisingly high levels of melancholy and yearning, as if Björk the great individualist had realized that humans must search for love and acceptance, otherwise they won't ever really be complete. 'Human Behaviour' had its dark side after all – you can be more disappointed in than entranced by people, as she also described on the bubbly but tense 'Crying': *'I travel all around the city, go in and out of locomotives all alone/there's no one here and people everywhere . . . here everyone is vulnerable and I'm as well.'* 'It's about being misunderstood in general rather than not having a boyfriend,' Björk explained. 'It's like you love people very much but they're just interested in something you're not interested in, and vice versa.'

'Crying' and the more dream-disco 'One Day' (*'and the beautifullest fireworks are burning in the sky just for you'*), were the oldest songs on the album, 'which you can probably tell because they're the most melancholic', she ventured. 'I've had the best times of my life in the last few years. It's probably more introverted than melancholic now'.

Björk maintained that her songs usually came from something that she was particularly into that month: 'It might be cinnamon and silvery, tingly things, and I can spot them everywhere. Last month it might have been muscular women. But it's always a relief to let it out. I decide on every detail and I get obsessed'. Love was unquestionably the overriding detail when she was obsessively formulating her lyrics, and *Debut* was overwhelmingly smitten by being smitten, to the point where the old surrealist version of realism was no longer pertinent. Take 'Aeroplane', full of moody, urgent longing, written about her trips to LA to see Dom – *'I cannot live peacefully without you, for even a moment . . . I'm taking an aeroplane across the world to follow my heart'.* 'Come To Me' was passionate devotion – *'jump off, your building's on fire/I'll catch you . . . destroy all that is keeping you back, and then I'll nurse you'.*

Or take the deliciously lush 'Venus As A Boy', also inspired by Dom, the shared passion heated by lust – *'his wicked sense of humour suggest exciting sex/his fingers focus on her/touches, he's venus as a boy'.* The line, *'he's exploring the taste of her, arousal so accurate'* doesn't have to suggest oral sex, though probably does, and is all the more sexy for it, while Talvin Singh's string arrangement (recorded in Bombay, to get that real Indian film-soundtrack timbre) dips and swirls alongside Nellee's sensual arrangement. Without Einar's disfigurements, Björk was free to illustrate beauty and romance. "Venus As A Boy" is about this boy I know who sees everything from a beauty point of view. And not superficial beauty, but the beauty of brushing your teeth and the beauty of waking up in the morning in the right beat and the beauty of having a conversation with a person. All this was new to me as I tend to look at things from an energy point of view.'

'There's More To Life Than This (Recorded Live In The Milk Bar Toilets)' was the album's truly offbeat, impish moment – an out-and-out dance track that suggests there is more to life than club life, sung live *in* a club (Central London's now defunct Milk Bar), in and out of the toilets, with cubicle doors banging and the crowd humming, and the whole shebang gently tweaked in the studio.

This was Björk's attempt to get closer to the source, to make pop music magic, but to keep it real. 'I'd already written the song, and I'd been obsessed with making an album live, as opposed to some artificial studio experience. I think a lot of pop music is written in reference to pop, which I think is a bit ridiculous, it's like writing a book on a book. You have to write pop music about real life, so I kept going on about that, and trying to change old songs and old styles to get more real life things, so that it would almost be like film music. Nellee came out with the idea to go to The Milk Bar. It was played on the stereo there and then what you hear is the music leaking on the microphone, and I sing, and I go inside a room, and into the toilet, and back out, and then out the door. People were in the club but it wasn't a very busy night.

'The idea is that I'm in the club and I go to the toilet. I'm not on the song, the song's just the disco. It's probably the most true to reality song on the album because it's very much what me and Nellee have been doing in between working on the album. You know the feeling when you go to a club and you've looked forward to it for a long time, and you end up spending the whole evening in the toilet? You get out of the toilet and everybody's getting into their coats and leaving.'

Her inspiration this time had been a different kind of love, encountered during a particularly vivid night out in Reykjavík. 'I went to a party with this big, exciting girl who I really liked and she was a bit daring, and I kind of sneaked off with her. So we got really drunk together by the harbour and had a really good time. Where I come from we don't have the choice of clubs you have in London. There's The Bar, The Pub, and The Disco that'll play hardcore techno, and then maybe Stars on 45. If you want to have fun, you have to make it yourself.'

The track was the only one on *Debut* with a distinct four-to-the-floor techno beat. People had been surprised at the lack of overtly machine-driven beats but Björk wanted her dance beats to have a life of their own. 'I think they're beats that are more reflective of daily life,' she told *Rolling Stone*. 'Like life in the middle of the day in a city, as opposed to the nightlife of the clubs.'

The euphoria of 'There's More To Life Than This' segued into the heavenly harp setting of 'Like Someone In Love', like E-cstatic club madness succumbing to a sublime, drifting comedown. The song was written by Johnny Burke and Jimmy Van Heusen in the mid-forties, and made famous by jazz saxophonist, vocal balladeer and the James Dean of his pre-war age, Chet Baker – 'the most beautiful man in the world', according to Björk. The 'Disney'-fication decoration Björk and Nellee had worked out was birdsong and sea swell, to accompany the sentiment, *'Lately, I find myself out, gazing at stars/hearing guitars, like someone in love/Sometimes the things I do astound me, mostly whenever you're around me.'*

The mood abruptly changed for 'Big Time Sensuality', Björk's ode to Nellee. The tone was passionate, but untouched by lust, as Björk explained: 'I think it's quite rare, when you're obsessed with your job, as I am, when you meet someone who's your other half jobwise and enables you to do what you completely want . . . so it wasn't about a sexual romance . . . it's about when you meet someone and you just want to do everything in the world and take off and fuck the rest and let's get lost and all that bollocks.'

The mood of the song was mirrored in the title of the album's last dance tune, the jittery 'Violently Happy' – *'since I met you/this small town hasn't got room for my big feelings . . . violently happy/come calm me down before I get into trouble . . .'* Written in autumn 1991, 'it's about being stuck on an island and in love with someone on the other side of the planet.'

'Big Time Sensuality' and 'Violently Happy' seemed to say it all for Björk. If nihilism and negativity are not only key motifs in rock music – the last rock action hero has to be Nirvana's Kurt Cobain, violently haunted by his complicated pain – but found running through all art, then Björk wanted to tap a vein of positivism more often than not associated with hippie idealism, 'the glass is half full' approach rather than 'the glass is half empty'. In doing so, she was achieving the near impossible, aligning the passion of punk with the hippie belief system.

'I never identified with the glorification of doom and gloom. Also, I really hate pop artists who exploit their own negativity. A lot of harm has been caused by rock stars who misuse their fans so that they can get rid of their own depression. I couldn't justify that kind of behaviour to Sindri. In many respects, a pop artist is closer to his listeners than their parents or friends, so that you have to have a positive influence, to allow two-way traffic. It is too easy to assume that in order to be fascinating, you have to have drama and suffering.'

Debut closes up shop with 'The Anchor Song', Björk's most positive statement of all, a love-song-lullaby of homecoming that could be interpreted as an open letter to Iceland, or just an affirmation of one's own sense of self: *'I live by the ocean/and during the night/I dive into it/down to the bottom/underneath all currents/and drop my anchor/this is where I'm staying/this is my home.'*

Björk had written the song in the summer of 1990, when she had left Sindri with a child-minder and set out across Iceland, 'on a freedom thing', riding her bicycle around with the express purpose of visiting all the churches built by each farm settlement in the country. Against expectations, her requests to play the church organ were granted, and she would play uninterrupted for hours before moving on to the next village. Songs invariably got written, and 'The Anchor Song' was one that she finished. If travel really is a search for the soul, then is the concept of home the knowledge of what has been found?

The inspiration behind the song's Nordic folk-jazz whale-song atmosphere came directly from her childhood. After *The Sound Of Music* had been laid to rest, her absolute favourite record was *De Seksten Beste*, an album of children's stories and songs by Norwegian writer Tornbjorn Egner, starring the two trolls Karius and Baktus, whose sound effects Björk likened to a simplified, child's version of Igor Stravinsky, 'with wind and brass instruments. There are happy songs and sad songs on the record, but they're all very dramatic. "The Anchor Song" is definitely influenced by this, a very simple song with silly lyrics, and wind instruments.'

The track had been knocked into shape by Oliver Lake of the World Saxophone Quartet. Having recorded songs with Icelandic brass blowers in 1990, Björk sensed that something was missing from her saxophone parts. 'Musically, it was the form I wanted them to be, but they needed arrangement. I sent Oliver the score and tape, and he kind of rewrote the bits for saxophone and made it come alive. He put attitude in it that I was incapable of . . . 80 per cent of saxophone I can't stand, like rock'n'roll sax. But Oliver's attitude is very modern. It's fresh. Saxophones tend to romanticize a lot, I like them being quite pranksterish, sounding rude.'

'My experience of Björk was very short,' Lake recalls. 'She was interested in incorporating the World Saxophone Quartet sound in her album, sent me the music, and I came to London, and rearranged what she had arranged. It was a very easy-going situation: she knew exactly what she wanted, so there wasn't much for me to say. I liked the song very much, and liked the final result even more. I don't work much with vocalists, especially pop vocalists of the exposure of Björk, but I thought her sound, and her vocal, was very unique, which is my signature on the saxophone too. Her voice calls you. I could see the way she writes isn't formularized, which is the pop way, so in that way, she's like a jazz writer. She breaks the norm of what the industry thinks will be a hit, puts together different rhythms and songs and colours, and people like it. That's great!'

Getting someone of the calibre of Oliver Lake to work on her music showed that London had been an ideal place to centre herself and explore outwards. 'These jazzy, funky people are in London, playing live, getting into interesting areas of music,' she raved, and she could have been talking about *Debut*. Björk's talent for styling was the equal of Nellee's, and it was hard to think of another artist who had lived outside the mainstream of indie-pop and dance, yet who had united them together so successfully. 'It's always irritated me when people try to separate the two. That dance music has to be brainless and simple while "serious" pop music has to be more difficult and lyrically orientated. I have always felt, even before I began to make my own music, that everything should be possible, all combinations. I want to be everything at once: clever, dumb, angry, sweet, ancient and childish, naive, experienced, happy and melancholy.

'I think not sticking to any particular musical style makes the album real. Life isn't always the same. You don't live in the same style from day to day, unexpected things happen that are beyond your control. That's this record. One song is about the mood you're in walking to the corner shop, another is about being drunk and out of it on drugs in a club and the next is about feeling romantic and making love.

'Pop is music for a particular moment. You should be able to throw it away the next day but it has to be real for that one moment so that as you're doing the dishes and hear it on the radio, you can relate to it, go deep into it, and know that it matters and makes a difference for you. It doesn't have to be some existential arty piece, it can be just a song that everybody can sing along to. But it has to touch you deeply for that moment!

As we know, *Debut*'s consummate brilliance was to deeply touch literally millions, for a lot more than a moment . . .

One such was Björk's mother. Hildur, who had listened to numerous demos over the years, expressed surprise when she first heard *Debut*. 'But for anyone who knows Björk, it is so very much her too. She got a lot from nature which she now puts into her music. It is a bit to do with being Icelandic, to do with the dark and the light, the dramatic contrasts. It is very honest music!

A viewpoint also illustrated by a glorious memory of Nellee's. After *Debut* was finished, Björk, Dom, Nellee and Marius had gone on holiday, to Phuket in Thailand. One night, they were dining in a restaurant with a cocktail bar and piano, whose owner discovered that Björk was a singer, and asked her to sing. 'She asked the pianist, "Do you know such-and-such?" and then sung a few standards. The place was full of people who'd never heard of her, mostly older people, American and European, and everyone just stood up and applauded. To the older generation, she came across as just as much of a star. She is the real deal. Thinking of all the hype around Björk these days, she just stood there, in a silver dress, and sung, relocated in a fresh environment, and won them all over. It was free champagne for the rest of the night. It was like Picasso, who'd walk into a restaurant, sign the napkin, and get free food and drink.'

Take the plaintive passion of Sinead O'Connor, the angelic whimsy of The Cocteau Twins' Liz Fraser, the flighty Nordic torch-folk of Stina Nordenstam, and the Canadian-born spirits of Jane Siberry and the incomparable Mary Margaret O'Hara, who both mix folk, jazz, torch-song and blues into more indedinably individual, rapturous styles. Björk had the lot, wrapped up in one five-foot-plus battery, with the added *x* factor of unpredictability, that feisty-punk-child-woman-sorcery *thang* . . .

Almost every music critic agreed that *Debut* was unique, daring, refreshing, seductive, enchanting, *complete. Time Out* called it, 'certainly the most original, *musical* music to come out of the dance-pop milieu since the disinvention of the human bassist . . . may turn out to be the first complete pop music of the decade.' Nellee Hooper's role was equally praised: 'He's produced it like a landscape, with depth, light, texture and weather.'

There had to be odd doubters. *Melody Maker*'s Chris Roberts, the man who first turned cartwheels over 'Birthday', thought *Debut* was, 'by turns frenetic, frothy and frustrating', while Nellee Hooper's production was blamed for making, 'a mere nightclubber of her guileless sealclubber.' What's more, 'the feral is pushed to the peripherals . . . when Björk stops believing that being an "alternative Kylie" is big and clever, she can walk and talk like a *driven* doll.'

The implication being that Björk was in danger of becoming to the nineties what Sade was to the eighties – the ubiquitous coffee-table 'heroine' on every suburban turntable, the epitome of 'tasteful'. Björk gave short shrift to any detractors who suggested that *Debut* was a commercial betrayal of her Icelandic/alternative roots. 'From my point of view, I was more commercial with The Sugarcubes,' she told *NME*. 'People think I'm selling out, but it's really the other way around for me. I'm following my instincts.'

'I've listened to PJ Harvey and she sounds sincere, but I'm not into getting out guitars and being angry anymore,' she told *Outlook*. 'It's the kind of thing you do when you're fifteen and you leave home. You can't scream and shout for twenty years. I'm more into real songs nowadays.'

But if *Debut* was destined to be a coffee-table album for the nineties, then at least it was raising the creative stakes for the cultural totem –

a record that doesn't fit conveniently, that revels in its otherworldliness, that demands more involvement than passive background reception. If there was a thirty-something hipster audience, who saw in Björk the kind of mainstream star they can willingly accept, then Björk was winning the war for pop.

Before the album was even released, she was already sceptical about its fantastic reception, having been burnt by the press turnaround on The Sugarcubes' second album. 'I'm just going to see what happens,' she decided. 'I'm down to earth about things. I've got quite comfortable in my own little misunderstood position. I grew up that way, like at school, and I learnt very early to turn it to my advantage, and I like that, so I'm not too worried about what other people say. But what I'm concerned about is the same as with The Sugarcubes. I'm just making my album, and I'm proud of it, but the press, especially in England, are very thirsty, very bored, and I'm not going to save them from boredom. If they think I am going to solve their problems, I will let them down. I'm just doing my album, and I don't want them to misunderstand me. For instance, my next album is not going to be like this album, it's going to be something completely different. I just want it to be right.'

Make way for the juicy metaphor! 'If I'm going over to someone's house to cook them a meal, and they think I'm great at cooking Russian meatballs, and I've never cooked it before . . . just don't have great expectations, or take me for something I'm not. I'm going to come to your house and we're probably going to have a great time, but I'm not going to cook Russian meatballs!'

Modest to the end, outlandish media support for *Debut* appeared to unnerve Björk. 'It sounded like they were describing a bowl of chicken tandoori more than a record!' she laughed. Even the likes of Eric Clapton publicly praised the album – an irony that didn't escape her, having a stepfather considered Iceland's Clapton – and Björk wasn't sure whether to feel flattered or wonder if she had done something wrong. 'I still have so far to go and though I think this album is alright, it's a bit of a rehearsal,' she said. 'I don't think I'll make a really good album until maybe three or four records down the road. There's so much that I still need to learn.'

Looking back from the vantage point of 1995, Björk told *Raygun* that she thought *Debut*, 'very good for when it was made but it was very much about me being terribly shy and deciding, "Well, it's now or never." It was just about baring myself for other people to see, and I was very insecure. I wanted to make perfect, immaculate pop songs, which was a result of my shyness, really.'

Shyness might have been intrinsic to the music but Björk was anything but retiring when it came to promoting *Debut*. After The Sugarcubes' latterday acts of bolshiness, she was willing to sacrifice her time on behalf of her songs. 'I've been doing press every day for two months now, twelve hours a day, every day,' she admitted. 'It's good because it means there are more possibilities for me to make an album any way I want. The more interviews I do, the more likely I am to sell records and do more the next time. Plus the best thing is that you get more mental strength from it.'

She needed that mental strength because the nature of the interviews themselves was still unsettling her. 'I've worked in factories for sixteen hours a day but this is a completely different kind of pressure, it plays games in your brain. It's alright for a while but it's a bit misunderstanding. If you read an interview, something will confuse the person. They're not going to take things as they are, they have their own ideas, and you shouldn't listen to music like that. That's the best thing is, like when you listen to music on a radio in a taxi, you know? Or in a club? It's the honest way of listening, because you have to take it for what it is.'

She joked of stickering the album with, 'WARNING: THIS INTERVIEW WON'T BRING YOU CLOSER TO THE MUSIC', but she was going to have to let the public decide that Björk and her music were two completely separate issues. 'In a way, there's nothing more to it than music,' she responded, weakly. 'That's where all the magic is and the messages, and all the creation.' To agree to talking so much, and then complain about it, seemed pointless. Of all the garrulous, camera-loves-me types, Björk seemed one of the last to try and downplay the cult of personality.

The Hardcore And The Gentle

'I want to prove that music can be happy and fascinating at the same time. That there is as much intense emotion in, "I feel fantastic", as in, "oh, I'm such a martyr."'

Even if she secretly despised the media process, Björk gave good quote, and of course the press lapped up every opinion, wild claim, joke, complaint . . . a star with boundless energy and stroppiness to boot was better than almost any other combination. The magazines and newspapers wanted all the facts – her age, her race, especially what she looked like, anything that the public might be seduced by. The music press adored her feisty spirit, weighty opinions and musical adventurism; the style press adored her for all that, and needed her as much, for how many singers were so keen to embrace fashion, with a face to match that to-die-for voice?

For her debut solo photo spread, in a February edition of the *Sunday Times*, Björk had made it clear that her clothes were as much a clue to her persona as her music, wearing an Indian prayer bead and chiffon scarf dress, with her hair in child-like bunches. Yet for the cover of *Debut*, she showed that she had an understanding of the power of understatement: the image was starkly simple, black and white, of Björk alone, from just the elbows up, in uncoiffured hair and mohair wool sweater ('I've always been for hairy things – and if you don't have a friend or a pet or you're away travelling, then it's nice to have cuddly things to wear', she once recommended). Your eyes were magnetized by hers; under each eye, she had stuck the traditional Indian decoration, bindis, which are traditionally applied to the forehead, echoing Man Ray's famous jewelled tears. Her fingers, dipped in gold paint, were held, prayer-like, over the mouth.

The back cover of the CD booklet was more experimental – hair pinned up with dangling threads at the side, a shrunken sweater over a dress with unfinished edges made by Belgian designer Martin Margeira, the newly crowned king of 'deconstructive' fashion (fabrics turned inside out, ripped, roughed up). In another photo, Björk was sitting down, hair strands delicately combed over her face, as she cradled a toy boat taken from her own collection.

The session was the work of celebrated French fashion photographer Jean-Baptiste Mondino. 'Right away, when I saw her,' Mondino says, 'I knew we were dealing with someone important. From her demo tape, it was obvious that she was a really important crossover, a mix between technology music and some kind of artistic, personal expression, for the first time. Just dynamite. When we met, she was already wearing Martin Margeira's clothes, which I didn't mind her wearing for the shoot, so we did the session and it was very, very pleasant. Because she comes from a different background to where we expect pop music to come from, it accounts for her fresh approach. She's not really conceptual, and there's a lot of freedom. She knows what she doesn't want, but at the same time, she thinks anyone can take a great picture or make a great video because she brings everything in – the style, the clothes, the attitude. And there is no fear. Most times, people are a bit anxious about how they will be portrayed but she is very easy because she doesn't pay attention to it. At the same time, she is herself, and will stay like that. For me, she is an iceberg, we only see a litle tip of it.'

TV performances and the video of 'Venus As A Boy' revealed more of her maverick spirit when the track became a single in August. Bindis now decorated her eyebrows as Björk wore figure-hugging orange and gold, revealing a sensual curviness – this was no child-like waif or pretend supermodel, but something organically sexier. In the video, Björk explores the lust-filled saga with a sex/food analogy, singing in a kitchen (a dayglo fantasy to match Michel Gondry's forest). Fondling an egg would have seemed bizarre to anyone who didn't know her obsession with George Bataille's *Story Of The Eye*; in this three-minute potboiler, the egg gets rolled over her face and upper body, butter sizzles in the pan, then burns as Björk absent-mindedly swoons, eyes and mouth a flutter. The egg is subsequently fried in oil, salted, and taken off camera to . . . eat? *Voila*, the world's first sex-cookery-music promo video is born.

The video director, Sophie Muller, had worked closely with ex-Eurythmics singer Annie Lennox, whose cross-gender role-playing and tightly scripted pop had made her the definitive eighties female icon alongside Madonna. Björk thought Muller was right for the close-up format she had in mind, and gave her a copy of *Story Of The Eye* two days before the shoot, though she didn't insist that she read it. Muller ran out of time, and subsequently missed the point of the storyboard in Björk's eyes. 'She kept on about the egg being fried,' she told *Details*. 'I was saying, "No way is that book about a fried egg. I'm sorry. Poached? OK. Boiled O-kay. Raw? *Okay*. But not fried. It's too hard. It's rough and it's greasy. It should be about being sort of liquidy and wet and soft and open.' In Björk's mind, *that* was sex and sexuality.

Though *Debut* had been put to bed, Björk was still looking to explore musical diversions and collaborations, and the continuing pattern of releasing two CD EPs for each single gave her the room. The first CD of 'Venus' included a mildly clubby mix by Mykaell Riley, a 'non-toilet' mix of 'There's More To Life Than This' and Björk's own reverential, 'domestic mix' of 'Violently Happy', comprising just voice and church-style organ. The second turned through 360 musical degrees. There was one of the long-lost Elgar Sisters tracks from 1987, the spellbound *'Stígdu Mig'* (which loosely translates as 'Step', as in, 'get me going', says Árni Matthíasson. 'It was one of Björk and her friends' private jokes'); a second excerpt from the Corky Hale sessions, 'I Remember You', written by Tin Pan Ally supremos Victor Schwertzinger and Johnny Mercer; between the two, Björk's beloved Sheffield technoids Black Dog turned 'The Anchor Song' into underwater music, with much probable use of the 'oceanic dub sensarround' button. But leading the CD off was a '7 inch Dream Mix', in a bass-heavy mix with a beat half way between trip-hop and reggae, the work of one of Björk's newest admirers, Mick Hucknall of Simply Red.

'She's the Billie Holiday of the nineties and beyond', Hucknall gushed. 'That voice deserves a vast audience.' Derek Birkett met his request to do a remix by sending him a preview tape of the album. Though Birkett might have been thinking of the commercial possibilities, Björk certainly wasn't, but she wasn't going to deny Hucknall just because of his popularist streak. 'Some people have got a lot of snobbery going on, and arrogance', she frowned. 'They think that some people are better than others, which is bullshit. Mick Hucknall had a sincere interest in working with me and my voice, and I've always been a bit soft on sincerity'. In any case, Björk accepted the mix but relegated it to the second CD: 'I didn't think it improved on the original because that's the way I wanted it to be', she said, diplomatically. 'Mick Hucknall's mix is Mick Hucknall's mix.'

Birkett didn't even want 'Venus As A Boy' as the next single, thinking it wouldn't be a hit, but he liked the remix, as did national radio programmers. They preferred it to Björk's own mix, gave the single daytime exposure, and subsequently boosted it chartwards, and Björk onto *Top Of The Pops* for the first time.

The media train was now running under its own steam. Dance music lacked amazing graceful faces, and only the rapidly rising Suede was injecting pop with a palpable sense of glamour and panache. Björk was a heaven-sent combination of both attributes. Even the tabloid press joined in, witnessed at its misjudged, facile finest by the *Daily Star* comment, 'Pop sensation Björk has revealed how she fled to Britain with a trendy American DJ in a last-ditch bid for stardom.'

Björk had the chance to ingratiate herself further into the murky mainstream when Levis Jeans approached her with the flattering offer to use 'Venus As A Boy' in the label's forthcoming commercial. According to Derek Birkett, Björk had already turned down Pepsi and Coca-Cola on principle but Levis had got a stage further because of its historical association with music. But Björk felt that any product link coloured people's perceptions of her songs, and Birkett couldn't convince her otherwise. 'It was our next scheduled single, so it was an incredible offer, but she gave me all the reasons why not. They even came back with the creative suggestion that they run Björk's video, and then put, "Sponsored By Levis Jeans," at the end, but she still wouldn't agree. I was convinced that she was going to do it at one point but I've never been able to talk her into anything.'

With or without sponsorship, *Debut* was selling steadily in and out of the UK, to Derek Birkett's surprise. 'He'd expected it to sell about a third of what The Sugarcubes did because it was just too eccentric, Björk grinned. 'But I said, "Listen, I gotta do this. At least I'll die with a happy face." So it was a complete surprise how well it did.'

In Iceland, she was more shocked than surprised to find politicians sending letters of congratulations. 'The last victory we won this big was in the Disabled Olympics years ago, when this girl won a lot of gold medals.' In a cover feature in *The Face*, Björk relayed a story of how she had been called at home by Iceland's foreign minister. Before the elderly Icelandic operator put him through, the woman got in a few words of her own: 'I'm a big fan of your music. And by the way, would you like me to pass on a message to your granddad? I see him every day at the swimming pool.' That's how it is in Iceland. They don't know how to treat me. When I do interviews there, they ask questions like, "Are you famous?", "How much money have you made?", "Have you met Michael Jackson?"'

One Little Indian's then press officer Christina Kyriacou recalls a photoshoot around Reykjavík, which included the famous, serene Blue Lagoon. 'We were there first thing in the morning, as it's mainly Icelanders there, not tourists. There were these old people, taking in the medicinal benefits, and Björk hadn't got her bathing costume, so she was running around trying to get one, and these old ladies were clasping her hand, going, "Oh Björk, well done, it's so wonderful," acting like her grandma or a relative, but Björk had never met them before. That's how people are towards her there. They all feel they own a part of her, and that Björk is a part of Iceland.'

Gling-gló, however, still proved more popular there than *Debut* – ironically, the record that kept *Debut* off the top of the Icelandic charts was ex-Sugarcube Siggi's *Bogomil Font* album! Björk was still a little bit of an acquired taste at home. As Björk's best friend Joga saw it, 'Everyone is proud of Björk here. But to them she is like a little girl.'

Björk was still as suspicious of fame as she was when a little girl of eleven. 'No one's a star in Iceland because it's too local,' she reiterated. 'You see stars buying toilet rolls in the supermarket. I'm suspicious of fame. Anyone can be famous – just walk down the street naked once.'

Her fame had spread far enough to fuel rumours of potential duets with Bryan Ferry, Duran Duran's Simon Le Bon, Mick Hucknall and uprising Brit-soulman Omar, but they seemed more like PR jokes than serious opportunities. She did actually meet Omar and discussed a collaboration, but otherwise it was the Björk office getting inundated with requests. Björk's mind, of course, was approximately 900 miles away. Dealing with the concept of surrendering the studio's cosseted environment and embracing the dynamics of the stage again, to be exact. The problem lay in translating *Debut*'s textures into flesh and blood. The majority of the album's backing tracks had been played on synths and drum machines and she hadn't even thought of playing the tracks live when she wrote them. 'The two ways of doing it were just having tapes and DATS and sequencers and just me, or doing it live and consciously trying to create a new sound,' she decided. 'And no fucking way I'm going to tour with a cassette.'

Björk's first solo live appearance had been on the BBC music show *Later*, backed by British dance act D-Influence but a permanent band was essential. She initially thought that she would have to assemble a fifteen-piece band. 'I knew immediately that the people I had to find would be musically from all sorts of different directions,' she said in her 1994 video *Vessel*. Eventually, she settled on six – Ike Leo (bass), Leila Arab (keyboards), Guy Sigsworth (keyboards and programming), Dan Lipman (sax, flute, tambourine), Tansay Omar (drums) and Talvin Singh (tablas and percussion). Dan, Tansay and Ike arrived via audition; Talvin had played with Guy backing Nokko (the Japan's Madonna), while Acid Jazz guru Gilles Peterson had sent over DJ/keyboardist Leila, Guy Sigsworth recalls, 'who fitted in after about two minutes. I couldn't play all the parts myself, and Björk wanted to get a girl in. Leila had a homegrown jazz piano technique and a genuine creative energy. She had something instinctively modern about what she did.'

Which sounds just like Björk herself. 'I was looking to do more studio work, and nobody else but Björk could have persuaded me to go back off on tour, except Bruce Springsteen offering me shitloads of cash,' Guy laughs. 'I'd heard a lot of her stuff but I didn't know if that amazing vocal style happened after a hundred takes, or whether she could just do it. It was obvious from the start that she could. It was fascinating working with her because she taught me that there are no boundaries, that you can take from free jazz, techno, classical, and draw it all together. I'm from a more classical background and she found a way to fit that in. It was a fascinating band, and a very international band too. We all learnt a lot from each other.'

It had taken a while for all these people to mesh together, Björk admitted, 'because they were almost puritanical in what music they like, but for us to come from such different cultures, different musical styles too, was very fascinating.' This was cosmopolitanism in practice: you had Indian (Talvin), Iranian (Leila), Turkish (Tansay), St Kitts Island in the Caribbean (Ike), two Brits (Guy and Dan) and one immigrant Icelandic housewife. That was London's music community for you, while Björk's choice more strongly reflected the city's funk undertow than *Debut*'s more site-unspecific temperament.

'That to me is England today: all these different races, so many immigrants,' she told *Time Out*. 'I can't put my finger on it because it's still in the making, but the diversity is incredible. The idea today of people from Brazil only making Brazilian music doesn't exist. No way do people in London hear "Greensleeves" and The Beatles. People worry that they'll lose their individuality if they share their ideas with other people but if you've got a strong identity, you could hang out with aliens. You can't be stingy with your ideas because the more you give, the more you get back. It's arrogance to think that all the ideas you get are yours, it's bollocks. People who get a lot of ideas are those who've got their antennae out. People say, "You're mad, Björk, you're back in your dream world," but honey, this is what life is about.'

Björk was doing that David Attenborough thing again, narrating the action between scenery/music and the audience, 'to introduce the two together.' Her debut date was at London's 3,000-capacity Forum on 19

August, to coincide with the release of 'Venus As A Boy'. The support acts were an Indian bhangra and Spanish flamenco band, followed by Björk's self-styled, 'Indian disco pop band'.

In truth, the music was more of an ethnic, Acid Jazz disco band, which wasn't Björk's intention, but as Guy Sigsworth points out, 'You play dance music on normal instruments like keyboards, sax and flute, then it ends up sounding Acid Jazzy, which I know Björk wasn't very keen on. She wanted to avoid sequencers, because she was used to having a live band around her, but she was determined not to have a guitarist.'

The stage decor was pretty serene, with backdrops of water ripples and rushing clouds, model sailboats on pedestals and aquatic mauve and turquoise lighting. The aim, says lighting designer Paul Normandale, 'was to create a stylish, animated look with a classic, library-book feel, something you wouldn't normally see on stage.' The mellow effect was perhaps a premonition as the band sound was too quiet and the rhythms too polite. The audience seemed restless with quieter material like 'The Anchor Song' and 'Like Someone In Love', only coming to life with the dancier dynamics of 'Violently Happy' and 'Big Time Sensuality' towards the end of the set. Björk, though, was energized, rushing all over the stage, her hair in top-knots, her arms akimbo and her bod encased in a stunning, white paper maxi-dress. This was the work of Cypriot-born (and London-dwelling) designer Hussein Chalayan. For the tour, Björk had bought several of his paper-fabric outfits (a kind of 'envelope' paper, a washable, untearable material called Tyvek), with little messages or poems sewn into the collar (another of his idiosyncrasies was to bury the paper clothes in soil for up to six months before they were deemed 'finished').

The dress caught all eyes but without Einar to help fill up a whole stage, Björk had to work overtime. *Melody Maker* pinpointed, 'the inner child's voraciousness, insatiability and wilfulness letting rip like a supernova. She's a Kid's Lib Guerrilla dolled up like a disco diva.' It seemed that Björk either needed a more intimate venue for her funk-jazz-folk collusions, or to head for a much more hard-edged momentum, in line with her dance remixes. To play her second show at Wembley Stadium, supporting U2 (as The Sugarcubes had ended up doing) seemed suicidal but the reviews were enthusiastic. When Björk pulled out of her scheduled support slot to U2 in Dublin, it wasn't out of musical fear but to spend time with Sindri who was returning from his summer holiday in Iceland.

Björk agreed that her debut shows were lacking in pizzazz. She later admitted that she had initially refused to tour with *Debut* but had acquiesced under pressure. 'I thought I was unprepared and perhaps the performances would be a little forced – in hindsight, I was proved right,' she said, but thought that matters improved as the tour progressed. 'The first show was a rehearsal and it was 10 per cent,' she told *Vox*. 'And it's gone obviously like 20 per cent, 30 per cent . . . the show in Manchester I'm really proud of, and in many ways it was better than the record. I've always been a big fan of live things. Then again, I'm a big fan of synthesizers.'

The tour supports were drawn from the dance fraternity, like folk-techno duo Ultramarine and the singular Speedy K. The Dutchman enjoyed the experience, and like everybody else, had only good words to say about Björk: 'My first impressions of the tour were that she travels with a lot of people, and she wants everybody to be happy, so she tries very hard, which I liked about her.'

Guy Sigsworth remembers Björk's first tour being, 'a back to basics, back of the van type affair. We had no real idea how well the album would sell.' The camaradery was already there, but when Talvin bought a pocket-sized Yamaha QY 20 sequencer, which enables you to write songs on it, everyone ended up buying one. 'Everyone would put their headphones on, and write, and then we'd later see who had written the best tunes. We'd have back-of-the-bus Eurovision Song Contests – I got everyone their national flag – and play the songs. When Björk would hear a funny noise or tune, she would spring to life and get going. Some of the noises on the second album are from that little box.'

As the tour progressed through Europe, Björk would get psyched up for the shows. The band would settle into the 'Human Behaviour' groove, and she would scuttle around the stage below the spotlights, and then suddenly pop up to catch the opening verse. After shows, and on days off, she would meet up with friends from Kukl and Sugarcubes days, getting drunk and partying madly. Meanwhile, back on the ranch, her theme track to a new film, the Harvey Keitel-vehicle *Young Americans*, was released in the UK. 'Play Dead' was co-written by bassist Jah

Wobble, a founder member of PiL, and a master bassist with 'world music' leanings, who had been brought in by the film's incidental composer and arranger David Arnold.

The film's director Danny Cannon had wanted to make a film about London in the nineties: like Björk, he found England, 'too hooked on Victorian times . . . It's like English people are ashamed of England today.' He brought in David Arnold, who was suitably new to the world of film soundtracks but had an old-fashioned belief in cinematic scores. Arnold's main drive was to have a human voice to 'top and tail' the opening and closing credits. 'It had to be female,' he emphasized. 'I think it is far more disturbing when you hear a female voice in anguish or in pain and I think it creates much more of a sense of hopelessness and despair than would a male voice.'

Björk was his very first choice: 'For me, there are very few singers who I felt could tap into that kind of emotion and have it heard without the use of a lyric. I wanted something far more primal than a song. Listening to early Sugarcubes records, everything I heard in my head came out of Björk's mouth, and I could see the potential in doing something unique with her. I think she was quite pleased with that – originally she was under the impression I wanted her to do a rave track, and when she realized she could put far more creative input into the score, she became very excited about doing the film.'

Once she was convinced about Arnold and Cannon's intentions, she got the latter to write out a page of phrases that represented the character's emotions. 'It was very difficult for me because at that time I was very happy and all the lyrics I've done lately have been happy and hilarious,' she told *Vox*. 'To do something so painful, I had to get help from Danny.' In the end, she only used the title and the phrase, *'sometimes, it's just like sinking.'*

When Björk started doing her Icelandic improvising to the orchestral score, Arnold saw that she was giving voice to his dreams. 'It was a goose bump moment and the combination of her voice and the orchestra sounded completely natural. I thought to myself, "I can't believe no one has done this before with her," and I was glad to be there first. I think when an artist with a talent like hers is given a freedom away from the constraints of a song or solo career and is kind of "dared" to do something different working like this, then when they pull it off, it is quite extraordinary. And that has certainly been the reaction of everyone who has heard it.'

Arnold's mega-ballad mightiness – sawing strings and a weighty rock pulse – was matched by Björk's opening wails, while lyrics like, *'I play dead, it stops the hurting/it's sometimes just like sleeping/curling up inside my private tortures'* kept the emotional flame burning. As 'Play Dead' became her first Top 30 hit, the attendant fuss kept Björk's flame equally hot.

Björk was uncomfortable about the idea of adding the track to *Debut* but Derek Birkett persuaded her that, instead of ripping off the fan base, many more people would buy the album to find it wasn't there, so they would feel equally cheated. 'She was proud of the track and didn't feel artistically compromised, so it went on,' Birkett says. 'I reckon we sold another 500,000 to 600,000 thousand on the back of it too. And those who wrote in to complain, which was about a hundred, we sent the new record as compensation.'

Yet again, it was ironic that a rock song should break Björk commercially, but even 'Play Dead' was to be eclipsed by Björk's already scheduled single release of 'Big Time Sensuality' (it was originally intended to come out first). Wrapped in a striking black and white photo of a giggly, hair-knotted Björk set against a shimmering glass chandelier, the single's now standard two versions presented another cornucopia of Björk to date.

Like playing live, Derek Birkett admits that she was also reluctant to follow the standard marketing practice of releasing multiple singles off an album in order to promote it but that she compensated with all the different mixes. 'By reworking the tracks,' he says, 'she was hardly ripping anyone off.' The first CD included two more Elgar Sisters tracks, 'Sidasta Eg' (meaning 'The Last Of Me', not as in, 'you've seen the last of me,' more 'the last copy of me,' according to Iceland-opedia Árni Matthíasson) and 'Gloria' (a Björk flute solo) while Black Dog turned 'Come To Me' into the Indian pop disco ambient techno that should have been the staple of Björk's live sound. The second CD contained no less than seven remixes of 'Big Time Sensuality' – three floor thumpers by London-based technoids Fluke, two by DJ Justin Robertson and one apiece by Dom T and American DJ/mixer David Morale. Björk saw the exercise as not just a way to embrace the dance market but to collaborate with some of her favourite people.

'I was really excited with a lot of things that were going on here and a way to work with a lot of people that is quite a modern way is to get them to remix you,' she elaborated. 'We did a lot of remixes because there's a lot of remixers I respect. I like different points of view, I love the thrill of being in control of one song and then giving it to someone to get their view of it. Even before *Debut* was finished, me and Nellee would start picking and sending and getting remixes done for excitement, and then we'd put them out for the clubs.'

Justin Robertson had previously remixed The Sugarcubes' 'Birthday' for 1992's *It's It* album. He remembers Björk appearing when he was running the Most Excellent club in Manchester: 'She once had the crowd captivated there, when she was down there with 808 State. She went into this strange girlish skip around the club, with the rucksack on her back. There was lots of gawping and general amazement.'

Jonathan Richardson had relentlessly hounded Derek Birkett to let Robertson and his other charges Fluke have a go at a Björk remix, to which Birkett agreed, though at reduced fees – Birkett only had £7,000 left in the budget due to the number of remixes Björk was commissioning, there was only so much money to go around. Ironically, the biggest fee had gone to a garage-style remix by the hot American DJ David Morales, but not only did Björk love the Fluke 'Minimix' so much that she made it the 7 inch single cut in place of her own, but even house/garage-style British DJs like Pete Tong championed the Fluke remix over Morales.

The video was handed over to Frenchman Stephane Sednaoui. His portfolio included lavish – if highly individual – treatments like U2's 'Mysterious Ways' and The Red Hot Chilli Peppers' 'Give It Away' but Björk scaled him right down – to just the singer, in white sweater and silver skirt, on the back of a lorry trailer in New York. Back and forth she danced, gleefully clutching herself, shivering with delight, drunk on wonder, evidently bewitched by sensuality. It was another stark, highly personable image that stood leagues apart from the MTV-sanctioned decorations which pervaded most soloists' video treatments.

'I saw her on a poster, such an amazing face,' Sednaoui recalls. 'I listened to her music, loved it so much, thought her voice was so fresh and so pure, and managed for her to see my showreel. When I saw her perform, I thought that she had been doing acting, dancing and mime because of how she used her body. The reason I wanted to meet her the most, was the way she was moving her head in the "Human Behaviour" video, in such a personal way, with all those little tiny moves. I love her intonation. Like with musicians and stylists and photographers, she's very good at choosing the right video director. She would never have used me for "Human Behaviour", for example, as Michel Gondry was right for the fairytale vision. I think she liked the energy of my videos. She's determined to get what she wants, she doesn't hesitate. She's been doing this since she was eleven, and from eighteen to now, so she knows what it takes to make a record cover, a photo session, a video, design, everything. She observes. She is very sharp.'

As much as the video positively promoted the single, which went on to sell 150,000 copies in the UK by Christmas, Sednaoui's penchant for fish-eye close ups and Björk's intoxicated performance were also major causes of the media's persistent 'she's cute, but a bit mad' frenzy that followed (when Brit-comics French and Saunders did their Björk parody in 1996, this was the clip they copied). But who was thinking about drawbacks? Björkfever was escalating and *Debut* kept climbing the charts five months after release.

The single's success led to Björk being invited to the annual *Smash Hits* Pollwinners' Party, held in early December. She, in turn, invited Fluke to back her, and 'Big Time Sensuality' and 'Violently Happy' were subsequently thumped out to multitudes of impressionable teen screamers. 'We just stood there behind our instruments, staring out at 7500 Take That fans, with our jaws down, as Björk mimed,' was how Jon Fugler of Fluke remembered it. 'She just gives it hell and entertains people. She was very together, and we were impressed by that.' Here was a star whose impishness appealed to kids, teenagers, older indies, post-indie yuppies, club kids and discerning thirtysomethings . . . the perfect pop star!

For every mention of her music, there was equal billing for Björk's fashion sensibility, which spread her name and image just as quickly. Her combined wild-child dresses and fuck-off mountain boots, a look that first originated in her teenage mind, was being increasingly mimicked. Mix that with the buying power to pick and choose more extreme and arresting clothes, with the ability to align herself with cutting-edge designers like Margeila and Chalayan, and Björk became equally popular with the *couture* catwalk designers. Not content with her musical achievements, Björk was now leading female fashion victims like a dizzy Pied Piper.

Her secret was that mix-and-match sensibility – blend genres, obey no boundaries, mix nostalgia and futurism, and one plus one equals something new. A Chinese dress in red embroidered silk reinforced the Asian Lolita look but the baggy magenta tracksuit bottoms and hi-tech trainers subverted the image completely. Paper dresses buried for six months until they decompose into a semi-plastic, vellum-like state, had an unearthly sheen. Top it with an extraordinarily vivid face and hair that goes places and you have the makings of something sensational. 'A cross between earth mother and otherworldly angel,' was *Looks*' devotional verdict.

'When I was growing up in Iceland, I thought the clothes shops were completely pathetic, so I guess I've always been a bit of a flea-market chick,' Björk recalled. 'Even now, it's very rare that I find something in a shop which is exactly right. My taste has always been extreme – for some reason, I always either like things that cost fifty pence or fifty billion pence, and I don't like the in-between stuff. The way I resolve it is that most of the clothes I buy, both for Sindri and myself, are second hand – so I buy ten things for £10 and then I buy one expensive thing.'

Björk was certainly more aware of her public image than Stephane Sednaoui suggested – it was just that she didn't need the bolstering of make-overs and retouched photos in the MTV/Hollywood tradition of overkill. She was her own stylist (though Mondino associate Judy Blame did lend a hand during the *Debut* session). At a fashion shoot for the *Independent* newspaper, the journalist excitedly relayed the fact that when the strands of hair wouldn't lie down, as she was assembling her now customary top-knot style, in the absence of hair grease she made do with some cream cheese left over from breakfast.

This freeing-up attitude was a definitive sign of the times: if Sade and *couture* elegance epitomized the eighties, then Björk and rag-bag deconstruction was the key to the nineties. Björkettes would consistently pop up at her concerts, with top-knot hairdos, little backpacks and feminine tom-boy gait, and you had to admit that she was becoming a role model. By determining a singular fashion sensibility, Björk was unwittingly making a statement on feminism in the nineties. Madonna had stressed the overtly feminine line, milking the institutionalized virgin/whore ambivalence (a role subsequently replayed by Courtney Love), while Annie Lennox stressed the overtly anti-feminine escape into masculine role-playing; typically, Björk avoided such contained statements for a boundary-free mix.

In this new decade, Björk was joined by Polly Harvey, who stressed the confusion between those two opposing poles, and, operating in a decidedly glamour-free zone, the fleetingly notorious *Riot Grrl* punk movement, whose mostly teenage protagonists stressed the suffragette-born and seventies-defined style of activism that argued for equality on a more pragmatically political scale. Björk, as ever, was stressing individuality, subverting the constraints of gender altogether by ignoring them. By reflecting innocence and experience, fusing the traditional and the experimental and placing such importance on self-representation, Björk was showing that sisters were truly doing it for themselves.

Björk acknowledged her appreciation of Courtney Love for her intuitive, strong femininity, Madonna for her sense of humour and, 'the fact that she made it look good to control your own life when that was something that was not supposed to be very sexy for a woman. She's one of the few women who has remained true to herself and been a character.'

She also respected the fast emerging *Riot Grrls* for their committed efforts but disagreed with their brand of feminism. 'What they're doing for the rest of the world is brilliant but what they're doing for themselves is shit,' she responded. 'They're closing themselves in corners. Feminism shouldn't be about making things more difficult: it should be about the *other* thing. I believe in a more positive approach, not whining "Waah, I'm a girl and I don't get to do anything." 'Cos then your life is gonna be like that. By now, people have realized that it's not a question of being a boy or a girl – it's a question of what you do. If the *Riot grrls* had been born in the thirties or fifties, then they could moan and whine. But thanks to all the brilliant feminists this century, writers, artists and politicians who've said, "No, we don't want to live in this cage," the cage has been removed. Now it's time to prove yourself.'

Short of world domination, Björk could only be violently happy at the way she had proved herself that year. *Debut* ended up topping several Albums Of The Year lists, including that of *Melody Maker*: 'With a unique, playful and beautiful voice, a boundless imagination and the helping hand of producer Nellee Hooper, Björk ditched The Sugarcubes and her indie-rock past to emerge this year as a glistening pop princess,' it trumpeted. Women's style/fashion magazine *Elle* voted Björk 'sexiest newcomer' of the year. She, Sindri and Dom could fly to Iceland for Christmas knowing that each single had sold progressively more (a vinyl remix of 'One Day' had been released on a club promotional white label just after 'Big Time Sensuality', causing a clubland stampede) and that there didn't seem to be one publication that hadn't saluted her genius. But like The Sugarcubes at the outset of their career, Björk had overdone the promotional stint, and had no problem showing it – again.

In the Christmas edition of *The Face*, she said, 'It was alright for the first six months; seven months was a bit tricky; eight months was when I started hitting people. I've been telling this hideously pathetic, stupid joke that the Bible in England is different, God created the world in one day and then he talked about it for eight days.'

Maybe the press had run out of things to say, but their old xenophobia was back on the agenda. 'If I was from Newcastle, I wouldn't get any of this elfin bullshit,' she snorted. She hated the predictable, 'Why are you so weird?' line of questioning, because to her, wearing paper dresses, rolling eggs around her face and dancing on the backs of lorries were just ways to enjoy yourself. 'I don't think I am weird,' she groaned. 'Everybody sees things from their own viewpoint. Because no two people are the same, that, in a way, makes everybody weird. It means that what is normal to me is not normal to you and vice versa.'

Generally, the press are suckers for caricature, and Björk's individual mannerisms were ripe for exposing. Her habit of wrinkling her nose, à la the late, great Elizabeth Montgomery in the sixties sorcery sitcom *Bewitched*, made her irredeemably cute; off-the-cuff comments like, 'If the sun had loads of hairs and you could hug it, it would be really nice,' made her irredeemably, 'cute, but a bit mad'. Perhaps, but refreshingly mad compared to the stuffiness of her presiding British judges. Björk clearly wasn't mad, just playful. Such a violently happy persona was evidently too much for those who had long ago lost their inner child.

'I've got the right to be an idiot and I've got the right to be clever, both at the same time, and I refuse to be only one or the other,' she told *Details*. The same with her music: 'I insist on being happy, mad, sad, stupid, brilliant, genius, imbecile, horrible, mean, happy. I make an effort not to forget all those different colours: to get hilariously drunk sometimes and to pay my electricity bill and to forget what time it is and run a band without a fault.'

Being treated as a piece of exotica, 'an ice princess', she saw as a cop-out, not just a harmless piece of star-gazing. It made her laugh, she said, but saddened her too. 'I don't see why people can't take things as they are,' she complained. 'What is wrong with bread and butter and tube stations and cinemas, all these things around us? I think they are the most interesting and exciting and crazy things, the real things. So why do people have to put on some pink sunglasses? Reality is much more exciting than fantasy, if you want my opinion. Much more absurd. Ridiculous things happen – meeting people accidentally, that kind of thing. I look at myself as this basic, down to earth, simple person who likes the simple things in life, and I get spoilt by journalists who try and make it all very complicated and mystical.'

Björk also contradicted herself when she admitted to quite liking the weirdo tag. 'It's quite flattering because it makes me more interesting than I think I am. I look at myself as a down-to-earth person who happens to be obsessed with pop music.'

What she truly objected to was having to justify all facets of her behaviour, to analyse intuition. In Iceland, she had been embraced or misunderstood but no one constantly forced her to use the head to explain the workings of the heart, her favourite organ (probably . . .). 'If you went out somewhere and had a really good time, you don't wake up the next morning and try to figure out *why* you did,' she argued. 'It's just the atmosphere, the people, the chemistry of friends, the mood, what happened before, what will happen after. And you can't explain it, and I don't understand why you should. And it's the same with songs.'

Björk had managed to say no to fashion shoots, even turning down a request from Stephen Meisel, best known for photographing Madonna's

Sex, for Italian *Vogue* and Gap shoots. 'It's against my principles,' Björk said of the Meisel's request. 'Besides, I think they're more into models than eskimos.' So why couldn't she shut up, avoid the media glare, disappear for longer than a week? What made the press different? Was it that Björk felt more at home with them? Or that she recognized where her real power base lay? That the press gave her some control over the finished article? One thing she wasn't going to be was a coffee table ornament, or a class A pop star. To this end, she even declined an offer of dinner from Prince: how much more divorced from real life can you be than dining with a stranger with a God complex?

'She's far more down to earth than I imagined,' says Jon Fugler of Flex. 'We didn't talk about the music when we met, but how shit Iceland is, and London is, and how difficult it is to find good schools for your kids. She's more concerned about that than all the crap of being in a band. She's one of the lucky people who's been through so much, it doesn't affect you anymore.'

Björk still felt the need to appeal against the belief that all pop stars had to be ego-maniacs. She would go to great lengths – too great sometimes – to confirm that fame itself meant next to nothing. Just as Hussein Chalayan said he was interested in clothes, not fashion, she maintained that there was a clear difference between a musician and a pop star. 'I definitely haven't got the ambition to be bigger than everyone,' she told *NME*. 'I don't want to sound like I'm arty, like I didn't pick to be here, because I think that's a pathetic attitude as well, but

I've actually started to think a bit about it all. It's just so . . . *untrendy*. I'm not moaning but as far as I'm concerned, all that bullshit comes with the job, and if you want to make a big record, you've got to take part in all that. I've come a long way. Most of it has been in Iceland, but it's the same game, only a hundred times bigger.'

Could Björk claim not to be ambitious? Having felt misunderstood and sung in misunderstood bands for so long, was there not a drive (the need for justice, or even revenge) to see recognition for her talent? Her message was clear either way: don't expect me to be an Annie Lennox or a Sade, or to be anything approaching a role model. 'A hundred years ago, if you were a singer, it was a crap job. It just happens that today, if you're on stage and you've got a microphone in your hand, you become a spokesperson for a lot of people. That has nothing to do with what I do.'

Björk's personal highlight of 1993, she claimed, was nothing to do with success, but the formation of her band. 'It was very emotional for me, something I couldn't have imagined even a few months before that it would happen, getting six top musicians that have a lot of character themselves, playing my music. You can't really ask for more than that.'

Her own album of the year was Black Dog Productions' *Bytes*. Her description of it summed up the appeal of her own album. 'It's hard to describe why you like things,' she began, 'but their music is beautiful, original, very simple and direct, with a lot of intuition. It's privately happy in a very intimate way, and also very modern pop music. The music managed to be modern, as is techno, but mystical at the same time. It proves that 1993 can be mystical without being antique.'

Could Björk maintain this precarious balance between the mystical and the normal? Looking back, Jon Fugler wonders whether Björk was portraying an image – 'the biggest professional image that anyone has portrayed in her life,' he thought. 'I mean, you can see that she is a professional, that she switches on and does her show, but it might even stretch through to meeting people. But somehow,' he concludes, 'you get the feeling she is sound. You couldn't keep it up anyway: she'd end up blasting her head off with a harpoon.'

Lately The Things I Do Astound Me

Q: 'What is, "something Björk?"'
A: 'I make Björk music, and Björk music is very flexible, very intense and very rich, but also very whimsical and inconstant. I get bored very easily. I think . . . yes, I think that is the reason I do what I do: I get bored easily.'
(From the *Post* book)

Coincidence or fate? With her musical ambitions temporarily satisfied, Björk began to experience domestic upheavals at home. As she worked closer with Stephane Sednaoui, on the outline and filming of a long-form live video release, their relationship became more than a working one. At first, Björk would only say that her new boyfriend was a secret but after several reports in the tabloid newspapers naming Stephane, she confessed that they had become lovers.

The relationship with Dom had gone the way of that with Thór and Óskar – a slow drifting apart over time. Dom knew that Björk's career could take off more emphatically than his could, 'because when you DJ in a new place, you have to start from the bottom all over again. Hers went ballistic, but it was more exciting than scary, and I was very happy for her. Of course she was busy but that wasn't the problem.' He is less than happy to discuss what the problem was, but says that the separation was down to, 'an amalgamation of different reasons. As with any relationship. There were times when it was hard to communicate, but I'd like to think we've always remained friends. But I guess I'm not the Venus as a boy that I used to be!'

In the *Daily Mirror*, Björk was quoted as saying, 'It's not working anymore. Let's call it a day.' The ubiquitous 'independent source' was quoted as saying, 'they are both cut up about what happened, but in the past few months they realized their romance was going nowhere and they were drifting apart. It's particularly sad for Sindri because he has come to see Dom as a real father figure. They got on fantastically with each other. They say there is no one else involved.'

Given the fact that Björk and Stephane Sednaoui had been working so closely together, it seemed unlikely that the two events had no connection: another (the same?) unnamed source confirmed that meeting Stephane had something to do with the split from Dom. The story eventually broke in the middle of March 1994. Another unnamed source, this time from America, reported that, 'she and Stephane just hit it off. They have become very fond of each other very quickly, Stephane is very dashing and has a bit of a reputation as a womanizer. He's very flamboyant.'

Another anonymous contribution made claims that, under the same roof, Dom's more laid-back qualities and Björk's franticness didn't properly mesh; Sednaoui was a more hot-blooded presence, and a fresh one at that – there was no reason why feeling easily bored and craving newness couldn't transfer to matters of the heart.

Sednaoui was obviously infatuated with Björk. 'She reminded me of an actress like Anna Magnani, the wife of Roberto Rossilini, where all inside, her emotions, shows on the face,' he gushed at the time. 'But it's not tortured, just everything is real, all pure.' Were they romantically involved? 'Let's keep this professional!' he laughed. 'She is a great artist to work with. She is fantastic.'

The pair's working relationship flourished when Sednaoui started filming *Vessel*, the proposed live video. Aside from the planned concert footage, he wanted to add some face-the-camera interviews, which Björk, somewhat against character, allowed. Maybe Sednaoui was too charming to deny. 'We're not trying to make it look like an interview because she has done so many, but more abstract, dreamy portraits,' he explained. 'She doesn't want to be specific, to talk about subjects like morality or pollution, or Björk herself, which would be a bit boring. Sometimes she talks, sometimes not, but it's not reportage, following her everywhere, but more her being natural and simple. When people catch just a simple moment of somebody, that shows ten times more than when they are asked questions. She could be on the subway, or talking about waiting at airports or a dream. I just like to see her expressions. I did my best to show her enjoyment of life, that energy she has. Different images open other doors.'

Music aside – but only just – image was the commodity by which most multi-million sellers sold themselves. Björk was no exception, except that she wanted no part of the industry establishment. At the annual music industry BRITS awards, she was approached by the organizers to join in their PR-polished plans. Björk was about to win both Best International Female Artist and Best International Newcomer awards, so the organizers felt that a duet, preferably with a male, was highly desirable. Both David Bowie and Mick Hucknall had approached her independently, both requests being politely denied, while the BRITS' own suggestion of Meat Loaf was met with total derision. 'Of course, I was very flattered,' Björk told *Musician*, 'but I've worked with enough people in my life to realize that even though you've got ingredients that function quite well on their own, like, say, ketchup and chocolate, sometimes it's not very good to mix them together. So I said, "Listen, there's this person that I just know I'll meet and it will be completely relaxed, and we won't have to explain everything or take nine months bonding or whatever."'

Feeling brave as usual, Björk initially asked avant-classical percussionist Evelyn Glennie to join her, but Glennie couldn't do it at such short notice. Björk then forwarded the name of Polly Harvey, a fellow wilfully independent, siren-tongued spirit, who proved to be the most willing and perfect of foils. The BRITS agreed, but the organizers probably didn't expect the duo to sing and play without a band, or to pick The Rolling Stones' '(I Can't Get No) Satisfaction'. 'It was very important that we do it with just the two of us onstage together and be able to play all of the instruments,' Björk stressed. 'I had my little organ noise, Polly played guitar, and we played it really, really slow and quietly. I just knew that me and Polly would click immediately. It was magical. Polly's brilliant: every inch of her is true.'

At the ceremony, Björk was photographed alongside supermodel Naomi Campbell, who Nellee Hooper was presently producing, which was the first time she had been seen cavorting in famous company. Björk's mother was playing the starstruck role, trying to track down her old hero Van Morrison. The various Icelandic dignitaries at Björk's table were just as overwhelmed. One of them was Jakob Magnússon, newly ensconced as Iceland's cultural attaché in the UK. He admitted that Björk's award winning had turned her into a national hero and made the front page of the Icelandic newspapers. 'But she was remarkably relaxed about it, with no nervous hysteria. She was very humble and balanced, which are her main strengths.'

Björk could celebrate with two London shows inside three days in February – a 'Björk On Legs' club-style show at the Brixton Academy and a 'Björk On Seats' show at the Royalty Theatre which was filmed by Stephane Sednaoui for the forthcoming video. She scooted on, in her now ubiquitous white, arms outstretched like aeroplane wings, and carried on that way: the *Independent On Sunday* wrote that she, 'danced like a tipsy child, unselfconsciously and winningly graceless.'

The combination of press coverage, live shows and awards saw *Debut* rise to number three in the album charts. Having reached a commercial high, Björk's decision to release 'Violently Happy' as the fourth (and last) single from *Debut* in its original, erratically undulating form – despite numerous bracing dance remixes on the second CD by Fluke, Graham Massey, American duo Masters At Work and Nellee Hooper – accompanied by a video centred on the gleeful mutilation of dolls was an act of terrorism worthy of Einar. The video was left to the imagination of Jean-Baptiste Mondino, who built a silver-blue padded cell, in which a bunch of model-agency 'inmates' took scissors to dolls while Björk unstuffed the cutest of teddy bears. Daytime TV took five steps back, and when MTV did show the video, it received a formal warning from the Independent Television Commission. But it would take more than a banned video to stop her from making the charts.

A more realistic type of violence surrounded the making of the video. Björk had flown to LA for the shoot in January 1994, just before starting her Australian and Japanese tour. When the famous earthquake hit, the video production office in the San Fernando Valley was reduced to rubble. Björk, never having experienced such a natural phenomenon before, naturally thought it was brilliant. 'I always thought it would be this really nervous thing. But it was this really deep, big bass in your guts. I thought:

'Yes! This is what I've wanted to feel ever since I was born! It's funny, it's like your body is thirsty for it and it satisfies you in a strange way.'

According to her co-manager Nettie Walker, 'Everyone was trying to get hold of Björk to see that she was okay, but she had gone to the video shoot, dead on time, ready to start. When Björk is committed to something, she is committed.'

A more mental style of violence surrounded her return to the UK from Australia. In her absence, and out of the blue, she was served with a high court writ in February. The instigator was Simon Fisher, the English computer musician she had first met in Iceland, who claimed that he had had a hand in the writing of four songs on *Debut* − 'Crying', 'Aeroplane', 'Venus As A Boy' and 'Human Behaviour'. Since the album had sold one and a half million copies by that point, Fisher − or Simon Lovejoy, to give him his stage name − would stand to make up to £200,000. His evidence was a demo tape made by the pair, which would be studied by expert witness. While Björk didn't deny the existence of such a tape, she denied the charge outright. She could not win either way, as Fisher was using Legal Aid, so she would have to face half the legal costs even if she won. But she was determined not to settle out of court − that could be interpreted as a partial admission of guilt. Björk was never one to back down . . .

The amount of money being contested meant that the case had to be submitted to the High Court, which delayed the hearing for months.

Björk was able to concentrate on writing. The Royalty Theatre set in February had been but an hour long, and she had apologized to the audience for not having written new songs. She had initially wanted to record a new album as soon as *Debut* was finished, a plan delayed by the live shows, but her way of compensating for her dissatisfied state of mind regarding the live sound was to jump straight back into recording. She already had two songs, 'Army Of Me' and 'The Modern Things', both co-written with Graham Massey in 1992, and then shelved. Between other commitments, she would try to write at home, on a cheap Casio keyboard, and almost always at night, after everyone had fallen asleep, 'which is very precious to me, like a little relationship between me and myself.'

The simplicity of her demos could be gleaned from live versions of 'The Anchor Song', 'Come To Me' and 'Human Behaviour' on the first CD of 'Violently Happy'. The session was recorded for Spanish radio and featured Björk and Guy Sigsworth on harpsichord. Sigsworth says that the live band had introduced more ethnic sounds and early keyboards like the harpsichord, in order to 'de-Acid Jazz' the music. The mutating Björk sound had a chance to seriously expand when she accepted an offer from MTV to record a live *Unplugged* session, which would provide a stop-gap between *Debut* and the next album.

Before the show was broadcast, Björk contributed some vocals (alongside Sinead O'Connor) to Jah Wobble's new album, then teamed up with O'Connor and Marianne Faithfull for a cover of the latter's composition 'Dreaming My Dream' on behalf of Women Against AIDS. Björk was also charitable toward London's new club-wear emporium Sign Of The Times, agreeing to open the shop (it was one of her favourite outfitters, staffed by the young and the keen, who she felt an empathy with). She also took to the catwalk for Jean Paul Gaultier's show in Paris, while Thierry Mugler's creations were influenced by the Icelandic diva.

'The more no one could look like me, the better I felt,' she said. 'I'm much more relaxed about that nowadays.' Not that you would think so from Björk's various photo opportunities, where she would embrace all manner of outfits, in all manner of locations – one time, in a silver raincoat, Walkman headphones on, playing a video game by the side of the open road, another time surrounded by domestic chaos, cassettes and books (Hermann Hesse's *Siddhartha*, short stories by Bataille, a biography of German electronic composer Stockhausen) in a satin miniskirt, lacy patterned cling top, woollen tights and suede platform boots, all various shades of red (the domination of white was coming to an end). 'It's no use pretending you aren't expressing yourself with clothes, because you are,' she said. 'The visual side really matters. If I look the way I sound, that helps me, because people are much more trained visually than they are audio-wise. This is to show that I'm an extremist, that I take things to the top.'

It seemed inevitable that Björk's visual impact and all-round dynamism would attract Hollywood, though the film project she was offered was based on the British comic strip heroine Tank Girl (from *Deadline* magazine). Music press reports announced that Ice-T, Courtney Love, Iggy Pop and Björk had either confirmed, or expressed a desire, to appear in *Tank Girl*, with Björk strongly tipped to play Jet Girl, Tank Girl's sidekick and pretend lesbian lover. Liz Naylor was one who feared that Björk would make movies, 'like, "this beautiful creature, let's bang her in a movie", which would be embarrassing,' but Björk was too sussed to risk the pitfalls of further acting ventures. She soon confirmed that she had never even expressed any wish to be included – wisely, as it happens, as the film proved to be a commercial and critical disaster. 'I think I should stick to singing,' she decided.

Björk had taken said voice and band to Australia for the first time, where she had appeared at the Big Day Out festival, and had valiantly stood out from grunge rock kings like The Smashing Pumpkins and Soundgarden ('like a little pink dot among all the guitars, as Björk said!' Nellie Walker laughs). The following dates in Japan had been equally successful, and though the combined shows delayed Björk's plans to record a new album, eschewing the hedonistic aspects of 1993's jaunts and striving for healthiness – out of bed early, lot of swimming and reading – certainly put her in the right frame of mind.

On her return, she was greeted with the ultimate accolade, a Björk puppet on the satirical TV show *Spitting Image*. The skit involved a Björk puppet singing along with a fax machine, a hump-back whale and *Star Wars* robot R2D2, but rather than be embarrassed or angry,

Björk was delighted, and thought the makers had been unnervingly accurate. 'The fact that your average English person perceives me as someone who sings along to a fax machine, it couldn't be better,' she told *Dazed & Confused*. 'They actually got very much to the pin there, like what I am about. I prefer a fax machine any day to a guitar solo.

'Most people in Britain have telephones, they know the sound you make when you put in a video. They know car alarms, fire alarms . . . I believe these things affect us. A day in my life is car noises, the toaster, but it's also in the wind, the rain, the cold, the human voice – the greatest influence on us all. That's why, in my music, I want the humanity, the sun and the moon, the ocean, the earth, because you could live in the middle of fucking Manhattan and you'd still have all these things.'

There were greater accolades to come. In comedian Rob Newman's debut novel, *Dependence Day*, Björk's name became an adjective when he wrote, 'she had on raggedy jeans and a jersey of the softest, björkest wool'. This kind of deep cultural penetration meant that Björk was a national figure in the UK as well as Iceland; in a huge colour spread, the *Sunday Times Magazine* even went as far as proposing that, 'her fans herald her as the new Madonna'. In other words, an *icon*. Playing a song with Talvin Singh at the London Jazz Festival was more in Björk's line, though in a three way interview with Tori Amos and Polly Harvey in *Q* (the trio had met up backstage at the BRITS), Björk admitted a little touch of the megalomaniac. 'You might attack some innocent room service people sometimes,' she confessed.

The national heroine returned to Iceland in June, to play her first homecoming show in two years. It was Icelandic Independence Day, and before her show, Björk was advertised to appear at a family festival. Thousands of people turned up, and in a mad act of joky megalomania, she parachuted on to the stage, 'which caused a sensation', remembers Árni Matthíasson.

'I wanted to give the fans something extra special', she said. 'The organizers suggested it and before I knew what I was saying I agreed. It all happened so quickly that I didn't have time to be nervous or scared. As I was floating down, all I could think of was what songs I had to sing, and in what order.'

Björk had got her memories mixed, because she wasn't even scheduled to sing at this appearance, although she acquiesced and did a solo rendition of 'The Anchor Song' on piano. She sung it in Icelandic too, which set the tone for the evening's show proper, in front of 6,000 people. Opening with 'Human Behaviour' as usual, the crowd were as bouncily dynamic as Björk on stage, except when they realized that she was singing the whole set in Icelandic, 'which threw them off a bit because they had never heard the songs that way', says Árni Matthíasson. 'Björk said that she would have felt stupid singing in English, that it would be like talking to your grandmother in another language. But it was a pleasant surprise.' As was Björk's request for a minute's silence half way through the show, in memory of her hard rocking faves Ham, 'the best band in the world', she cried, who had just split up. Which must have thrown the crowd yet again.

It was summer festival season. Björk headlined Scotland's T In The Park and played a prominent slot at Glastonbury. At the other end of the scale, in September, Björk's MTV *Unplugged* session ran. This was the perfect opportunity to elaborate on her 'remix' mentality. In this orgy of collaboration, she roped in Oliver Lake, Evelyn Glennie, a gamelan orchestra, a set of wine glasses, tablas, double bass, tuba and flute. *Debut* deconstructed. The set climaxed with Corky Hale dueting on 'My Funny Valentine', shedding the instrumental setting and singling out the voice for the most lasting of impressions.

Derek Birkett wanted to release the *Unplugged* session, but Björk's stringent aesthetics stood in the way. 'She considered it an audi-visual experience, and that the music didn't stand up without the visuals,' says Birkett. 'I would have given it away free with the forthcoming remix album as well but she wouldn't have it.'

Unplugged was the last reinterpretation of her old repertoire that Björk could reasonably expect to make, so the news that she had been recording was welcome. She had finally secured time with Evelyn Glennie, whose boundary-breaking work (where did the classical end and the ethnic begin?) was all the more intuitive for the fact that Glennie was clinically deaf. Glennie hadn't worked with anyone in pop before but since she believed that, 'everything, in my mind, had to be spontaneous, immediate, unrehearsed and raw,' the pair seemed perfect for each other, and they immediately hit it off. Marimba, steel drums, clay drums, car exhaust pipes laid on a frame . . . Björk would go round the room, picking up instruments, Glennie would pick out patterns and Björk welded on chords and melodies. This was not the path Sade would have taken after a spectaular debut; the Liz Naylor's of this world could start to sleep soundly.

September was a busy month, with the long-form video *Vessel* on general release. If *Unplugged* and the Glennie sessions captured the wild, adventurist Björk, then Stephane Sednaoui's work captured her comparatively adequate stage show, but worse, captured the hair-twiddling, child-like, off-kilter Björk that she maintained in interviews was a caricature and a cliché. Like the 'Big Time Sensuality' promo, Sednaoui used plenty of fish-eye lens close-ups and time-frame trickery to create an avant-psychedelic playground, through which Björk gurgled, giggled and squinted, uttering naive asides like, 'I couldn't hear without my ears.' She also repeated many of the comments she had made to the press, which hardly adhered to Sednaoui's wish to catch her in an off-guard, improvising mood.

As Bragi noted at the time, 'Sometimes she tries to hide behind some infantile, naive look when doing TV interviews, which disturbs me. But she is a very wholesome person, very honest and straightforward, very 100 per cent.' Even knowing the fact that Björk wanted to be silly and childish as well as serious and organized, it was a curiously one-sided approach.

At a press conference, Björk was more succinct. The title *Vessel* came from a desire to collect her thoughts and ideas and transport them to us – but of course she needed something to put them in. And then she sung 'Human Behaviour', 'Come To Me' and 'The Anchor Song' with just Guy Sigsworth on harpsichord, to reiterate the real essence of the video.

After a year of rumoured release dates, Björk's remix album finally appeared in October. The proposed title *Björk's Affairs*, which One Little Indian had preferred, was again jettisoned in favour of the playful *All The Remixes From The Same Album For Those People Who Don't Buy White Labels*, so that people couldn't possibly mix it up with Björk's second album proper. She also made sure that the album was priced as a 12 inch single, so as not to exploit those who might want to buy the album having already bought the singles.

'Listening back to all the remixes, I had got this sudden idea for a remix album. At first, my record companies abroad were like, "We want a remix album out before Christmas," to pump out more money, and I told them, "No way, fuck off, I'd never do anything like that, and no, I'm not putting out all the remixes, just six out of twenty, the ones that I thought were timeless. That I didn't want to be lost or forgotten."'

Short of an avant-garde explosion, Björk had just about covered every front. Now she had inextricably woven herself into pop's rich tapestry, with enormous kudos being handed out by the musical dignitaries around her. No other rock/pop industry artist could genuinely touch her credibility – as a certain Madonna had evidently recognized . . .

La Ciccone would not have requested Björk and Nellee to write and produce all of her new album on the grounds of cred-by-assocation alone; she wanted some of that big time, divine dance sensuality, and this was indisputedly the hottest pop ticket in town. When the approach was made, Björk initially reacted as she did with Prince's dinner date; despite the respect she held for Madonna, it was too loaded and forced an association. But over time, she saw a way of making a point, by putting words into Madonna's mouth. 'The lyrics just sort of popped into my head,' Björk recalled. 'I thought of a collection of words that I always wanted to hear Madonna say, which was, *"Let's get unconscious, baby"*. She needs more unconscious. She's all on the outside. So I wanted her to say, "Let's be impulsive for a change, instead of so clever". Then I formed the song around those phrases. I decided it could be the most personal present I could give her.'

Thus 'Bedtime Stories' was born. The melody was one that Björk felt wasn't really suitable for herself, and got Nellee to offer it to Madonna, who gratefully accepted its slinky, lush tonality. Björk then drew the line at Madonna's additional request to make it a duet. 'I had written the song specially for her but my intuition told me that it would be wrong for me to sing on the song,' she told *Rolling Stone*. 'I also refused to meet her officially when she asked. When I meet her, I want it to be by coincidence, when we're both drunk in a bar or something.'

Björk wasn't completely adverse to a brush with A List celebrities. She subsequently accepted an invitation to attend the launch party of Quentin

Tarantino's epic – and epically hyped – *Pulp Fiction*, donned a glamourous frock, and arrived in a limousine. 'It was very, very funny – it felt like Christmas or a Halloween fancy dress party,' Björk grinned. 'I can live without that for another year, but I might like it again in another year's time.' Real fame, she said, was as much the property of a female food scientist in Iceland as it was a pop star, as the former worked just as hard as her. 'Why am I more interesting than her, just because I work with a microphone instead of a microscope? I'd much rather read about people who make films or homeless people.'

Sadly, TV awards for science are few and far between, which is why MTV's inaugural European Video Awards at the Brandenberg Gate in Berlin starred the likes of Björk alone. She sung 'Big Time Sensuality' with Fluke's assistance again, and rolled around on the floor, dressed, as the *Financial Times* said, 'like a raspberry mousse' (one of Hussein Chalayan's red paper ballgowns, as it happens). As Fluke manager Jonathan Richardson recalls, Björk nearly didn't appear, after throwing 'a massive fit' during rehearsals when she discovered that she was being filmed without permission, and threatened not to perform. 'She can be seen as difficult, and demanding, and is prone to tantrums,' Richardson vows. 'People don't always agree with what she wants.'

Despite claims that Björk could be manipulative, bloody-minded and petulant, it was only those who had known her for years – Bragi and Siggi of The Sugarcubes, and naturally her mother – who didn't treat her as some kind of deity. Perhaps it is their continuing willingness to work with Björk that stops some from painting the whole picture, but to counterbalance any criticisms, there are a host of comments claiming that Björk is essentially honest, fair and considerate. Anyway, don't you need a certain amount of selfish bloody-mindedness in order to fulfil a vision? 'I very very rarely argue with people,' Björk said. 'Once every five years or so. Well, it used to be that way. This year has been very drastic. There's been a lot of people trying to force things down my throat they think they know all about. They don't realize that I'm doing something for the first time and I want it to be done different from before.'

As Björk planned pre-production for a new album in November and December, she would have understood the pressure of following a hugely successful album like *Debut* but she also understood that she could never listen to advice to form any consensus agreement, to play it safe. 'I think one of the reasons my album is the way I wanted it to be is because I could do it in my own corner without anyone poking at me, and Derek let me do anything I wanted. I'm probably not going to get tne same peace next time around unless I do it totally on my own and don't let anybody hear it for a year.'

Björk's pre-production work was done with Graham Massey, Howie Bernstein (a DJ pal of Nellee's who had part-engineered *Debut* and worked on his own trip-hop-style fusions primarily for the Mo Wax label – he had become one of Björk's best friends in London) and Leila Arab. But she sought out Nellee Hooper when it came to starting the finished recordings. Surprisingly, he initially told her that he didn't want to get involved. 'Björk was experimenting on her own and found it all a bit tricky, so she approached me, but I didn't feel as excited over doing another record. I thought Björk knew enough to do it herself this time but she felt she needed some kind of coverage. Why did I agree? I guess I was once again seduced by Björk.'

Unusually for Björk, she had become a bit dependent on their musical relationship, and she recalled leaving his house, 'really pissed off, thinking, "You don't love me anymore", and things like this.' She subsequently wrote a series of songs, played them to him, and in a drunken haze, got him to promise he would be around. 'He said he'd be my safety net,' Björk said, and later wrote 'Cover Me' about the incident. *'While I crawl into the unknown, cover me/I'm going hunting for mysteries/cover me/I'm going to prove the impossible really exists.'*

Satisfied with the work in progress, Björk and Sindri decamped to Reykjavík for the Christmas holidays. All the exposure she had enjoyed in 1994 had seen *Debut* make twenty-seventh in the best-selling albums of the year chart – achieved with only one single ('Violently Happy') behind it. Violently happy to the end, she threw a huge New Year's Eve party, and looked forward to a new album.

Let's Get Unconscious

12

With all the mania of her working life, Björk's love life was seemingly destined to proceed with matching volatility. Both Björk and Stephane were hot-headed and hot-hearted, and words apparently confided in tabloid journalists again suggested that this combustible formula was never destined to last. The couple split in November 1994 but there was no acrimony as they continued to keep in contact. A new song, 'Possibly Maybe' was written about their affair: *'mon petit vulcan/ you're eruptions and disasters/I keep calm/admiring the lava/I keep calm . . . how can you offer me love like that?/my heart's burned/I'm exhausted/leave me alone.'*

Then again, the lyrics could just as well have been about her next liaison . . .

As usual, Björk kept quiet about her private life. She was never caught by photographers, and always replied, 'It's a secret,' when asked about her new lover, until months after the fact. Björk had thrown herself into pre-production work but later admitted that she had been disturbed by the fact that she didn't have a boyfriend, for the first time since the age of sixteen (which supported the claim that she hadn't split with one before meeting another). 'When we broke up, I thought I might as well enjoy this, which I do and I don't,' she told *Interview*. 'It's scary at times. The best bit is that you're kind of skinless, you're more vulnerable and emotional and on edge. Then there are all these things saying how brilliant it is to be self-sufficient and not needing anything or anybody and getting all these tools so that you can do everything yourself. Everything is geared toward self-sufficiency. Fuck that. For me, the target is to learn how to communicate with other people, which is the hardest thing, after all.'

Abstaining from sex was tough too, as she outlined in *Details*. She called herself 'outrageously greedy' when it came to sex – so much so that, 'it's, you know, a problem . . . I sort of do karate and swimming and working out and masturbate all morning every day and then I'm OK.'

Perhaps it was the uncertainty that plunged her into a new affair that was always going to be unpredictable, because the man in question undoubtedly was. Once again, Björk let a working relationship flourish beyond the drawing board; having fallen for a film-maker, a DJ and a photographer since Thór, it was another musician who stopped her in her tracks – a certain Adrian Thaws, who had earned his nickname Tricky Kid on the run-down streets of Bristol. Tricky, as he was now known, later joined the city's burgeoning music mafia, contributing to both Massive Attack's albums, 1991's *Blue Lines* and 1994's *Protection* and, in between, forging his own fiercely heated, darkly troubled work (the 1993 single 'Aftermath' and the 1994 single 'Ponderosa', which Howie B assisted on). It was only a matter of time before Björk would meet this brilliantly intuitive, rhythmic alchemist. Under a nightclub roof, they got drunk together and immediately started plotting how they could work together.

Björk had returned to Iceland for Christmas, to see her friends – her real friends, that is, because, 'where I come from, you don't say you're friends with someone unless you've known them for ten years, delivered their babies and gone to their funerals,' she said. But she soon shocked herself to discover that she missed London – or at least the friends that now constituted the framework of home. After two weeks of increasing restlessness, she called her new tricky mate, and over he flew.

'Tricky was getting a lot of pressure from his record company, because there was a real buzz about his album, so he was a bit naughty and escaped to Iceland,' she told *Interview*. 'We drove around in a four-wheel drive and saw the glaciers and swam in the hot springs and wrote two tracks. It was brilliant working there, with twenty-four hour darkness and snow up to I don't know where.'

As Tricky saw it, 'We said we'd work together, and the next thing I know, I'm in a hotel room in Iceland, having a drink, running a QY20 [sequencer] through a beatbox, then the next day you have a song.' Two actually – 'Enjoy' and 'Headphones', both composed with noises made by that pocket-sized Yamaha QY20 and both quickly added to the stockpile for the new album.

Tricky was an ultimate $1+1 = 3$ sparring partner, somebody who Björk had to use her stealth and patience with in order to get the best out of. 'At first, it was very much a case of him being the eccentric who finds the world is not a very fascinating place, you know?' she told NME. 'He's the kind of guy who has his own kingdom, he doesn't go to peoples' houses, they come to him – he's a bit of a hermit in that way. So you have to enter his house, his chaotic little world, and get lost for a moment, to pretend you have nothing in your pockets, no ideas, and then he comes up with something and you just "happen" to have something that fits. I like Tricky – he got that nickname at school and it's no coincidence, you know. If you want Tricky to go right, you ask him to go left. If you want to do an aggressive song, you suggest that you do something tender, and if you want to do something tender, you suggest something very aggressive.

'But Tricky's true talent is as a poet. He's a born street poet and he's got such a gorgeous, impulsive, intuitive mind. Me, I'm not a poet at all, my talent is for music, and I basically translate the music into words. So my words cannot stand on their own – they are a translation into language of what is happening in the music. That's why it doesn't matter whether I sing in English or Icelandic because it's all just a translation of what is there already.'

So a new love affair began, but one that was as unstable as the last – Tricky was about to release his debut album masterpiece (no other word for it) *Maxinquaye* and thus embark on a crazy year, and this was one tempestuous, moody misanthrope to begin with. Anyway, Björk had an album to make. But where? It was Nellee Hooper who came up with the idea of recording Björk's skyscraper tonsils outdoors, and so suggested Capri, where there was a clifftop studio with a terrace, and no cars on the island. Björk relished the chance: she had always had it in mind to record in a more organic manner after *Debut*'s more rigid disciplines, to get back to nature, to be closer to the ocean, as if she was in Iceland. But when it was time to organize the trip, it was already winter, and the weather too unpredictable, so a short conflab later, Nassau in the Bahamas became the chosen destination for the A team of Björk, Nellee, Marius De Vries and Howie B.

The location wasn't chosen for purely exotic reasons but for mundane tax purposes too. In order to register her newly formed company Björk Overseas Ltd outside the UK, having changed the name from Bapsi Ltd (according to Árni Matthíasson, Bapsi was her childhood nickname, a derivative of the name Björk), she had to record half the album outside the UK. Not that the record would suffer for the move: Nassau's Compass Point Studio had an exemplary track record and cost no more than a London-based studio of the same quality.

The majority of Björk's vocals were done on the beach. To leave her free to wander off if she wanted, she would wear a tiny tape recorder powered by a lightweight battery, on a long lead, singing as she went. 'It was a very sentimental thing, to sing outside, because I knew everything would fall into place,' she told *Interview*. 'Nellee made it happen. I'd just sit there at midnight. All the stars would be out, and I'd be sitting there under a little bush. I'd go running into the water and nobody could see where I went. In the quiet bits, I'd sit and cuddle, and for the outrageous bits, I'd run around. It was the first time I'd done a song like that in twenty years. I was crying my eyes out with joy because it was something I so deeply wanted all those years. Almost like you had sex lots of times, and it's gorgeous, and then you couldn't have it for twenty years, and then suddenly you have it. It was completely outrageous.'

With their machines rolling, the production team diligently slogged away, working from prepared demos or from scratch, as 'Cover Me' was done (the original version was recorded in a cave with bats flying around). With hindsight, Björk declared *Debut* too controlled, too much on the surface – this time, she wanted to focus more on the energy of the music. 'The emotions are more definitive, because I feel braver,' she told *Raygun*. 'The aim was to express myself without complications, to be more direct.' She took this to extremes, such as singing 'Possibly Maybe' in the nude, which was a bit of a rites of passage experience even for this child of nature. 'It's hard because you are very concerned that everyone is looking at you,' she claimed.

The album was supposed to be delivered the day after the party returned from Nassau but on arrival, Björk had a panic attack, fearing that she hadn't truly achieved her aims by making the music too machine-based. Björk embarked on a new round of re-recording, with trumpet, sax, bagpipes, harpsichord, a symphony orchestra, a brass band, everything but the kitchen sink . . . 'I just wanted to bring the album alive,' she told *Raygun*. 'I still find it ten times more natural for me to deal with live instruments than programmed ones because that's what I've been doing all my life. Electronic instruments are harder to grasp for me, but of course that's the reason why I need to tackle them.'

Derek Birkett says that he couldn't see what was wrong with the original sessions – 'I think you'd have to be incredibly close to the record to see any big changes' – and even Nellee thought that she could easily get away with overdubs rather than outright re-recordings. 'She thought material like "Hyperballad" and "Possibly Maybe" sounded too soft, but with Björk, she makes it all sound a lot more drastic. She could say, "It all sounds far too soft," or too programmed, and you'll change one thing, like the treble on the hi-hat, and she'll say [puts on Icelandic accent], "it sounds *brilliant*".'

'Björk tends to pull things to pieces,' Marius De Vries reckons. 'She had extreme reactions to things, which is a virtue as well as a fault.'

Despite the air of panic, Graham Massey admits that the sessions he was involved in, 'were not laid back as such but a really good atmosphere, without that kind of, "we must get it right" pressure. There was lots of, "shall we go for dinner?" or, "shall we go clubbing?" atmosphere, with work concentrated in small bursts, which gets the job done a lot faster, rather than torturing yourself. She has an incredible amount of experience in the studio now, and that makes the difference between having an artist in charge of the session rather than an engineer in charge of the session.'

The reworking brought back some old faithfuls – Guy Sigsworth to add harpsicord to 'Cover Me', Gary Barnacle and Talvin Singh to add sax and tablas respectively to 'I Miss You', a track co-written with Howie B. The latter track had been pulled apart and reworked since the days of *Debut*, when it was titled 'Gail Biffen' (after one of Björk's Nordic-jibberish phrases). It was left off the album because Nellee couldn't get a good enough chorus out of Björk to match the Chic-style house backing. Björk later retitled the track 'I Miss You' and wrote new lyrics but Nellee declined to work on it, and so Björk went off with Howie B, ending up with a programmed but raw Latin feel that she chose to leave unadorned.

A new face to appear on the album, though an old face in musical terms, was the legendary Brazilian composer/arranger Eumir Deodato. He was best known for his late sixties arrangement of Richard Strauss's 'Also Sprach Zarathustra' (usually recognized as the theme to Stanley Kubrick's sci-fi classic *2001: A Space Odyssey*) but Björk had contacted him because of his work on a little known track 'Travessia' by Latin musician Milton Nascimento. Deodato was of a different generation, but had worked inside the pop industry, though he hadn't experienced the whirlwind that was Björk. Surprise, surprise, he was deeply smitten by the effect, and ended up scoring strings for three tracks, 'Isobel', 'Hyper-ballad' and 'You've Been Flirting Again'.

'She has developed a style and music that I've never heard anything like in my life,' he told *Rolling Stone*. 'When I heard her material, I freaked out and I said, "What are you doing? This is crazy, this is so difficult, to propose this kind of style to the people." But she does, and she's successful at it! There's the liberty she takes with melodies and with harmony that sometimes apparently leaves clashes that are not really clashes, they're concepts. It's an acoustic principle, but she instinctively goes into that vein, and she blends all these things with a beautiful voice.'

As if to test Nellee's faith in her, Björk's reworkings of 'Cover Me' and 'You've Been Flirting Again' were done alone, and became her solo production credits. She also made other vital advances, co-writing the string arrangement on 'You've Been Flirting Again' and writing all the brass parts on 'I Miss You'. In the end, only a third of the twelve tracks were produced by Nellee Hooper and Björk. The new album was as important a rite of passage as *Debut* had been, as Björk had to prove to herself that she could keep progressing without losing nerve or direction. Cohesion was going to be a lot harder to maintain; though *Debut* had been assembled from songs composed over a decade while the new songs that made up the newly titled *Post* were culled from just two years of volcanic creativity, the new collection felt like a greater *mélange* of elements, using all the lessons she had taken from her post-*Debut* collaborations, reflecting all the different phases of recording and the newest collaborators.

If *Debut* was rooted in London's clubland, as Björk delighted in the freedom of dance music, then the new record was Björk foraging all over the world, taking mental notes, discovering new fauna and flora and performing little aural experiments. She saw the theme of the new album as rootlessness. '*Post* is very much influenced by being away from home, particularly in a country where everyone thinks you're mad,' she told the *Irish Times*. 'The English, especially, can't relate to me. As post-colonial people, they think they can own things, and laugh at them. That's how they deal with different cultures. And the fact that I'm not very English deepens the sense of isolation that's at the heart of *Post*.'

She had called the album *Post*, 'because all the songs on the album for me are like saying, "Listen, this is how I'm doing," because I always address my songs back in my head to Iceland, like a letter,' she told *Rolling Stone*. 'Like I have a love affair with someone, and it goes horribly wrong, and I go, "Dear Iceland, Possibly Maybe". Because it was such a big jump for me to move away from all my relatives, all my friends, everything I know. Also, *Post* is an international word, that everyone can understand.'

Björk saw the new album not so much as a major departure from its predecessor but as a sequel. 'In a way *Debut* and *Post* are the same thing, but before and after,' she said in the *Post* book. 'Basically I don't think of *Post* as more diverse than *Debut*. It's just that the mad songs are more mad, and the delicate songs are more delicate. I could exaggerate all the things better, because I'm better at what I'm doing.'

Graham Massey could only agree. 'There's very little music left that comes from the true spirit of adventure,' he said in the *Post* book. 'There used to be much more. For me, a lot of the songs on Björk's new album have that quality to them. There's strong music that comes out of adventurousness. There are songs like "Cover Me" which could come from any time – they're timeless. *Post* is even more special than the album before and I think has even more longevity to it.'

Derek Birkett, however, was more doubtful. Though he loved the finished album, he rightly deemed it more difficult than its predecessor, and wondered if it would sell as well – but since he originally reckoned *Debut* would sell around 25,000 copies in the UK, what did he know? But even he agreed that Björk would not benefit from doing so much press this time around. The management had the feeling that the press were a bit bored, and were looking for some dirt. A little bit of mystery needed retaining, to keep an artist fresh, so the decision was taken to only talk to the cream of the magazine crop, the ones Björk really liked, and to hold press conferences around festival appearances so as not to alienate the rest of the faithful.

Having returned from the Bahamas to pick up her 1995 BRITS awards – Best Female and International Artist for Björk; Best Producer for Nellee – her profile was hardly going to suffer for it. Any press she did consent to was invariably a front cover feature, so there was no noticeable dip in Björk Around Town. The PR machine started turning in April, while Sindri was back in Iceland with Thór over the Easter holidays, leaving Björk twelve days of family-free frolics. To break the deadlock of predictable interviews, she started with a two day jaunt on the Orient Express, London to Venice, and then settled in a French hotel, L'Abbaye Des Vaux De Cernay, a converted twelfth century abbey. Luxury all the way. Faced with a cavalcade of the world press, she ironically contested the idea of overexposure. 'Because people find my music quite unusual and they find me quite unusual, they don't really know how to picture the whole me and I quite like that,' she told *The Face*.

As Jean Cocteau once said, 'The more visible they make me, the more invisible I become . . .'

At the end of April, 'Army Of Me' became the first track to be released off *Post* as a single. With its military, stomping beat and grinding atmosphere, it seemed a curious choice for Graham Massey and Björk to have conjured up, but as Massey says, 'We'd come up with this rock-monstery groove which obviously triggered something off in her mind in regard to the lyric, and then it became a solid thing rather than just a riff.' It seemed an even more curious choice as a back-in-the-fray single, and it certainly lacked the heightened magic of the Björk we knew.

But the track prooved more hypnotic over time, and remains a bold reintroduction of intent – a strident, unforgiving Björk, inspired by being angry at a friend prone to self-pity, fights on the behalf of positive action. '*"So if you complain once more, you'll meet an army of me,"* is me saying, "Just get to work, stop this, please"," she told *Melody Maker*. 'You come to a point with people like that where you've done everything you can do for them, and the only thing that's going to sort them out is themselves. It's time to get things done.'

Because she felt that she rarely got angry, Björk and sleeve designer Paul White decided that the anger would come from a cartoon figure, Astro Björk, modelled after Japan's cartoon hero Astro Boy. On the sleeve, Astro Björk flies around, surrounded by tiny polar bears, while the second, remix CD switched the characters, promoting the cutest angry polar bear. 'I identify with polar bears,' she claimed. 'They're very cuddly and cute and quite calm but if they meet you, they can be very strong. They come to Iceland very rarely, about once every ten years, floating on icebergs. So I am a polar bear and I'm with 500 polar bears, just tramping over a city.'

Derek Birkett didn't share Björk's concrete certainty. He hadn't wanted 'Army Of Me' as the first single to be released from the new album, 'because it wasn't what people were going to expect,' he reasoned, and the majority of the press acted accordingly. Björk was perplexed: 'I thought it was a natural continuity of *Debut*,' she told *Melody Maker*. 'I purposefully didn't sing with any emotion, because it was supposed to be quite sinister, right? So I wasn't trying to shock people, but I seem to have.'

The song was still a hit in the UK, and Björk appeared on *Top Of The Pops*. To reinforce the song's musical and lyrical force, she asked fellow One Little Indian labelmates, metal-soul renegades Skunk Anansie, to back her (a collaboration already initiated on the second 'Army' CD). 'Imagine you're in a club full of heavy metal types and grunge people,' she told Q. "Army Of Me" is like somone's granny blasting out over the PA and saying, "Snap out of it! Stop whining! Wash your hair! Smarten yourself up!"' Proof, then, that guitars needn't be a total anathema if a message could be secreted in there. Björk wasn't going to always neglect the punk rocker in her system. She was subsequently criticized for this manoeuvre too. 'I do a heavy metal thing on *Top Of The Pops*, which I thought was quite shocking, and most people go, "Oh yes. Of course. I've lost the plot, to be honest. Not that I ever had it".'

At least the B-sides were comfort to Björk traditionalists and the anti-Sade squad. 'Cover Me' could have been Björk playing the church organ all over Iceland, with a liturgical calm that could have been Brahms or Messiaen; 'You've Been Flirting Again' (in Icelandic) was a soft-as-snow ballad of just voice and Deodato's strings; 'Sweet Intuition', from her sessions with Black Dog, was intoxicating futurist ambient jazz funk.

'Army Of Me' needed a tongue-in-cheek video, so who better than Michel Gondry, who came up with a dream-surreal sequence to end them all. In a sub-*Blade Runner* urbanscape, Björk drives a tank, gets a gorilla dentist to take out a diamond before she plants a bomb in an art gallery to free a human exhibit. Come again? 'The video is about me grinding my teeth,' she explained. 'My car breaks down and I've got the biggest car in the world because I'm so angry – it's like a truck – and because I'm so mad and the car's teeth are broken, I have to go to the dentist to get new teeth for my car.'

One Little Indian's video commissioner Kenny Addison described the part where Björk has to jump out of the giant tank, on wires, 'which is when she freaked out, and we discovered that she has a fear of heights. She got a bit woozy but was okay.' That parachute jump in Reykjavik must have taken some guts then. 'Björk suffers for her art,' Addison muses.

'Army Of Me' was included in the Tank Girl soundtrack, which was released in May, a month before the film. Asked about what soundtracks she would like to be involved in, Björk said that she was keener on a film project she could empathize with, like one directed by New Zealander Jane Campion, whose three-hour *An Angel At My Table* or the more recent *The Piano* had won fantastic notices. 'Anyone who loves my music should go and see *The Piano*,' Björk raved. 'I wrote her a very polite letter saying that if she ever needed someone to write the score for one of her movies, I would jump at the opportunity. She does with film what I do with music: she takes elements from someone's life – without resorting to science fiction or implausible plots – then gives them a kind of magic resonance. Or if Gabríel Garcia Márquez was ever to write a book which would be filmed. He also sees the fantastic in the ordinary. I think it's fantastic that I should have developed the same sensibilities in Iceland that he did growing up in the exotic, tropical South America. In Iceland, that feeling for magic stems from our recent past.'

Coincidentally, Björk appeared on a new album that month from French composer Hector Zazou, *Chansons Des Mers Froides*, or *Songs From The Cold Seas*, singing a traditional Icelandic song 'Visur Vatnsenda-Rósu' (other contributions came from the likes of Jane Siberry, John Cale, Suzanne Vega and The Balanescu Quartet). She had originally wanted to do it in the original, choral arrangement, and sing all the parts, but the collaborative attempt with Guy Sigsworth didn't work well enough, and they were forced to do just a vocal-and-harpsichord version. Unbeknown to them, Zazou amalgamated both the Björk-choral and solo versions, which pleased her no end.

She also took part in the Pagan Fun Wear fashion show organized on behalf of the Bosnian War Child charity. It brought her more national press but it was the anticipation of the new album that saw a *Daily Star* feature under the headline 'BJÖRK'S A BJERK' appear a week before release date. The piece was illustrated with a photo of Björk looking angelically loopy, her knees locked together, feet pointed in: the eternal child caricature, in other words. 'SHE wore a duvet to school,' the piece exclaimed. 'SHE licks walls of buildings. SHE believes she can fly.' It was claimed that Björk didn't go out under a full moon because she was superstitious, that she was allergic to the colour purple, that she licked the walls to get the greasy layer of London's pollution off. What a strange coincidence that, in an *NME* cover feature the previous week, Björk had discussed the freedom she enjoyed as a child, her mother's purple colour scheme, the thought of joyfully leaping off a roof in a blizzard, violently happy and drunk . . . 'I was sorta born on drugs,' she owned up, playing at metaphors, whilst the tabloids could only be pathetically literal.

Derek Birkett probably thought Björk was still on drugs when she scrapped a £24,000 photo shoot with Jean-Baptiste Mondino because she wasn't satisfied that the results (Björk surrounded by large, silver polystyrene balls, an idea repeated on the 'Hyper-ballad' single sleeve) suited the mood of the album. Maybe it was too hyper-modernist, too technological, so she set up a second session with Stephan Sednaoui. 'Now I know what I want,' she laughed. 'Okay, I admit it! I'm a pop star!'

According to Paul White, her record sleeve designer, the effect that Björk was after approximated awe. The idea had come from the image of a house of cards interlocking, so a series of intersecting, vibrantly-coloured flags and banners were hung up in a courtyard in London, with a Chinese parasol behind her head. She wore a Hussein Chalayan white crepe paper jacket, with red and blue 'airmail' piping around the collar – Venus as an envelope. And quicker than first class post, the album went straight to the top of the UK chart.

Like 'Army Of Me', *Post* took several listens to sink its seductive claws in, but the results were more courageous, dramatic and satisfying than even *Debut*. Odd critics felt disappointed by the lack of the smoothly syncopated lushness that decorated *Debut* but it was still there, in the stunning shapes of 'Hyper-ballad' and 'Isobel', except more extreme as Björk had intended. Both tracks were born out of typically Björkian whimsy, inspired by her desire to tap into the same root as novelist Gabríel Garcia Márquez, the greatest of all magic-realists.

'Hyper-ballad' was about the idea of permanence and pressure in relationships, about hiding frustrations and the negative side of our lives and minds in order to preserve love, a story which Björk wanted to tell in a quasi-fairytale or fable, 'like something that happens over and over again,' she told *Interview*. 'It's about this couple who live on a cliff in the middle of the ocean, they live in a house, just the two of them, and she wakes up really early, about five in the morning, before anyone else wakes up . . .'

'Hyper-ballad' was inspired by the fact that, 'when people fall in love, they make this kind of drug in their bodies, so they become physically dependent on each other,' Björk supposed. 'And this drug lasts for three years. That's how long nature gives people to find out if they want to spend the rest of their lives with each other. But sometimes people wake up after three years, and go, whoops, what am I doing here? . . .'

Hadn't Björk fallen out of love with Dom after three years? With Thór after three or four?

'. . . So you're really sweet on the front, but – growl! – you've got all these dragons behind you and they make you go the pub without your partner for ten hours, and so you have to do something really gross to get the monsters out. You've got to really shock yourself; dance topless on top of a bar, snog somebody you don't even like, maybe even go to bed with them. There's too much preciousness in relationships. People should be more honest and do things that are spontaneous and provocative.'

'There's a beautiful view from the top of the mountain/every morning I walk towards the edge and throw little things off/like: car-parts, bottles and cutlery/ or whatever I find lying around . . .'

'. . . So she goes outside and throws things off the cliff, then imagines what it would look like if she herself were to jump off. Then she sneaks back into the house, back into bed, then her lover wakes up, and it's "Hello! Good morning, honey!" And she's got rid of all the aggressive bollocks.' If this story was true to life, Björk was admitting that she hadn't managed to vent her frustrations enough to keep a relationship going.

'Isobel' was as much a fairytale as a fable. The inspiration was born out of her period of being single. Björk had been working very hard on pre-production, with no reward in the shape of a boyfriend, and with that thought, she glanced down, and saw a moth on her nightshirt. Eager to discuss the metaphysical implications, she called Sjón in Iceland, the pair concluding that the moth was coming from, 'The Unexplained', 'and it's telling you, don't even try and understand it!' She asked Sjón to write lyrics about the incident, and 'Isobel' was born – the name coming from Isobel Griffiths, the orchestral conductor of Deodato's strings.

As Björk saw it, Isobel was a mythological figure, born out of a spark in the woods, who symbolized intuition and instinct. As she grows, so do the pebbles on the forest floor which she realizes are actually baby skyscrapers, which eventually take over the forest and she finds herself in a city. Knowing no better about morals and behaviour, she goes to a party naked, she falls in love with a married man . . . recognizing her mistakes, Isobel withdraws into herself and eventually marries herself.' Hence the name Isobel, not Isabel, 'because it's about a girl who lives a very isolated life,' she told *Melody Maker*.

Was that the story of her life, leaving Reykjavík the forest for London the city, and withdrawing? 'I really felt that when I came to London,' she confessed. 'I would work all week like a lunatic, eighteen hours a day, and when I go out for the weekend, to have a laugh like they do in Iceland, I would find myself on top of a table, taking my top off, jumping and screaming, and I just realized that everyone in the whole club would go like [impersonates sucking a lemon] and just sit there polite with a little . . . pint. I'd go like, "Oh, ahem, sorry." I know they think I'm completely mad and a lunatic, but in Iceland, believe me, I'm the quiet one.'

Isobel was Björk's symbol for intuition, 'which is something everybody's got. You stand up one day and you've got to do something. There's no logic to it. Just pure instinct. That song's about all the battles you get into when you have to do something and all the clever people are saying, "No, you can't do that," and you go, "Why?" "Because you're not supposed to". Damn it, the battles of her childhood were still her battles of today . . .

The second Björk/Graham Massey collaboration, the giddy, spacious 'The Modern Things' was *Post*'s third storyboarded chapter. Björk wrote it on a train visiting Graham Massey in Manchester, as a form of revenge against those detractors who suggested that she had sold out her alternative roots. She was drinking some wine, looking out at the hills, appalled at the idea that people were so terrified of the future, of change. Remembering a friend's observation that modern machinery actually looked old, Björk was sparked into imagining that all the 'modern' things in life - cars, computer games, blenders – have always existed, hiding inside mountains, waiting to emerge, *'at the right moment'*.

'That a computer would sigh, "Damn, listen to that tyrannosaurus moan," whereas I have to wait here for another thirty thousand years,' she said, delighted at the ludicrousness of the idea.

Besides 'Army Of Me' and 'Cover Me', the remainder of *Post* was concerned with the different phases of love. 'Possibly Maybe' was about the heat of the affair; the first Tricky/Björk collaboration 'Enjoy' examined the heat of the moment against the fear of commitment; 'I Miss You' looked at the idea of love's rapture to come; 'You've Been Flirting Again' was harder to describe but seemed to explore the dynamics of trust in a relationship. The second Tricky/Björk collaboration, the closing abstract drift-athon 'Headphones' explored the simple love and restorative powers of music itself, as Björk listens to one of Graham Massey's compilation tapes: *'my headphones/they saved my life/your tape/it lulled me to sleep/and nothing will ever be the same'.* Even if love will break your heart, music will mend it . . .

The successor to 'Like Someone In Love' in the forties cover version stakes *was* the big-band romp of 'It's Oh So Quiet'. Björk had always enjoyed the over-passionate but coolly observed romanticism of Chet Baker, which this cover perfectly mirrored. Chosen for its exhaltation of the intensities and extremities of love, it was delivered with gleeful wonder – if Björk had been a forties starlet, she could definitely have written it. Originally titled 'Blow A Fuse', the song was written by Messrs Hans Lang and Bert Reisfeld and was a hit in 1948 for blonde Hollywood bombshell Betty Hutton. Guy Sigsworth had first played it to Björk, and it rapidly became her favourite song. 'Isn't that the best song you've heard for five years?' she asked *Details* a year earlier. 'In a way, it was against my principles to do an old cover version because I'm so anti-retro. But it has this story, this narrative: there's a beginning and something happens in the middle, and the ending is different. So many pop songs, especially with English lyrics, are just nine hundred different ways of saying, "she left me!" Which I actually love because it's pop, just one idea, very simple but it doesn't mean it's cheap. I can relate to it, but I belong to the storytelling group.'

Ever the musicologist, Björk had been listening to pre-war pop, 'with one microphone in the middle and a fifty-piece band, and it's completely dynamic,' she told *Rolling Stone*. 'It was like punk. It has this complete hardcore energy.' Her own version faithfully followed Hutton's, with a full-scale orchestra and dynamic extremes. 'People think my version is over the top but hers makes mine the ambient version!' she told *Sky*. 'I guess the song describes pretty well what being in love feels like because it's in and out, innit?'

As for love, and the falling out of it, 'it all just tumbles, doesn't it?' she said, a belief that ties back to 'Hyper-ballad'. 'In one week. Even less. You end up saying, 'What was it we did the last three years? I forgot.' Really? For most people, love was alarmingly quick to fall in to but then agonizingly slow to fall out of. But falling out of love quickly fitted Björk's way of thinking. People and friends were not disposable but very precious but when it came to relationships, Björk didn't like to hang around. 'I don't like in between stuff,' she said, although she admitted that she had gone off the rails – albeit momentarily – when she and Dom had split up (sadly, no one can, or is willing to, corroborate this fact!). 'I guess I'm a very over-emotional person,' she said. 'I'm very, very happy, or I'm very, very this, or I'm or very, very that. I have a hardcore, Viking, don't-feel-sorry-for-yourself attitude.'

Björk had even dedicated *Post* to her grandmother Hallfridur out of love. 'She is my only true idol, because she has really been the centre of the family, love-wise. And everybody turns to her if they need love – in one way or another, whether it's a question of wanting some chocolates or to be quiet or whatever. And she is a genius because she is so good at being unselfish when it comes to love and at the same time she is good at being selfish – like she'll just go for a week into the middle of the countryside with several bottles of wine and just paint. She just knows when to be selfish and when to be unselfish and that's such a brilliant balance to have.'

Even as late as July, despite the rumours, Björk wasn't naming Tricky as her paramour in press interviews ('it's a secret', etc.) but admitted that she had never experienced the feeling of getting ready to go on a proper date, and nervously changing her outfit five times before going out. Björk the unstarstruck teenager would just wear her little punk outfit. 'He's ever so sensitive about sound and music,' she said about this anonymous boy. 'He's got, like, a motor running inside him. And then you feel like you've got the same kind of motor yourself, and we're the only people who can hear it really.'

Tricky was also busy setting up a series of collaborative ventures as well as starting out on his debut tour; *Maxinquaye* had received the most superlative of reviews, and the press were just as demanding as they had been with Björk. The pair had little time to spend together, so when they were caught together, it was an unlucky accident. There was one notable incident, outside a London club – photographer Ray Newton claimed that Tricky had sprayed gas in his face when he tried to take his photo, while a spokesperson for the singer said that Tricky had spat at the photographer when Newton had ignored his request to desist.

The tabloids got a buzz out of it, the music press dutifully followed in their wake, and the incident got forgotten.

With the Simon Fisher case still to come, Björk had been wrenched into the public domain again by another legal dispute just days before *Post* was released. The intro to 'Possibly Maybe' used a loop of a mobile phone dialling tone, sampled himself by Scanner's 1994 album *Mass Observation*. Scanner a.k.a. Robin Rimbaud – Robin Aspel to his parents – was an electronic experimentalist delving into people's communications systems and conversations. 'It was really clever and interesting', Björk thought, and borrowed the thrity-two seconds, 'like an atmospheric beginning.'

She subsequently informed Derek Birkett of this, and numerous other, samples, none of which were eventually used except Scanner's, which Birkett had forgotton to clear – of the different versions of 'Possibly Maybe' that Björk had recorded, Birkett admits that he thought that the one that she finally chose for the album contained no sample on it. Scanner and his manager were informed of the error just weeks before the album release, and although Scanner asked for a payment of £500, Björk insisted that he should get £1,000, in line with previous payments to Quincy Jones for the sample used on 'Human Behaviour' and One Little Indian's payment to Nirvana over another sample for use by UK rap trio Credit To The Nation.

It would have stayed that way if Scanner's publishing company Beechwood hadn't argued that the thirty-two second sample was, in fact, an intrinsic part of the track's atmosphere, and if Beechwood hadn't felt aggrieved that, out of the forty-nine samples that might have appeared on the forthcoming Björk remix album, Scanner's was the only one not cleared. Feeling that Scanner had been mistreated, Beechwood pressed for a royalty payment instead of the usual flat clearance fee (say the album sold three million copies, then Scanner would stand to make between £60–70,000).

The irony, as Björk pointed out, was that Scanner's work was based on the premise, 'that all the noises in the world are for free,' and Scanner himself that his work dwelt in, 'the negotiation between what is legal and what isn't.' But Beechwood weren't about to be swayed by matters of irony, and while the dispute ran, One Little Indian was forced to release *Post*, then instantly delete the album, and re-release it within an hour without the offending sample (Birkett had distributed two million copies worldwide, and would be hard pressed to retrieve them).

Scanner himself had initially colluded with Beechwood's stance – he was planning to release the track that the sample originated from as a single, and was upset that people would think that he was copying Björk. Stuck in the middle of the dispute, he suddenly decided that neither he nor Beechwood should be money-minded and even said he was ready to drop his claim. 'I was getting so messey and involved, I was getting completely sick of it,' he told *NME*. 'All these worms were crawling out of the woodwork looking for a slice of the money, so I decided to let them have it for free.' Beechwood, feeling that they were not being supported by their own artist, dropped the royalty claim, and eventually an independent sample clearance expert set a payment of £2,000.

As it happened, the Björk vs. Simon Fisher/Lovejoy case was held in the same month as the Scanner controversy. Lovejoy had already dropped his claim on three out of the four songs before it reached court, leaving just 'Crying' to be adjudicated on. Björk didn't have to appear in person but she wanted to; once there, she said that she had been very quickly disappointed with the collaboration. 'The magic of music,' she told the judge, 'is that one plus one equals three. My expectations were so high I would have tried everything, but nothing worked.' She admitted that Lovejoy had a similar song to 'Crying' on his computer disc but that she was responsible for the music. The judge concluded that Fisher's version wasn't a substantial reproduction, that his evidence was, 'diffuse and vague' in many respects, and rejected allegations that Björk had acted dishonestly. 'Where there's a hit, there's a writ,' was the judge's sage response. The victory left Björk and One Little Indian with £50,000 court costs, but the point had been made.

July was a busy month for controversy, and if you didn't know Björk better, you'd think that she was enjoying the notoriety. *The Daily Star* reported an incident when Björk unleashed that usually controlled temper flooring a thug who started wrecking her favourite hot-dog stall because he was fed up of queueing. Björk, who was said to be a karate expert, forced him to apologize. 'I've never even heard of that story,' says Derek Birkett.

'I was in a restaurant with Björk once, and she threw two olives at me in play, and it was in the papers the next day.'

It was harder to deny the fact that, on live national breakfast radio, when she was asked what the hardest part of a song was, Björk replied, 'the lyrics take a fuck of a long time.' She reiterated that lyrics were 'a headfuck' and talked further about 'the fucking lyrics'. She was more than probably conscious of what she was doing, and couldn't care less. What a little boot boy.

The Devil Cuts Loose

Dean (9): *'She's an idiot. My whole family hates her.*
She plays rubbish songs. She can't sing. She can't dance.
She hasn't got the voice or the face.'
Kelly (10): *'Or the hairstyle. Or the legs.'*
Dean: *'She's like a baby.'*
Charlene (11): *'I think she's mad.'*
Janine (10): *'She's stupid. Not exactly stupid but the way*
she goes on, it's as if she's abnormal.'
(from childrens' interviews in *Q*, 1995)

Björk had always planned to tour with *Post* so she was able to escape any more potential timebombs by hitting the road. The lessons of the *Debut* band had been taken to heart, and Björk wanted a more extreme sound, more machines and more of the organic instrumentation of the *Unplugged* show. She leaned on Guy Sigsworth to help organize it. He began by resequencing the *Post* tape masters for use on stage, then suggested to Björk that she avoid using sampled strings to replace Deodato's sublime scores, and to use an accordion instead. 'It's one of those old and creaky instruments, with bellows and lungs, that really appeals to Björk. It also had no Acid Jazz connotations, which is also why she decided not to have a bass player, but to have the bass lines from the sequencers which Leila would manipulate.'

It was decided that Leila was more suited to sound manipulation than routine keyboard duties, so they took the unusual step of having her control an on-stage mixing desk that could alter the sequencers – 'A DJ world view,' as Guy puts it.

Björk was thrilled at the idea of having spontaneity as part of the sound mix. 'When you're doing the ninety-seventh gig, it becomes really important to get at least one surprise. Leila was our security. We'd never know what was going to happen next.'

Guy: 'She certainly surprised us many times, bringing down choruses to almost nothing where we expected something big, radically distorting and manipulating the sound of certain parts, and so on. In many ways, her role was the most spontaneous of us all - she was probably the only one who never played the same on any one night.'

The last pieces in the jigsaw were the vastly experienced drummer Trevor Morais, replacing Talvin Singh who had commitments elsewhere, while the accordionist was the singularly named Koba, from Japan. Björk had seen him advertised to play at London's South Bank arts centre, and asked him to join. Koba had never heard Björk's music, but said he would if he liked it. Months later, he was on tour . . .

She road-tested some *Post* songs on TV's *The White Room*, in a billowing black crepe dress, dayglo trainers and a T-shirt with her favourite cartoon characters Ren and Stimpy ('I wish I could marry them: Polly and Tricky and Ren and Stimpy, those are my four favourites'). The first tour date was in Dundee (they denied the press access, claiming that it was technically a warm up show and potentially not up to scratch, but charged the audience nevertheless). In support were string-based avant-classicists The Bronsky Quartet, playing Shostakovich and Stravinsky and confusing the audience, who perked up when Björk joined in for lavish versions of 'Hyper-ballad', 'You've Been Flirting Again' and 'Isobel'. The quartet cleared the way for the full band, and off Björk went, on another fantastic voyage. The gulf between the *Debut* shows and these was vast; here were the extremes she was after, with more rhythmic propulsion, but more intimacy too. Having enjoyed the one-on-one parts of the *Unplugged* show, Björk wanted to repeat it with each member; she and Leila fashioned a version of 'Enjoy', Trevor worked out 'One Day' with gamelan sounds triggered from his electronic drum kit; Koba did 'The Anchor Song'; Guy did 'Venus As A Boy' on harpsicord.

The mixing console and drums were woven into a design that echoed the rusty-futuristic aesthetic of The Modern Things, with organic steel tendrils, mummified trees, tubular coils and speakers on stalks, with the added aura of projection screens and drapes. Björk could dance and dream through this techno-organic forest like Isobel herself. Armed with dresses specifically designed by Hussein Chalayan for the shows - 'flowing silks with crystal beading, materials that worked well with the lights – she was in scampering mood, revelling in all the dynamics and diversity of the music. She would often kick off her shoes, like a small child, then sing a ballad with such expressiveness that she seemed as old as time. The fluidity of the approach was the polar opposite of the rigid dance routines and poses of Madonna, whose work always suggested what effect the world had on her, whereas Björk's work was about the effect she had on her audience.

The press reviews were predictable. The *Glasgow Herald* got it absolutely right: 'Her charisma swamped Barrowland, the show by far the most adventurous, both musically and stylistically, you are ever likely to see from an artist who has sold so many records.'

In August, she returned to Iceland to play the country's first music festival, UXI, organized by her old sparring partner Einar Örn. Held in Kirkjubæjarklaustur, a small town on the tip of Vatnajökull glacier, the festival had been part-funded by the Icelandic tourist board, which paid for some press to be carted over when it became clear that Björk would perform. She ended up flying in alone, singing only four songs 'Hyper-ballad', 'The Anchor Song', 'Enjoy' and 'Violently Happy' – in her native tongue of course – and just as quickly flew out again, in time for the release of 'Isobel' as a single.

Yet again, One Little Indian didn't want the track released – Derek Birkett thought 'Enjoy' and 'I Miss You' were the two most natural singles on the album, but Björk got her way. The two CDs presented the by now expected extremes – the rare reggae-based excursion 'Charlene' (recorded with Black Dog) and the techno-bubbly 'I Go Humble' (written with Mark Bell, one half of Black Dog's Warp labelmates LFO), with remixes from Deodato, Sugarcube drummer Siggi Baldursson and British junglist Goldie. Michel Gondry created another stunning video, filmed in the mountains of North-west Wales, a shoot notable for its pouring rain and mosquito attacks.

'Isobel' was a typical Top 20 entry, but surprisingly for an album seller of her stature, and someone who was headlining the Saturday night slot at the annual Reading Festival at the end of August, Björk still lacked a Top 10 hit. Dressed in her red, patterned Chinese satin dress, she took to the Reading stage as darkness fell, playing seventy-five minutes of freewheeling torchsongtechnocabaret and finishing off on a sensational quasi-gospelized 'Big Time Sensuality'. Unbeknown to her, as a celebration, the Reading organisers set off fireworks at the end of her set, spelling out her name – it cost £5,000, and took ten weeks to arrange. Someone must love her . . .

Including those who placed her at nineteen in 'The Hundred Most Influential People in Fashion' feature in *The Face* (number one was the Quantel Paintbox, the computer software which had revolutionized the art of retouching; number two was Ralph Lauren). Björk was the top musician by far, for her influence was putting paper dresses in every magazine and newspaper fashion spread in 1995.

If it was all going swimmingly on the surface, Björk was having trouble in private with Tricky. It seemed that the pair never had a conventionally settled relationship to begin with, while Tricky was always living up to his name. Tricky had been having some sort of a relationship with his co-singer Martina; they lived under the same roof at one point, and in March 1995, they had a baby (named Maisie), but there was no mention of any of the above when Tricky won his initial avalanche of press. It was unclear what kind of relationship Tricky and Martina had, and certainly by the time Maisie was born, Tricky felt free to pursue a relationship with Björk, though even this never got off the ground.

Tricky was the first to admit that he wasn't the most stable of co-dependants, and while both he and Björk were off on tour so much, it meant they hardly had any grounding for stability in the first place. Though there were no confirmed witnesses, there were press-fed rumours that Björk had been angry that, while she saw Tricky's show at the Reading Festival, he was ensconced in the bar during hers. Another rumour was that Tricky had told Björk the relationship was over just when she was about to go on stage in New York (this was a month after Reading) and that Björk had retaliated by walking off stage during the show and thumping him in the chest. If Björk and Tricky weren't going to give a public performance of confrontation, then the press would present it for them, daring the couple to waste time for the sake of their pride by suing for libel.

According to one observer, 'Tricky was always very aloof. He's very insular, and doesn't see much outside of himself.' In the April 1996 issue of *The Face*, an interview with Tricky found its inevitable way around the subject of their affair, and the following exchange:

Face: There were a lot of rumours about you and Björk.

Tricky: There were a lot of rumours.

Face: Were they true? (long pause)

Face: At Reading last year, she appeared to imply that they were.

Tricky: I'd left by then. She probably said, "Why can't he love me?" or that I was too scared to love. The kind of things she always says about me.

'With me and Tricky, I don't think we ever knew if we were going out together or not,' she later told *Dazed & Confused*. 'I mean, we were going out together and then we weren't. Because, basically, the way our relationship functioned was that we were a support system for each other, and we can still have this kind of, like, permission to call each other in the middle of the night. It's a very strange job we've got, and we don't have to explain it: we know. And we know the pressure. And I think the relationship didn't last a long time before we realized that this is why we'd met and sucked like a magnet to each other.'

The tension of the split and the pressures of touring after three years of total creative outpouring probably accounted for the exhaustion that finally caught up with Björk. The tour had successfully crossed Europe and then America, until, in California, she caught flu and lost her voice. In San Diego, she was shocked to discover that she had lost three octaves, leaving her just one and forcing her to adapt melodies and pull through. What annoyed the perfectionist spirit in her was how the crowd continued to adore her. 'They clapped for encores and I was so offended,' she told *Time Out*. 'Like, How dare you, this is the worst gig I've ever done. Can't you throw tomatoes at me?' I ended up apologizing that I wanted to sing them nine hundred songs, and then, typically over-emotional of me, I started crying. It was like *Little House On The Prairie*! And of course, we're in California, so they all fucking cried with me. They were all waiting for me outside, to give me nine hundred throat medicines.'

For the first time since 1987, Björk was forced to cancel shows – actually four in all, including LA and San Francisco. But it was the first time she had ever lost her voice, and she admitted being more scared than at any other time in her life. There was good news to come; although she was diagnosed with throat nodules, it was her body that had collapsed on her. 'I've been singing professionally since I was eleven,' she told *Time Out*. 'I've been spoilt rotten - I could shout and scream and my voice was always there. I had to rethink something I've always taken for granted. I had to make choices, like did I want to socialize or sing? I've always been the biggest rebel ever, but on this tour, I was only out of my cabin for two hours a day, while I was on stage. There were all these special things I had to eat! I had such a disciplined schedule, I felt like one of the Olympic people. Coming out of that, I feel like I've just done an Indiana Jones – I fucking killed the tiger, killed the Nazis, I've done everything and now the titles are rolling. It was a happy ending and I'm just ecstatic, in heaven. I've got my voice back, and I'm tripping, big time.'

Tripping big time perhaps, but still forced to live 'on the monk tip' as she termed it. On doctor's orders, she even had to stop talking, but there were benefits to be gleaned. 'It's amazing, the amount of energy that goes into communicating is just outrageous,' she discovered, with time to appreciate new music, films and books.

And time, too, to find a new boyfriend . . .

The press now expected Björk to have an affair with just about any male musician she was working with or photographed alongside, and the latest (mistaken) rumour was of a dalliance with 3-D of Massive Attack. But they were right when the word spread about Goldie. Just as Tricky was the first bona fide star of hip-hop, so Goldie's debut album *Timeless* had made him the first bona fide star of Britain's jungle scene. Like Tricky again, Goldie could be classified as a street kid, brought up in the Midland town of Walsall, and making a name as a graffiti artist before heading down the drums'n'bass route of jungle. Björk had loved jungle's fractured speediness – 'It's about fierce, fierce, fierce joy. The sort of . . . I'm just too happy, I want to explode. Aaarrggh!' she told *ID* – and had wanted to meet Goldie for a while. She did so at the London club Speed, which led to a Goldie jungle mix of 'Isobel' and him joining up as support on her American tour. His cutting-edge cavalier style, beatmaster leanings, street suss, sense of humour and louche sexiness was to take him from mere musical collaborator to swooned-over bedpartner.

Dazed & Confused asked her if she fell in love very easily. 'I think my reputation has gone a bit funny, because I've got a lot of friends, but I get very precious when it comes to love things, you know? I guess everyone thinks I fall in love every five minutes, and I have nine boyfriends. This [Goldie] is definitely the strongest, though, for many many years. I'm on natural E; I don't even want to drink, because that would make the feeling go away.'

The high would have helped overcome October's exhaustion, as Björk skipped right back into Icelandic-workaholic mode. That said, November press forecasts that she would be recording with Scanner on her new remix project and contributing to an album inspired by the American TV phenomenon *The X Files* turned out to be more hearsay than fact, while the – correctly reported – plan to play a one-off show with underground techno activists like Scanner, Plaid (Andy Turner and Ed Handley from the now fragmented Black Dog) was put off when the press started reporting it as an electronic supergroup. The proposed remix album *Telegraph*, a project that had been talked about even before *Post* was released didn't appear either, as Björk kept putting it back, with various collaborations turning up on B-sides instead.

Two projects that did materialize came from typically diametric poles. One was a recording of 'You Only Live Twice' for an album of James Bond themes that David Arnold was compiling; the other was the forty-minute score *Pierrot Lunaire* by the classical modernist Schoenberg, for which Björk anticipated needing three months of rehearsals to prepare for a performance in 1996. She had obviously revised her earlier opinion that, 'My biggest strength and my greatest weakness is that I can't do the same thing twice. It has to be spontaneous. That's why I'm doing pop, not some contemporary modern minimalist shit. I have to click into now in general.' It seemed that she could now do pop and serious 'shit' because she was still writing new songs, to add to five more completed tracks, and thinking of depending less on collaboration and more on finishing songs alone.

With a couple of days off in Iceland for her birthday, it was back to rehearsals for the second part of her UK tour and a single release of 'It's Oh So Quiet'. Unlike any of her previous singles, the track had picked up airplay even before it had been released in its own right, and daytime and nighttime radio continued to respond to its exhuberant jitterbug melody and novelty dynamics – a series of whispered verses and jubilantly yelled choruses, with arguably the most delicious screams you could find on a pop record. Five year-olds and 65-year-olds could equally love it, and any range of people in between, which made it the perfect Björk single, even if she didn't write it herself.

'Army Of Me' and 'Isobel' hadn't even broken into the UK Airplay Top 50 but 'It's Oh So Quiet' became Björk's first ever single to cross over to the playlists of mainstream radio stations like Capital and Atlantic 252, and it continued to assault the charts. It was assisted in its forward trajectory by a brilliant video directed by Spike Jonze, with dance routines straight out of a forties Hollywood musical (though located first in a tyre depot, then Björk dances with a letter box . . . an offbeat musical then). She had filmed the video in LA between cancelled shows; despite illness, she had learnt the dance steps in two days, then filmed it all in 115 degrees heat. What a gal.

The Christmas market is traditionally more supportive of fewer records, helping 'It's Oh So Quiet' eventually reach number four in the charts and rack up sales of half a million copies. Her unexpected arrival at Mainstream Central was confirmed when she was asked to co-present *Top Of The Pops* with comedian Jack Dee – 'Jack's deadpan delivery and Björk's eccentricity make an ideal match,' reckoned the show's producer, and millions of viewers on Christmas Day were treated to the cutest Icelandic-Cockney accent on earth.

I Walk Towards
The Edge

14

Björk and Sindri eventually got home for a Christmas holiday but they had been denied their traditional Icelandic Christmas dinner, and life might never be the same again. The new year began with more awards, and engagements that would have worn out an Icelandic fisherman. She sung with Brazilian superstar Flora Purim for a future Red Hot And Rio AIDS charity album; she would sometimes put in eight hours a day training for the Schoenberg piece; she played four shows in the UK, in Sheffield, Manchester, Bournemouth and, finally, London with Goldie and band in support (as were ex-husband Thór Eldon's new band Unun). In the meantime, she had won Best Female Artist at the MTV Europe Music Awards, and world domination seemed much more likely than death.

Domination of Goldie seemed pretty much in the bag too. 'I listen to Björk perform, every night, all the energies she puts into her voice, and it's like a glass,' he told *Ikon*. 'It makes me feel so vulnerable. I think, "Shit, she's going to break the glass!" She pushes it so hard, every night, and it's so solid yet so fragile . . .'

By February 1996 *Post* had sold 900,000 worldwide and 'Hyper-ballad' became the fourth single off the album, with another magic-realist Michel Gondry video (Björk as a video game figure). The track was never going to repeat the success of 'It's Oh So Quiet' but it maintained the profile, and the extra B-sides were more evidence of an exhaustive series of collaborations. Though there were numerous dance remixes on her singles, Björk was keen to do the opposite of *Debut*, and take away the rhythmic elements and enter more free-floating territory. This was invention on a scale that no other artist, major or minor, was attempting. The 'It's Oh So Quiet' CDs came with ambience (treatments of 'You've Been Flirting Again' and 'Hyper-ballad'), string quartets ('Hyper-ballad' via The Bronsky Quartet), vocal improvisation (the church organ-led ballad 'Sweet Sweet Intuition' and Evelyn-Glennie-on-exhaust-pipes collaboration 'My Spine'). The 'Hyper-ballad' CDs were no less varied; 'Isobel' got turned into molten metal by Carcuss, 'Cover Me' was disassembled by Plaid while 'Hyper-ballad' itself received no less than seven foraging remixes, including Outcast Productions' jagged, tumultuous 'Over The Edge' mix which Björk reportedly felt was the finest piece of music she had ever been associated with.

A life-long dream came true when Björk set off for Asia. Ever since she had been nicknamed China Girl at school, she had wanted to head East. 'I've always identified with those people for some reason,' she said. She was equally thrilled to take Sindri along for the six-week duration: 'He's one of the most interesting characters I've ever met. He's never felt like an anchor on my thigh.'

The tour started with four dates in Japan, followed by a show in China's capital Beijing, at the Workers' Stadium; people were aware of Björk because of a radio DJ's support, and because one of China's biggest stars Fay Wong, had modelled herself quite closely on Björk circa 1993 (hair-knots, long sleeves, long satin skirts). During the Hong Kong show, Björk was thrilled and even more shocked (she dropped her microphone) when an unexpected Goldie bounded onto the stage to hand her the 1996 BRITS Award for Best International Female Artist, which she scooped for the third year running (Madonna wasn't really competition by this point, and even though Annie Lennox won Best Female Artist, the accolade was rightfully Björk's too).

It was then that rumours that Goldie had asked Björk to marry him began. But if it all seemed too much of a fairytale, then the wicked witch got her way just days later. From Hong Kong, Björk flew on to Thailand. Netty Walker, who was travelling with Björk during the trip, reports that all polite requests not to take photos but to wait until there was a photo call were completely disregarded. Björk had been consistently asked for interviews, which she continued to turn down, and Sindri was now of the age when he could be approached too, which increasingly worried her – Björk always sought to shield him from public attention, from intrusions on his right to privacy. Though she was told otherwise, Björk came through Bakgkok Airport VIP area after clearing customs to be greeted by numerous camera crews, including those of cable station IBC's youth show *Fast Forward*.

The show claimed that it had been informed that Björk would do an interview, but as the camera footage showed, she didn't look up for the task. She emerged with Sindri on top of her full luggage trolley, her expression one of grimacing annoyance. *Fast Forward*'s 24-year old presenter Julie Kaufman beamed, 'Welcome to Bangkok', in Sindri's direction and Björk suddenly turned on her, hit her around the face an estimated seven times, dragged her to the ground, then banged her head on the ground an estimated five times before security guards pulled her off. According to Árni Matthíasson, 'She almost never loses her temper but she has one, and it can flare up.'

Björk did, after all, once say, 'Life is basic things . . .you need to eat, drink, sleep, fuck, get drunk, be happy, get angry, solve things and cause a catastrophe once in a while.'

Netty Walker: 'Of course it wasn't the right reaction by any means. But what people didn't realize was that there were about eight sets of cameras and lights on her, closing in on her. They'd all been told there'd be no interviews but we were stitched up. I was leading the trolley, with Sindri on top, and the camera crews were literally falling over each other. It was overkill. We were trying to get down the steps, off the tarmac, to the curbside, and it was like, "where's the bus?" because there was no bus or car to meet us. We were marooned. That's when the journalist approached Sindri. I had my back to her when she went full swing at her.'

Said Kaufman, 'She looked at me for a few seconds, then lunged. It was so scary, She never said a word.' The fight was captured on film, and the incident replayed on TV as well as freeze-framed in the newspapers. Björk was suddenly a worldwide pop star villain. Being un-villainous at heart, Björk phoned Julie Kaufman to apologize, telling her that the journalist had been, 'in the wrong place, at the wrong time,' that she, 'had been having a lot of problems' (the only problem discussed was how China's dry air affected her voice). Either impressed that Björk had apologized or because she was feeling compassionate, Kaufman decided not to press charges, which took Björk by surprise. 'I feel sorry for her,' Kaufman concluded. 'She must have a lot of anger inside her.'

And maybe some undiscovered naivety, in expecting that the people's, 'representatives', the media, wouldn't be fascinated by her enough to disobey her requests for privacy? Working on such a worldwide scale, a strong, wilfully independent spirit like Björk who wants total control is not going to get it all the time, and she was going to have to accept those pressures – without lashing out.

That she did lash out was proof of her need to protect herself from the outside world setting whatever boundaries it liked, and to protect Sindri from being, as she told *ID*, 'recognized for what I am' as opposed to what he was. 'I was protecting him from my demons, from the silly things that have to do with my job,' she concluded.

One Little Indian subsequently issued the following statement: 'Björk has contacted the journalist to apologize, and would like to use this opportunity to publicly apologize for any embarrassment that she might have caused. Björk is just about to complete an extensive world tour and is physically and mentally exhausted. She knows that this does not excuse her behavour but she hopes that it will help explain why she acted so out of character, Björk is continuing with her world tour, and completing existing promotional commitments, but she is too exhausted to do any more interviews.'

Too exhausted to even make the statement herself; Derek Birkett had written the words, 'expressing her sentiments on her behalf,' he says. 'It was a combination of an over-demanding tour and a bad day. It's tough for her, because this has all been a bit of a shock to everyone. She sells a lot of records but people think she is Madonna or Michael Jackson, which takes a bit of time to come to terms with, and for those people around her too. We've been friends and working together for a long time and I find it hard to be out with her in public, as she's not your friend any more, she seems to be like public property so I tend not to go out with her in public now.'

Björk's family had already seen the warning signs. Hildur reflected how, in the Christmas break, she had noticed even Icelanders, who Björk always claimed were far from starstruck people, treating her like the Icelandic Michael Jackson, 'like an alien or something. They were coming up and prodding her.' As long ago as Björk's teens, Hildur had worried that Björk was taking on too much; now she was worried that so much success, so soon, was truly too much even for her daughter's notoriously high stamina levels. Her father Gudmundur said that Björk's sign of being upset or nervous was to rub her nose. 'Normally, when she returns to Iceland, this habit stops, but at Christmas, it took her a month to calm down,' he admitted.

The irony was staring Björk in the face. The price of free expression, of being understood, of being loved, was a denial of the privacy and space that created the art that got her there. How could she go walkabout in Iceland now? Camping with Sindri?

Árni Matthíasson: 'She is inherently a very private person. I think it's hard for her to accept she is a superstar and everything she does can be of interest to others. Her car was clamped in London the other week and it even made the American papers. I think she realized when she came to Iceland at Christmas that she was attaining the same status here and it shocked her. She seemed very embarrassed and uncomfortable about what happened at the airport. It's something she would rather forget. But the predatory nature of journalism doesn't take kids into account. The journalists probably didn't know she had

Sindri with her but even if they did, they didn't think it affected things. They still had questions to ask.

'When Björk went home at Christmas, she felt she had gone beyond the state of being well known, into the state of being famous, and everyone wants to bother you. In Britain, there is this superficial cordiality, where everybody feels free to talk to you, but in Iceland, people are really hard to get to know, or to get close to, so even if people know you, they don't bother you or talk to you. So Björk has been able to go back to Iceland, stroll downtown, and though everybody knows her, nobody would dream of talking to her or following her or taking her picture, but she is beyond that now, and that is what people were doing here. She went to a gym to exercise, and all of a sudden, she realized that she had about a hundred people staring at her, which is something you don't want, and it shocked her. I don't know when she will be able to come back to Iceland and relax again. Iceland was her sanctuary, where she could hang out with her old pals and do stuff, and it won't be easy for her to do that any more. Now she has to buy an island in the Bahamas!'

Or in Tunisia, where she talked about the fact that you could buy an island for £50,000. 'I'm going to buy one, with a house and everything – it's cheaper than a flat in London!' she told a press conference. 'I'm doing that next summer, that'll be my base. I started thinking about it two years ago and when I decide that's something, that's it: it's a decision. Actually, I decided when I was a kid that I was going to move to an island – the ocean makes my head function better. I'll be going there on my own but you know what it's going to be like, don't you? A fucking health farm for all my friends. They'll come to me before they have that nervous breakdown.'

As for England, 'I hated it here until about two years ago when I discovered Steve Coogan, French & Saunders, *Have I Got News For You* and *Absolutely Fabulous*.' The cream of British comedy aside, she said, 'The rest of England can just fuck off.' Being near water in Little Venice hadn't satisfied her, 'because it's a canal so the water doesn't move. I'm only here for work, for a period, to get my little mission done, and once it's finished, it's finished. But after this little job is done, I'm living by the ocean. It doesn't matter where it is.'

She might need to go somewhere remote after the media fuss that followed the combined efforts of the Thailand incident, the success of 'It's Oh So Quiet' and her BRITS award; if anyone was to have a nervous breakdown first, it was Björk. She was prime-time material for a full exposé, which saw the tabloids delight in a fuller investigation than ever of what they termed a story filled with strange childhoods, weird characteristics, 'showbiz' relationships and aggressive behaviour. 'BORN TO BE WILD' was the *Sunday Express* headline, REBEL OF REYKJAVIK – 3 PAGE SPECIAL ON SHOCKING STAR BJÖRK ran the ever-sensitive *Sun*, both features accompanied by photospreads of Björk, as a baby, young child, teenager and fully-grown adult. Who had donated the photos? Icelanders still weren't acclimatized to the intrusions of the Western media, and Hildur confirms that Björk's half-sister Hallfridur was called and offered £5,000 for an interview, but that she didn't know enough about Björk to be able to talk. She also admits that those of Björk's relatives who were contacted by British journalists were flattered at the attention. 'I think they enjoyed the chance to say something, and to show the pictures, because they are very proud of her,' says Hildur. 'It all happened without anyone really knowing what was going on.'

The Thailand incident also triggered more than one media analysis of the renewed stroppiness of pop stars. One was 'The Angry Young Women Of Rock' in the *Daily Telegraph*, where 'Icelandic fruitcake' Björk was compared to Courtney Love, who had assaulted fellow singer Kathleen Hanna (of *Riot Grrrl* spearheads Bikini Kill) just months before, and women like Alanis Morissette, Tori Amos and Sinead O'Connor were contrasted with the post-sixties generational politeness of Joni Mitchell, Carole King and Joan Armatrading. Feminist rage, now a new musical category . . .

When her Asian tour was finished, Björk and Goldie disappeared on holiday to Vabbin, a private island in The Maldives. There was good news – at the UK's third International Dance Awards, she had won Best Female Artist and Goldie the Best Male Artist (the organizers reportedly flew a £1,000 video camera out to them to film a special message but Goldie dropped it in the ocean while fooling around!) and at the Music Week Awards, Björk won Best Female Artist. But there was some bad news: the *Sun* reported a 2 a.m. scuffle with some French tourists who had complained about the noise coming from Goldie and Björk's room. The manager apparently confirmed that an incident had taken place but that, 'Björk had apologized and everything was fine.' The incident might well have been fabricated but the effect spilled over; the teen weekly *Shout* wrote, 'Björk's well known for her unpredictable temper.' If the caricature fits, the media have no problem in wearing it (out).

On her return, there were no record releases and no concerts, so no reason to be interviewed. In fact, Björk went to the other side of the tape recorder, on behalf of *Dazed & Confused* magazine, who had asked her which people she would most like to interview. The answer being the pioneering, now octogenarian German electronic composer Karlheinz Stockhausen, one of her all-time favourites alongside Public Enemy and Schoenberg, a man who remade classical music in his own electronic, industrial musical image. As Björk arguably had with pop music . . .

There was otherwise no reason to be in the public eye until the summer festivals she had agreed to do, so, finally, it had all gone quiet. April only saw two Björk/Tricky trip-hop collaborations appear on the latter's album of collaborations *Nearly God* – 'Keep Your Mouth Shut' (featuring vocal samples from 'You've Been Flirting Again') and 'Yoga'. The only serious Björk-related news in May came from *Musik*, when the writer phoned Goldie, who admitted that the rumours were true, then said, 'See ya later!' and promptly put the phone down.

Nothing Will Be The Same

'The only thing that's going to last forever is pop music, just as long as it changes every day.'

How was Björk to face the future? Where would she turn next? And would she get bored with this pop life, the way that she got bored woth everything else? Only if pop was a fixed concept, which we know that it doesn't have to be. Björk at eleven was never going to be happy singing 'I Love To Love' when there was so much more out there to investigate, and the 33-year-old Björk is always going to keep incorporating any damn notion of music she wants.

Even pop can limit your expression, and after all, she has to keep surprising herself, so the Björkaphile won't be surprised to discover that she might be singing Schoenberg's *Pierrot Lunarie* with conductor Ken Negano and the Opera Orchestra of Lyon, or a second Schoenberg score *Ode To Napoleon* and Spanish composer Peter 'Master Puppeteer'. At the time of writing, Björk was planning to perform it in

Leipzig but Derek Birkett was adamant that, if it was good enough, he would do all he could to persuade Björk to release it.

Birkett also confirms that she had delivered Telegraph but that she was still working on numerous remixes (from the likes Goldie and Talvin Singh) and that she had started work on a new studio album, with contributions from Eumir Deodato and The Bronsky Quartet already in the can (and deemed, 'brilliant,' by Birkett).

Björk has talked about where she plans to head with the new album: it will be a digression from *Post* and *Debut*, 'the greatest hits of the last ten years of my life, and more about me . . .it will include extremities and perhaps me with a Latin jazz quartet, rather than me going to all these different places. They were like *Tin Tin In The Congo*, *Tin Tin In America*, Tin Tin in . . . fucking wherever. Now I'm going to invite people over to my place. Now it's time to get it out of me.'

Over what is still a remarkably short period of time in pop terms, Björk has gone a long way. Heartbreaking vocal acrobat, barrier-breaking musical innovator, fashion image-breaker. What must the transformation have done to her head? According to Jakob Magnússon, almost nothing. 'I've seen her go from a fairly introverted, shy child to an almost eccentric teenager to now being a very beautiful woman in her prime, and it hasn't changed at all. She's not gone big headed or snotty, she is really in tune with herself. I wouldn't be scared to say it if there was anything bad to say about her but there isn't.'

Graham Massey tends to agree. 'She's had to separate her public face from the private face, but she's not the type to have bodyguards. A lot of people in her position would have had to change to get to where she is but Björk is still basically the same person. She's still that independent spirit that I imagine is hard to control. She'll wander off still, and worry a lot of people when she does, but that's her. She can handle herself.'

Despite all the trauma, Björk was still connected to Iceland via an umbilical cord, and all her good work was paying off, as Bad Taste's finances were swelled by Icelandic sales of *Debut* and *Post*. The label had managed to resuscitate itself after its first wave of bands had faded away, and amassed over thirty new releases, including albums by Einar Örn and Hilmar Örn Hilmarsson (under the name Frostbite), Thór Eldon's new band Unun, his wife and fellow ex-Sugarcubes Magga Ornolfsdóttir and Siggi Baldursson's Bogomil Font (an album of Kurt Weill tunes). A new wave of Icelandic bands has emerged in the wake of The Sugarcubes and Björk – Looq, Gus Gus and Bong are all excellent dance projects which have new UK deals, as have Unun, while Bellatrix are one of Bad Taste's new ventures just getting noticed. 'Alternative' music even has a secure foothold in Reykjavík, with a new record shop, fanzines, radio shows and successful gigs by the likes of The Prodigy and The Drum Club.

Not that the ex-Sugarcubes bunch would ever be happy just releasing albums. Magga has been writing children's songs and working as a presenter on children's TV; Einar runs Iceland's first internet café Cyberia; Siggi is currently living in America (Madison, Wisconsin, where his wife is doing her doctorate); Bragi has, in fact, retired from music to concentrate on poetry. Everyone is still involved in decisions regarding Bad Taste, and Björk maintains that, 'The Sugarcubes people will suppport each other until the day we die. And we are also each other's hardest critics. Like, I'll send a record to the bass player and he will tell me it's crap, you know? And he sends me his poetry.'

And what extra-curricular activity did Björk imagine for herself in the future? She has expressed a wish to learn animation in Japan, and to open a music school for children, and tell them, 'Fuck the snobs. There are no boundaries! Express yourselves!' She wants another child, and to be married again, which Goldie might have a hand (and more) in. And unlike most people, and unlike all pop stars, she is also looking forward to getting older. 'I can't wait until I'm forty-five. I'm just doing my best preparing to be a good granny, really. Yeah, you have to train your characteristics. You know, there's a lot of things still to learn. I'd love to be like my granny, she's got loads and tons and tons of love.'

Björk always knew as a child that she would make a good kid because she was very self-sufficient and happy. 'Then the piece between fifteen and thirty-five would be a bit urgh, and I couldn't wait until I got to about forty,' she told Time Out. 'At twenty-five to thirty, you gotta sit down and make an effort, which is scary for a lot of people. Up to this age, you have so much energy, it's like a free ride. Then you suddenly realize you can't do everything. I love Nusrat Fateh Ali Khan [master of vocal-led, Pakistani devotional, "qawwal" music]. His music's got nothing to do with age, it's to do with guts and facing your emotions. It's that kind of courage of being alive that I'm after from music.'

And what of the musical future? Into the new millennium? 'It's funny because the last time we met, me and Polly [Harvey] were joking that we would be fucking eighty years old and still trying to talk each other out of stage diving because our bones are getting too old for it,' she told *Hot Press*. 'But I might not be on stage because, as I said, I get a very big kick out of working with other people and I can easily picture me writing songs for other people or producing other people – I mean, hopefully, I'm not being big headed, but I would love to do that, it's like a tangent or a dream. Or writing musicals, I would love to write a modern musical. I would also love to teach. But it will always be music, I think, because it wasn't like I picked music, it was music that picked me. Sometimes it's quite weird but no matter how far away I try to go – if I go on holiday or whatever – I always somehow get back to it. It's an obsession.'

'If I have any vision of my life,' she told *Interview*, 'I think I'll be singing until I die, about ninety years old. It's funny, all the attention I'm getting, but I don't think I'm hooked on it. I could just as well move to a little island and live by the ocean and be just the village singer or whatever. Singing on Friday or Saturday nights, writing tunes for the rest of the week. That's my role.'

And her target? 'I would like to be considered very human, and also very brave, fighting for my opinions in life. I think the bravest thing you can do in the world is be happy. Because there are always going to be problems, but if you can deal with them and you're still happy – that's a virtue I really admire. That's my target, even if I haven't been there all my life. It's a question of having the guts to face each moment.'

In Derek Birkett's eyes, Björk has taught him the benefits of having the guts to face each moment. 'I've been incredibly lucky to work with her, in times when she sold very few records and then the dizzy highs and lows of The Sugarcubes and her own records. She's avoided the emotional temptations you face with failure and success, with coercion by me, I might add, to compromise your artistic vision, to work with lots of people. She'll only work with people she respects as opposed to musicians and business people which would have meant she would have sold millions more records. I was approached by four of the biggest selling artists in the world to sing with her at the BRITS but she desperately wanted to sing with Polly Harvey. I don't want to build her up into a myth but I'm prepared to say she is uncompromisingly honest in the way she deals with music and business, which is incredibly rare. The highs and lows haven't wavered at any point. She's done business deals on moral accounts, and paid people she didn't have to, and credited people who didn't need to be, whether she had money or not. I've had some rucks with her, over remixes, sleeve designs, photos, and sometimes I think she's lost the balance between working with people because of their creativity and who they are as human beings. But she's true to her philosophy. She's possibly the worst business person I've worked with but she's never professed to be that.'

After months, years, of people trying to work her out, like a laboratory or field experiment, like her first crush-love David Attenborough, what did Björk make of herself? 'I'll never, ever, ever understand what I'm about,' she concluded. 'I'm still really rehearsing my instinct. I started when I was five. I'm still trying to train it because at the end of the day that's all I've got. My little antennae that connect me and give me the whole picture. If you close your eyes and believe in your instinct, it's fucking *Star Wars* – may the force be with you.'

It's instinct which continually drives Björk on – no labels, categories, no boundaries. This is what creates opinions before feelings, judgement before sentiment. 'My favourite thing to do would be to write music in my house and then sneak up behind people and put headphones on them and they wouldn't know what age the person who did it is, what sex he or she is, where they came from and not even understand the words,' Björk says. 'To be affected by it, because that is what it is supposed to do. The music is supposed to bring out some things in you that you didn't know you had.'

When Björk comes out for the encore and the rapturous applause dies down, she says, quietly, 'I don't usually like talking. I prefer to let the music say it.' The music usually does; this mix of pop, folk, classical, electronic, dance, ambient fuses to produce a quintessentially nineties music – liquid, mutating, evolving, a sea of possibilities. As Björk sings in 'Headphones', '*sounds go through the muscles/abstract wordless moments/they start off cells that haven't been touched before/these cells are virgins*'. When the final notes die down, she disappears, and heads back to think about putting Sindri to bed, making dinner, sorting out the electricity bill, rehearsing an opera, performing with her techno mates like Graham Massey and Plaid, hanging out with friends, letting off emotional fireworks, causing a catastrophe, and writing, writing, writing songs. Singing as she goes. Taking courage to enjoy it. 'Writing is about now,' she once said. 'The word "now" in Icelandic is *nuna*. Not tomorrow, not yesterday. *Now. Nuna*. Just being there. Open.'

Index

Lyric credits